DAS REICH

The March of the
2nd SS Panzer Division through
France, June 1944

Max Hastings

 ZENITH PRESS

First published in 2013 by Zenith Press, an imprint of Quayside Publishing Group, 400 First Avenue North, Suite 400, Minneapolis, MN 55401 USA

Zenith Press titles are also available at discounts in bulk quantity for industrial or sales-promotional use. For details write to Special Sales Manager at Quayside Publishing Group, 400 First Avenue North, Suite 400, Minneapolis, MN 55401 USA.

To find out more about our books, join us online at www.zenithpress.com.

Cover design: Kent Jenson

Photo credits: Cover: Bundesarchiv, Bild 101III-Zschaeckel-206-35 / photo: Friedrich Zschaeckel
On the back cover: UIG via Getty Images

Printed in the United States of America

ILLUSTRATION ACKNOWLEDGMENTS: The author and publishers would like to thank all those who gave their kind permission to reproduce photographs here. Among others, we are are grateful to Miss Vera Atkins, Mrs. Pilar Starr, The Hamlyn Group, Askania Verlagsgesellschaft, HMSO, Editions Daniel & Cie, Verlag K.W. Schütz KG, SOGEDIL, Sygma, Popperfoto, and Keystone Press.

For Anthea
who should have been here to read this

Contents

Foreword

I WROTE THIS BOOK more than thirty years ago, in an attempt to get to the truth of one of the remarkable and terrible episodes of the Second World War: the march of the 2nd SS Panzer Division to Normandy, and the efforts of the French Resistance and allied special forces to delay its passage. Nazis and guerrillas clashed amid some of the most beautiful landscapes in Europe. Both sides afterwards promoted rival legends of what took place. What is indisputable is that hundreds of innocents perished. On the battlefields of 1939–45, Hitler's Waffen SS showed themselves to be among the most formidable fighting forces of all time. But behind the front, they displayed a savagery which drowned in blood their own claims to be regarded as Teutonic Knights, men of honor and chivalry. In 1980–81, when I carried out my research, many veterans of the Das Reich division were still alive, and I was able to interview a significant number. Most evaded some questions, and lied in answer to others, about the awful deeds in which they were complicit in 1944. I was then still a young and relatively inexperienced historian, learning my craft. It was a chilling experience to sit in the homes of Das Reich veterans, listening to their stories.

I remember in particular Major Heinrich Wulf, a mild-mannered, white-haired old man who met me in Bavarian national costume, complete with leather shorts, outside his charming south German retirement home. Wulf commanded his division's armored reconnaissance battalion, which on 9 June 1944 stormed into the central French town of Tulle to drive out communist Resistance fighters who had rashly occupied it on D-Day. Wulf claimed to have found the bodies of scores of elderly German reservists who had surrendered, then been murdered by the Resistance when they fled before the Das Reich. I incline to believe this story, but I asked Wulf whether any atrocity by the Resistance could justify his response that day: as a reprisal, he rounded up the entire male population of Tulle, and hanged ninety-nine boys and men from the lampposts.

He stared at me for a moment in resentful silence, then said, "We let them have a priest. Where else do you hear of people being hanged in the war who were allowed to have a priest?" After another long silence, he added harshly, "In Russia, we did things like this every day." And so they did. If the atrocities committed by the Das Reich in June 1944 were unusual in France, throughout the Eastern war Hitler's armies committed unspeakable acts which eventually embraced the slaughter of millions.

But if the crimes of the Waffen SS were shocking, I also learned much that then surprised me about the murderous hatreds and feuds on the other side. France in those days was disfigured by profound anti-semitism. French police and militia did much of the Nazis' business in herding Jews towards the concentration camps. As I interviewed scores of old Resistance fighters in southern France, I noticed a hostility towards a man I much admired, Baron Philippe de Gunzbourg, one of the few French aristocrats to work tirelessly and at huge risk for the allied cause. Finally I asked a Resistance historian if there was something wrong with de Gunzbourg, or his wartime record. He spat out: "*Il est juif!*" (He is Jewish!) To me, as a rather naïve young Englishman, it was shocking to be confronted by such shameless hostility to Jews, which was characteristic of that French generation.

In the course of my research, I learned a lot about Resistance and the work of OSS and SOE in supporting it. My studies sowed the seeds of a skepticism which has grown in the intervening decades about the value of guerrilla warfare against such merciless foes as the Nazis. I am today convinced that the military value of Resistance was eclipsed by the dreadful retribution Hitler extracted—of the order of a hundred French lives for every German killed—throughout the Occupation. The legend of Resistance played an important moral role in enabling France to resurrect its national self-respect after 1945, but the price was high indeed.

In the immediate postwar era, the French people and British admirers of Special Operations Executive constructed a legend about the achievement of Resistance fighters in combating the Das Reich division in June 1944, which I fear was grossly exaggerated. Although it is almost impossible to produce a definitive account of episodes for which documentary evidence is almost non-existent and much of the oral testimony—on both sides—was willfully deceitful, I would like to think that my account remains as close as anybody is ever likely to get in placing the story in historical perspective. I shall never regret all those weeks of travel in Germany and southern France, interviewing participants. Even if some lied through their teeth, I was able to bottle for posterity the stories of some remarkable people, real heroes and real monsters alike.

The Das Reich division's march across France in June 1944 will continue to be seen as an epic of the period, both for the fine deeds done by some actors and the dreadful crimes committed by others. Anyone who reads this book should gain a clearer understanding of the labyrinthine complexity of the life of France at war, and of often clumsy British and American attempts to harness Resistance to the greater allied cause. Here also is an insight, perhaps as shocking to a modern reader as it was to me three decades ago, into the depth of depravity to which Hitler's creatures descended during their struggle to preserve the hegemony of his Third Reich.

Max Hastings
England 2013

London and France

5/6 June 1944

A T 9:15 PM ON 5 JUNE 1944, as the first ships of the Allied invasion fleet came within sight of the Normandy shore, the French Service of the BBC began to broadcast its customary *messages personnels*. Through more than three years of tragedy, pessimism, defeat and occupation, through the long struggle to create an armed opposition movement within France, the *messages personnels* had been among the most vital, emotion-charged weapons of Resistance. In flats and farmhouses in the cities and countryside of France, little knots of men and women clustered to listen, at risk of their lives, amidst the static and crackle of distance and German jamming, to the voice of London: "*Charles est très malade. . . . Marcel aime Marceline. . . . Il n'y a pas de bananes. . . . La guerre de Troie n'aura pas lieu. . . . Yvette a dix doigts. . . .*" ("Charles is very sick. . . . Marcel loves Marceline. . . . There are not any bananas. . . . Yvette has ten fingers. . . .") Some of these phrases were as meaningless as they seemed. But many others each night gave *résistants* from Brittany to the Pyrenees, from the Vercors to the Ardennes, their private, prearranged signal to expect a rendezvous with a Lysander on a field outside Paris, a parachute arms drop on a hillside in the Corrèze, or a new wireless operator's arrival in the Gers.

On 1 May 1944 a most unusual set of *messages personnels* were broadcast. They covered the whole of France, and indicated that the Second Front could be expected within weeks. On 1 June, a second series was transmitted, giving a warning of days. On the afternoon of 5 June, the chief of Special Operations Executive, General Gubbins, and the London chief of the American Office of Strategic Services, Colonel David Bruce, called together on General Koenig, the Free French officer designated chief of all Resistance operations in France after the invasion. They went through the formality of asking his assent to the transmission of the "Action Messages" that night.

For the rest of their lives, former Allied agents and *résistants* would forget much about World War II, but none would ever forget his or her "action message" on the night of 5 June 1944. George Starr's message was *"Il a un voix fausset"* ("He has a falsetto voice"). It was his wireless operator, a little English WAAF named Annette Cormeau, who came down from the bedroom where she kept her set to report the news to the little group in the kitchen of a farmhouse at Castelnau-sur-l'Auvignon, in the heart of Gascony. Starr—SOE's Hilaire—was sitting among the Laribeau family, with whom he lived. He was a laconic, iron-tough mining engineer from Staffordshire who in the past twenty months had built one of the largest SOE networks in France. He was not given to extravagant displays of emotion. He simply grinned and said: "That's it, then," and began to summon men from other houses in the lonely little hamlet to drive and ride into the night, passing word. Within a few hours, the first explosions on the railways indicated the opening of the attack on communications. As the night advanced, men began to arrive on foot, by bicycle, and charcoal-driven *gazogène*. Exhilarated chatter and laughter echoed among the houses as they broke out the arms hidden in the church and began to pass them out, filling magazines and stripping Brens and Stens of their protective greasing.

Jacques Poirier's message was *"La girafe a un long cou"* ("The giraffe has a long neck"). He received it among the *maquis* with whom he was quartered in the lonely dignity of the Château Le Poujade, high above the Dordogne valley. The Germans had relinquished control of much of the Dordogne many months before, confining themselves to occasional punitive sorties. Under his codename Nestor, Poirier was SOE's agent for eastern Dordogne and Corrèze, in which he had arranged arms drops for several thousand *maquisards*, most of whom were now bursting to make use of their weapons. Poirier immediately took to his car. That night of 5 June, and through the days that followed, he raced from *maquis* to *maquis* in the woods and hills, pressing on them the request he had been making for weeks. "Make as much mess as you can."

Most of the *résistants* to whom he spoke had never in their lives heard of the Das Reich, the 2nd SS Panzer Division some eighty miles southwards around Montauban in the Tarn-et-Garonne. It was only on the rarest occasions that SOE's agents, far less *maquisards*, had access to military intelligence from London. They had no means of communicating with other groups except with chronic delay, by courier or personal visit. On the morning of 6 June, the thousands of *résistants* gathering with their arms in the Lot, the Dordogne, the Corrèze and the south-west knew little except that "*Le Jour-J*" (D-Day) had come. They expected to fight but few guessed against whom.

Captain Marius Guedin, lately of the French 60th Infantry Regiment, was one of the few Resistance leaders who had been convinced for months what his men should do. He was a native of Brive-la-Gaillarde, the beautifully named town at the foot of the hills of the Corrèze to which he had returned in 1942 from captivity in Germany. Guedin had been one of the first to begin working towards creating a local Resistance movement, and although he had the bespectacled appearance of a diffident university don, he pursued his plans with fierce single-mindedness. He developed a close relationship with a succession of British agents who came to his area, of whom Jacques Poirier was the latest. He rejected the overtures of De Gaulle's agents who came to see him, and who sought to exert a measure of direction over the local *Armée Secrète*.

By June 1944, his chief in the departmental AS, Colonel René Vaujour, claimed to have some 5,000 *maquisards* and secret *résistants* under his control. Guedin was effectively their field commander. He was convinced that, when the invasion came, the Das Reich would move north through his sector to reinforce the German counter-offensive. In March 1944 he gave orders to his men: on D-Day, they would deploy company by company to cover the bridges of the river Dordogne in south Corrèze and northern Lot. In the early hours of 6

June, throughout the region men who had been secret *résistants* for months or years left their homes and their families and began to walk or bicycle to the various rendezvous. Guedin's *maquisards*, already living openly without the law, broke their camps and moved to join them as his couriers brought the news.

But many others who were to meet the Das Reich Division had no fore-knowledge. All through the afternoon of 5 June, at a splendid Georgian mansion in Bedfordshire named Hasell's Hall, a pretty, dark-haired girl and a cheerful young man in battledress chattered, laughed and pieced jigsaws together without knowing each other's names. The man was a twenty-two-year-old officer of the Special Air Service named John Tonkin, who had already fought in North Africa and Italy, and made a remarkable escape from German hands to rejoin his regiment. Now he was to be parachuted into France to prepare a landing ground for forty of his men to follow, and attack German communications from a base far behind the lines, south of Poitiers. The house, he wrote later in a letter to his mother,

> . . . was the "last resting place" for all agents to enemy countries. We were very well looked after by ATS. The only operational people there were Richard and I and the Jedburgh team for Operation Bulbasket, two of our officers for Houndsworth, two for Titanic, and four agents, of whom two were surprisingly beautiful girls. We had checked and rechecked everything and packed our enormous ruck sacks about fifty times. Finally, there was nothing more to do, so we spent the time very profitably with the girls, doing jigsaw puzzles.

It was an odd little fluke of war that Tonkin's men should within the week have directed an air attack on petrol trains intended to move the Das Reich, while the girl, twenty-four years old and with one mission to France already behind her, should have been captured and sent on the road to execution by the division. Her name was Violette Szabo.

Vera Atkins, one of the most celebrated of SOE's Baker Street staff, also spent the long day at Hasell's Hall, after the postponement of the invasion, and thus of their drop, for twenty-four hours. That night, she drove with the girls to the secret aerodrome at Tempsford. Violette Szabo, she said, ". . . looked incredibly beautiful, in white marguerite earrings and a marguerite clip that she had bought in Paris on her last mission. . . ." One of the SAS officers approached Vera as they waited, and asked her to take his cufflinks and send them to his mother. Then the Halifaxes taking the British officers and agents to their several destinations disappeared into the darkness at the end of the runway; Vera returned to her car, and at last to Baker Street. There was no celebration of D-Day. They were all much too tired.

At the headquarters of the Der Führer Panzergrenadier Regiment, one of the two armored infantry brigades of the 2nd SS Panzer Division, on the morning of 6 June a brief signal was received from divisional headquarters at Moissac: "Since the early hours of the morning, the invasion has been taking place on the Channel coast. Preparations are to be made for a march."

CHAPTER 1

2nd SS Panzer Division
Montauban, Tarn-et-Garonne

May 1944

IN THE EARLY AFTERNOON of 6 April 1944, in the conference room of his headquarters in East Prussia, Adolf Hitler and his staff discussed what further units they dared strip from the Eastern Front to reinforce France against Allied invasion. The transcript of their conversation is mangled, but when they begin to discuss the future of the 2nd SS Panzer Division, the Das Reich, the import is clear.

> WARLIMONT: This movement of the 12 SS Div in this area is also under way, though for the moment they can't be replaced. On the other hand, Student's paratroop replacement and training division, which has about 12,000 men, is going into southern Holland . . . being built up there . . . Reich has . . . Now the . . . please, that he should be able to do with tanks . . . because here . . . can be moved here . . . as well as . . . and the front on the south coast. . . .
>
> FEGELEIN: When contact to 1st Panzer Army has been established, the Reich Battle Group can presumably be withdrawn?
>
> THE FÜHRER: Of course it should be pulled out—it should move over here.

FEGELEIN: It could be put together quickly.

THE FÜHRER: How strong is this battle group?

KEITEL: Fifteen or sixteen hundred men.

FEGELEIN: No, it's a bit bigger: 2,500 men. They weren't too badly mauled. That's the hard core.

THE FÜHRER: For over there, it's nothing. But if they're put here, you've immediately got 15,000 men. Then in no time. . . .

FEGELEIN: The Das Reich Division has 15,385 men altogether.

BUHLE: The battle group and that?

FEGELEIN: No, that alone.

THE FÜHRER: Then it's ready! Then it's a division again—in fact an old division!

Thus it was that some 2,500 survivors of Battle Group Lammerding, rump of one of the finest armored divisions Nazi Germany had created, found themselves ordered to abandon the mud and floods of Russia in the spring thaw, and entrain for a move across Europe that would finally lead them to Tulle, Oradour-sur-Glane and Normandy. They left behind their few remaining tanks, vehicles and guns, together with the memory of countless thousands of their dead in frozen graves from the Pripet marshes to the Cherkassy pocket. With infinite gratitude for their deliverance, they began to roll away through East Prussia, on the long journey from the eastern to the western extremity of Hitler's empire.

It was the high point of German fortunes in the East in 1944. The weather had forced a temporary halt in campaigning. The Russians decided to defer their next offensive until the Allies landed in France. Hitler had a priceless opportunity to shorten his line, to withdraw to defenses in depth while he moved men to meet the threat in the West. Instead, as always, he held his ground. His shrinking armies straggled along a front of 1,650 miles. In the center, divisions averaging only 2,000 men were holding sixteen-mile sectors of the line. Between July 1943 and May 1944, Germany lost forty-one divisions in Russia—almost a million casualties between July and October 1943 alone, 341,950 men between March and May 1944. Even in the months following the Allied invasion in Normandy, German casualties in Russia continued to average four times the number in the West.

Hitler's *Führerdirectiv* No.51 of November 1943 gave first priority to strengthening the western defenses against the Allied invasion. Yet in reality the East continued to consume the overwhelming proportion of men and resources. Divisions sent to France had either been ruined in Russia, were untrained or medically inferior. Special battalions were formed from the deaf and diseased. The ranks were filled with Russian, Hungarian and Romanian subjects of Hitler's empire—even some defectors from POWs of the Indian Army. Von Rundstedt had demanded seventy full-strength divisions to defend the West. By 6 June 1944, he had only fifty-nine woefully under-strength ones—850,000 men and 1,552 tanks. By contrast, there were 156 German divisions in Russia and twenty-seven in Italy. "Often I would be informed that a new division was to arrive in France direct from Russia, or Norway, or central Germany," Rundstedt wrote acidly. "When it finally made its appearance in the West, it would consist, in all, of a divisional commander, a medical officer, and five bakers."

The 2nd SS Das Reich Armored Division was not quite such a shadow when it arrived in Bordeaux from the East, but it was nothing like the superb all-volunteer force that had swept into Russia with the Wehrmacht in June 1941. The High Command in the East had ruthlessly stripped its surviving "teeth" formations to strengthen the sagging line on the Dnieper. Only a few thousand support personnel had been sent to France, to wait re-equipment with every kind of weapon and vehicle. To fill the ranks, 9,000 replacements flooded into the division's barracks and lagers: untrained boys, almost all seventeen or eighteen, many of them *Volksdeutsche*—Hungarians, Romanians and a large contingent of Alsatians, twelve nationalities in all. Three months before they were plunged into one of the great battles of history, in the woods and fields of south-western France, the raw recruits were firing their Mauser K98s for the first time, practicing the naming of parts on the MG42, and receiving their introduction to the Pak 75 anti-tank gun.

In April, they moved south-eastwards to a rendezvous with the survivors of the division's battle group, at last released to join them from the East. They formed one of the three armored, one motorized and thirteen infantry divisions of General Von Blaskowitz's Army Group G, responsible for the defense of southern France. The point on the map that Hitler's forefinger had stabbed on 6 April was the town of

Montauban, just north of Toulouse. There, his staff suggested, the Das Reich could not only prepare for battle in a quiet area, but stand poised to intervene on the north or south coasts of France, when the Allies landed. If the disturbing terrorist situation in central France which was already irritating Von Rundstedt continued to worsen, the Das Reich could guarantee communication between Army Groups G and B.

Throughout the last two years of the war, the deployment of the SS divisions consumed countless hours at Hitler's Fuhrer conferences. His faith and pride in their power were unshakable. Again and again throughout the war in the East, SS units had defied his generals' predictions of the possible, broken through the unbreakable, or held the untenable. The Das Reich had fought with distinction through the great summer battles of 1943, above all in the slow fight back to the Dnieper in August. In November, the SS Leibstandarte Division spearheaded the counter-attack that smashed the Russian armored corps after its breakthrough near Kiev. In April 1944, it was the SS Panzer Corps under Hausser that launched a brilliant flank attack to save the 1st Panzer Army from certain destruction in the Cherkassy pocket.

The SS had become the fire brigade of Hitler's empire, rushed to every crisis. In the last two years of the war, the Leibstandarte Division moved seven times between the Eastern and Western Fronts. Himmler exaggerated only a little when he said in January 1944: "So far, the Waffen SS has never under any circumstances caused disappointment, and it will not—even under the most severe hardships yet to come—disappoint in the future." Since October 1943, seven crack Panzergrenadier units, including the Das Reich, had been redesignated as Panzer divisions. With an establishment of over 20,000 men and 200 tanks, each was almost twice the strength of a Wehrmacht Panzer division. These seven units, together with another five or six SS divisions of slightly lesser quality, were at the forefront of Hitler's operational plans until the end of the war. It is a measure of his strategic priorities that, until June 1944, only one SS division was engaged with the Western Allies, in Italy. The remainder of this vast personal army—thirty-eight divisions and 600,000 men at its zenith—was committed in Russia or refitting.

Of the ten Panzer divisions in France on D-Day, three were SS. The only unit in a position to provide immediate support for the weak static infantry divisions defending the Normandy beaches was 21 Pz.

Rommel had already protested repeatedly to Hitler against the policy of holding the bulk of the armor at least fifty, in some cases 150 miles behind the coast. When the Allies landed, it was evident to every senior German commander that their air power would create immense difficulties for German reinforcements seeking to move forward. The Das Reich Division at Montauban, like 9 Pz further east on the Rhône, was some 450 miles from the north coast.

But whatever the difficulties in the forward areas, it seemed reasonable to expect that it would be possible to move an armored division from southern France at least as far north as the Loire before encountering serious enemy interference. Even the British, with their huge program of transport bombing, assumed that the Das Reich would be available for a German counter-thrust against the beach-head within a few days of 5 June: "2nd SS Panzer Division will. . . . be concentrating in a forward area by D+3," argued a British Intelligence assessment of German armored capability, drawn up three weeks before Overlord. The Allies expected, and indeed greatly feared, that the 2nd SS and its 209 tanks and assault guns—one-tenth of the entire German armored strength in the West—would be playing a prominent role in the Normandy battle by 9 or 10 June. Most of the officers of the Das Reich Division were of the same opinion.

In this fifth year of the war, Hitler deceived himself when he spoke of the Das Reich as "an old division." The ranks of the units training around Montauban were overwhelmingly filled by conscripts of a kind the "old" SS of 1939 would never have glanced at. A veteran NCO laughed scornfully when Sadi Schneid, a young Alsatian recruit who joined them at Bordeaux in February, complained of toothache and appeared on his first parade with his front tooth missing, after a visit to the dentist. The old Waffen SS, the legion of pre-war National Socialist supermen, rejected every recruit with the slightest physical imperfection, even a single dental filling.

Schneid himself was a boy of seventeen whose mother, a fervent Nazi, had caused his father to be sent to an internment camp by denouncing him as a former Alsatian autonomist. His elder brother had already joined the SS as an alternative to ten years' forced labor for black marketeering. It is a measure of the confusion of Alsatian loyalties that one of his younger brothers later joined the French Resistance, and one of his sisters broke off her engagement to a German tank officer because of his ardent Nazi sympathies. An officer of the Das Reich wrote later: "It was a terrible mistake to send men from Alsace to fight in the West when they had such strong links with France.... The effects were not only military. There was a rapid increase in crime requiring severe punishment." From the moment that they arrived in Bordeaux, the young Alsatians were incited by local French people to desert. On his second day in camp Schneid was offered an escape route to the *maquis* (guerilla Resistance forces) by a French girl dental assistant. He did not take it, but, to the fierce bewilderment of SS officers who had never encountered such a problem before, others did.

Even the German soldiers lacked the passionate fervor of four years earlier. A Panzergrenadier officer named Major* Otto Weidinger wrote:

> With the increasing bombing attacks on German towns, and the heavy civilian losses, the morale of troops is badly affected. Every day, soldiers receive news of the destruction of their homes, the tragic death of wives and children. They return from leave depressed. The pressure is increased by the treacherous campaign waged by the *maquis*, which is not fought according to the Hague Convention, and which makes every man a target at any time. Every soldier lost through these mean and unsoldierly methods increases the unit's bitterness. The years of fighting bolshevism in Russia have also affected the men's nerves.

Yet despite the diminished quality of recruits and major shortages of fuel, transport and equipment that hampered training through the spring of 1944, the Das Reich was still a formidable fighting force. Whatever the ghastly record of the SS and of Hitler's Germany, nothing can diminish their military achievements. Unit for unit—above all in the last years, 1943–5—the German army proved itself the greatest fighting force of World War II. Neither the British nor the American nor even the Russian Army could have matched its performance

---

* Throughout the text, I have omitted the unwieldy SS ranks, i.e., Major-Sturmbannführer, except on rare occasions when they seem necessary to make a point. Ranks given are those held in June 1944.

outnumbered, starved of fuel and supplies, faced by overwhelming air power. Even in 1944–5, diluted by the *Volksdeutsche* recruits, the SS divisions performed miracles. "The military significance of the Waffen SS is to be found not so much in its accomplishments during the years of German victory, as in its victories during the years of German defeat," the most objective post-war historian of the SS has written. Germany's methods of manning her armies in 1944–5 were little worse than those by which the Roman Empire filled its legions. According to veterans, among the officers and NCOs of the Das Reich at Montauban in May 1944 10 or even 20 per cent were obviously inadequate to their task. But so were an equal or greater proportion of junior leaders in most Allied units. The overwhelming majority of the Das Reich's regimental officers and NCOs were experienced, battle-hardened veterans who would fight to the end.

To understand the officers of the SS, and some of the things that were done by the Das Reich Division in June 1944, it is essential to realize what Hitler's Germany had given them. Almost all were of lower middle-class or working-class origins, men whom the old German Army would never have considered commissioning. Fritz Langangke, a tank lieutenant, was a miner's son. Major Gunther-Eberhardt Wisliceny, commanding the Deutschland Panzergrenadier regiment, looked the image of a tall, stiff Prussian *Junker*. Yet in reality he had served for three years as a miner in Upper Silesia before joining the army. His family had lost everything in 1918, when his grandfather's estates near Posen (Poznan) became part of Poland. Major Weidinger's father was a post office worker. He himself was rejected by both the army and the police before being accepted by the SS. This tough, impressionable young man embraced his new life passionately, above all the emphasis on athletics. When he was commissioned, he and his fellow-officers loved the gentlemanly rituals of the mess, to which men of their class could never have aspired in the Wehrmacht. Weidinger met his wife Annelise, a pharmacist's daughter, at a regimental drag hunt ball in November 1938. He would end the war with a brigade command at the age of thirty—scarcely an officer in the Das Reich Division was over thirty-two years old in 1944. Major Heinrich Wulf, commanding the reconnaissance battalion, was the thirty-year-old son of a North German worker who died as a conscript in Flanders in 1917. His mother became a waitress in a cavalry mess at Lüneburg. He himself left school at sixteen, was rejected by the army, and became a clerk. In 1934 he joined the SS—as a ranker, like every recruit—and was commissioned four years later.

Those pre-war years had been a glorious time for all of them: the comradeship, the discipline and supreme shared physical fitness of the training camps; officer school and the affectations of the mess with full-dress uniform and the adulation of so many girls. Then came the triumphal sweep into Poland, the exhilaration of discovering that they could crush the best that the enemy could send against them. Wulf was on his honeymoon when he heard that the attack on France was to begin: he raced to his unit still in full-dress uniform with his ceremonial dagger at his hip, terrified that he might miss the battle. After France, Wulf remained an instructor at the famous SS officer school at Bad Tolz in Bavaria until July 1943, because of his wife's persistence in producing daughters. As the only male in his family, SS rules decreed that he could not return to the front until he had a son. In October 1943, this duty accomplished, he took command of the Das Reich reconnaissance battalion in Russia.

It remains a common delusion among the people of Britain and America that World War II was fought in conditions far less terrible than those of World War I, and indeed from their own point of view this is perfectly true. But the huge, primeval struggle waged for four years between the German and Russian armies exceeded in scale and horror the worst of the 1914–18 battles for France. New standards of brutality in warfare were achieved by both sides. To understand how the officers of the Das Reich Division behaved in June 1944, it is essential to remember what they had spent three years learning in Russia. Each man who emerged from that campaign to fight again in the West counted his survival a miracle of odds.

The conditions of war in the East defied description. In winter weapons, vehicle bearings, engines, horses and men were relentlessly destroyed by the cold. Soldiers trudged through the snow with their boots wrapped in straw, their bodies lined with straw and newspapers beneath their greatcoats, their faces almost invisible lest some chink in their armor allow frostbite to attack. The cold, the lice, malaria, frostbite, fever, hunger and partisan attack all took their toll of health and morale. Fritz Langangke once stood shivering beside a railway siding as a Panzer unit's train drew up and a contingent of young tankers jumped down, fresh from France: "They laughed at our rags. We shouted to them to cover their noses, their ears. They just joked and laughed and chattered. Then the tips of their noses and ears began to turn white before our eyes. . . ."

They abandoned shaving for weeks on end to protect their skin, forgot mail from home, for it never came, grew accustomed to seeing their own ranks shattered in battle, rebuilt and shattered once again until their old units were unrecognizable. Casualties provoked meteoric promotions to fill the gaps. Heinrich Wulf found himself commanding a battalion reduced to a tenth of its establishment, yet when he himself left Russia, only one in ten of those men was left. "Our only concern was not to be captured," he said. The two armies rivaled each other in ruthlessness. One night Wulf's young ordnance officer, Hubseh, was captured by a Russian patrol. At dawn, as the light revealed the Russian lines two hundred yards away, they saw the German lashed to a haystack. A few moments later, a Russian loudhailer broadcast simple terms: surrender within ten minutes, or watch the haystack fired. The haystack was fired. Karl Kreutz—by June 1944 the Das Reich's artillery commander—remembered the discovery of an ambulance column, with forty German wounded systematically butchered by the Russians with their doctor. The order came down from division to take no prisoners for eight days. Was the order obeyed? "Of course."

There was no peace in darkness, for the Russians were masters of night-fighting. After the first months of the 1941 campaign, when herds of bewildered, untrained Russian soldiers were driven by their leaders on to the German guns, Stalin's commanders learned quickly. Every German who fought in the East returned with a profound respect for his enemy. There was no German tank to match the Russian T-34. By 1943, the Germans were awed by the huge artillery barrages laid down before the Russian attacks. Red infantry, sometimes stupefied with alcohol and driven on by their commissars at gunpoint, pressed home their assaults with the fury of despair.

Nor were the Russians always ignorant slaves. Fritz Langangke remembered a night in a hut, huddled over a little "Hindenburg light" stove, when two Russian girls who spoke German talked to them for hours about the war: "They were so intelligent, they said with such certainty that we lacked the fervour to match theirs. . . . That night I almost became a bolshevik," said Langangke wryly. He was a man of unusual imagination and sensitivity for an SS officer. But another Das Reich tank man, Otto Pohl, was also deeply impressed by a badly wounded Russian sergeant whom they blew out of his bunker with grenades: "We asked him his unit number. He replied simply: 'An NCO of the Russian Army does not give information.'"

It was the iron toughness of the Russians that they admired, and later compared so favorably with the qualities of the Americans. Some Russians were fighting just as doggedly beside the Germans, against their fellow-countrymen. Every German unit had its contingent of "Hi-Wis"—Russian prisoners or renegades who served as batmen, stretcher bearers, ammunition carriers and scouts. Hi-Wi patrols would slip out of the German lines every night, returning at dawn with often vital intelligence, until the inevitable morning when they failed to come back. They were utterly expendable, easily and casually replaced.

Through those years in Russia, few German fighting soldiers expected to come home. There was a catchphrase among them about "Living like God in France." The West came to seem almost a dream world. To the men of the Das Reich who emerged from the East in 1944, the rich fields and vineyards of south-west France brought them back to the glorious, happy memories of 1940. Yet they found that much had changed. Those who served there in 1940–1 had found most of the French people astonishingly relaxed and friendly. They now discovered that in public civilians addressed them coldly, or not at all. There was less to eat. The terrorist threat meant that it was impossible for vehicles or men to travel alone outside city centers. Even in Toulouse, the officers' messes and the *Soldatenheim* (Soldiers' Quarters) were faced with wire mesh against grenade attack.

Almost all of them took it for granted that within a matter of months they would be committed to battle against an Allied invasion, probably in the north. Over wine in the cafés, the officers reminisced endlessly about Russia, and speculated about the British and Americans whom they had never seen. "We thought of the Americans as children," said one of them. An officer who had been in North Africa with the Wehrmacht described how the British would sometimes surrender simply because they had run out of petrol. "But we knew that their air forces would be a terrible problem. We were not frightened of their men, but of their materiel. . . ."

Ever since the first winter in Russia, 1941, when the German Army suffered privations of Crimean proportions because of supply failures and military misjudgments in Berlin, many even among the SS had been puzzled by the High Command's omissions and failures. By 1944 some, like Wisliceny, had long since abandoned hope of winning the war militarily, but still hoped for some political settlement at tolerable cost. Others, like the twenty-four-year-old veteran Otto Pohl, not only loved their tanks and their division, but cherished ambitions to reach high command, and never thought of defeat. "Until the very end in 1945, I was sure that it would be all right for us," he said. Pohl was a son of one of the old German elite who had transferred his allegiance very early to the new aristocracy. His father had been an officer in the Kaiser's navy who joined Hitler in the 1920s, and was now an SS general. Young Pohl was educated at one of the special Young Socialist cadet schools, volunteered for Russia in 1941, and somehow survived there for three years. Some officers, like Otto Weidinger, had been troubled about the logic of invading Russia, but not Pohl: "A soldier never asks himself whether an operation is a good idea. Fighting is his business." When they asked themselves why they were sent the wrong type of ammunition, why there were desperate fuel shortages, why they were sometimes compelled to suffer terrible losses to no purpose, scarcely a man in the division considered fixing the blame on Adolf Hitler. Some said that the Fuhrer simply did not know of these things. Others, that he was badly advised by those around him, above all by Bormann and Ribbentrop.

But it is essential to perceive that, in many respects, these young soldiers of the SS—and the divisional commander was their only officer older than thirty-two—had much in common with the men of other armies. The SS newspaper prided itself on the freedom with which it criticized the failings of the organization. Officers and men shared a far closer relationship than those of the British Army. They inflicted their arrogance upon the outside world, not upon each other. Among junior officers, there was a hoary joke whenever some supreme organizational disaster was inflicted upon them: "... *Wenn der Fuhrer wusste!"*—"... If only the Führer knew!" When they sang, it was seldom the *Horst Wessel* song, more often a number like *Waldeslust*:

> I don't know my father,
> I'm not loved by my mother,
> But I don't want to die so young. . . .

In the privacy of their billets, most of them enjoyed a reasonably civil relationship with the French civilians who were obliged to house them. A Frenchwoman who provided quarters for six men of the Das Reich in Montauban in 1944 described how one of them with punctilious correctness brought her a 1,000 franc note that he had found in his room. It was a matter of pride within the SS that no man was permitted to lock up his possessions in barracks, although some of them stole petrol from the unit stocks to get to the brothels in Toulouse. The SS officers were elaborately, Germanically courteous to the wives and daughters of their enforced hosts. They considered themselves, indeed, to be the very pattern of chivalry. An officer of the Das Reich cited to the author an example of his division's gentlemanly code: in Russia, a colleague was found to have committed some aberration with a Russian woman, and was at once ordered to go to his quarters and shoot himself. He did so.

Yet these young men, so careful in their private courtesies and honesty, were also profoundly flawed. It is unnecessary to review in detail the principles of National Socialism, the anti-semitism, the uncritical devotion to Hitler—it can be taken for granted that almost every officer of the Das Reich shared all these, not least from practical gratitude for what Hitler's Germany had done for his career. The only acceptable salute in an SS unit was "*Heil Hitler.*" Otto Pohl readily forgave his father-in-law and two brothers-in-law dead in Russia, Karl Kreutz his home in Berlin destroyed by bombing and his family refugees in Silesia, Ernst Krag his six wounds, and the half of his class comrades at officer school already dead.

The aspect of their conditioning that is most relevant to this story is the extraordinary respect with which they had been imbued for the virtues of strength, of ruthless dedication to the task in hand, and the equally extraordinary indifference to the claims of the weak and the innocent. All their virtues were reserved for others within their closed society. They possessed neither charity nor mercy for any who were not deemed to have deserved it by their own code. It is striking that when the survivors of the British First Airborne Division at Arnhem found themselves in the hands of the SS, they expected to be shot. Instead, they were treated with the respect due to heroes. According to the SS code of chivalry, these were fellow-knights worthy of their highest honor. Yet as we shall see below, those whom the SS did not deem worthy of its respect—above all, enemy civilians—were treated with unflinching ruthlessness. The young leaders of the SS had been educated and trained to believe that only one principle mattered—the interests of Germany as they themselves and their commanders saw fit to interpret them. They did not spurn morality or justice or process of law—these were simply forgotten or unknown concepts to them. If the *Einsatzgruppen*—the SS extermination squads—or the concentration camps ever passed through their consciousness, they never allowed these mildly distasteful matters to linger. They were part of the natural machinery of the state, and no concern of theirs.

The greatest fear of an SS officer was that he might be considered guilty of weakness or cowardice. He could never be wrong if he adopted or accepted the most drastic solution to a problem. From the first appearance of the Waffen SS in the war, it had been made apparent that superior officers would always pardon an excess of zeal in the right direction. In September 1939, a member of an SS artillery regiment in Poland herded fifty Jews into a synagogue and shot them. The prosecuting officer at his court martial appealed for the death sentence, and the man was indeed sentenced to a term of imprisonment. But then Berlin intervened. An appeal hearing was held, at which the presiding judge said that the accused ". . . was in a state of irritation as a result of the many atrocities committed by Poles against ethnic Germans. As an SS man, he was also particularly sensitive to the sight of Jews and the hostile attitude of Jewry to Germans; and thus acted quite unpremeditatedly in a spirit of youthful enthusiasm." The sentence was quashed. The SS never looked back. Throughout the next four years of conquest and struggle, above all on the Eastern Front, the Waffen SS shot whomsoever they wished, whenever they wished. Within two weeks of the invasion of Russia, the SS Wiking Division had killed 600 Galician Jews "as a reprisal for Soviet cruelties." The Leibstandarte Division found six of its men brutally killed by Russian troops, and shot every prisoner for three days, a total of about 4,000 men. In September 1941, a support unit of the Das Reich assisted an SS extermination squad to kill 920 Jews near Minsk. Mass killing in pursuit of state policy never became the professional business of the Waffen SS—the *Einsatzgruppen* looked after all that sort of thing. But there can have been few experienced officers and men in the Waffen SS by June 1944 who did not regard it as a perfectly legitimate exercise to carry out mass reprisals and wholesale killings if the situation seemed to justify them.

The qualities that the SS most signally failed to foster were intelligence and imagination, probably because these characteristics would have rendered their possessors unfit for service in its ranks. Throughout its history, the Waffen SS produced an extraordinary corps of soldiers and regimental officers, but failed to throw up a single outstanding higher commander. At divisional level and above, the Waffen SS was lamentably directed. Only Paul Hausser, the venerated Panzer commander who once led the *Verfügungstruppen* from whom the Das Reich derived, has any claim to military brilliance, and he was a product of the old German Army. The SS fought and died bravely, often fanatically. They can expect no higher epitaph.

General Heinz Bernard Lammerding, commanding officer of the Das Reich Division in June 1944, was a typical product of the new Nazi aristocracy. He was born in Dortmund, qualified as an engineer, and became an early convert to National Socialism. He took a job as director of an SA engineering school, and worked in various capacities for the organization until 1935. He then became SS member no. 247062. He was a Waffen SS engineer captain at the outbreak of war, served on the staff of the *Verfügungstruppen* division from November 1940 to August 1942, then took command of an infantry regiment. After a brief period on an armored corps staff, in July 1943 he became chief of staff to General von der Bach-Zelewski. This officer was directing with legendary ruthlessness anti-partisan operations in the rear of the German armies in Russia. Lammerding's signature appeared on several appalling documents, ordering the wholesale destruction of entire villages and towns which were judged guilty of assisting partisans. At the end of 1943, Lammerding took command of troops of the Das

Reich Division operating against partisans in its rear areas, and on 25 January 1944, of the division itself. On 22 May 1944, while the division was at Montauban, it was announced with suitable celebration that Lammerding had been awarded the Knight's Cross for his work in Russia. He was still only thirty-eight.

Few of the surviving officers of the Das Reich Division have much to say in favor of Lammerding as a commander. He lacked personal presence, and possessed none of the obvious gifts of a leader of men. He was a curiously colorless, forceless figure, whose greatest merits were administrative competence and friendship with Heinrich Himmler. It was rumored in some Das Reich officers' messes that it was this personal alliance which had secured him command of the division. Himmler paid them a personal visit in the spring of 1944: "It was obvious that Lammerding and Himmler got on well, although I couldn't say whether this affected Lammerding's career," said his senior staff officer, Major Albert Stuckler. "After all, Lammerding had been a good engineer." But the impression emerges of Lammerding from all the accounts of June 1944 of a man overpromoted and quite unsuited to a fighting command, who would have been much more at ease on Himmler's staff.

In May 1944 Fritz Langangke was suddenly ordered to carry out a major rail reconnaissance for his tank regiment: "I had always wanted to have a railway since I was a little boy, and suddenly I was given one. I was provided with a special train with a saloon car and a carriage full of Russian soldiers as escort, and ordered to check every possible rail route for the division to the front." For two idyllic weeks, he coasted comfortably around southern France, measuring tunnel heights, checking bridge capacities and road connections. The train was commanded by a major who had been a pre-war wine merchant, and used the trip to shuttle hundreds of cases of black market wine hither and thither about his domains: "These fellows, they had already forgotten about the war. For me, coming from Russia, it was a revelation. For the first time I thought—'Oh yes, this is going to go. . . . We can lose. . . .' "

Langangke found most of the French railway officials almost unctuously friendly and hospitable, complaining bitterly about the damage being done to the nation's transport system by Allied bombing, which was indeed provoking passionate hostility to the Allies in many great cities of France. But in the house where he was billeted with an elderly aristocratic lady, her nephew sometimes called to talk. One evening this man said to Langangke: "You poor devils made a big mistake when you joined the Waffen SS, you're going to be the first to catch it when the time comes." The man offered to smuggle him to Algeria. Langangke said: "What would you do in my place?" The Frenchman remained silent. Langangke never saw him again.

The Das Reich's training program was lamentably behind schedule, yet all that spring it was continually interrupted in order that units could take part in sweeps and punitive operations against the French Resistance. Week by week, around the huge area in which the division was encamped in its fifty barracks and lagers, the campaign of sniping, roadblocking and sabotage intensified. For a vast fighting machine such as an armored division, the terrorists represented no substantial threat. But they obliged every unit to put its quarters under guard, every man to carry a weapon at all times, every ration truck to travel with an escort. Otto Pohl became so exasperated by the need to keep a four-man picket on the house in which he was billeted that he moved into quarters in the center of Caussade with his men. Sadi Schneid's anti-tank platoon found themselves the subject of a furious unit investigation one morning when it was learned that a stock of mines had been stolen from their store. Even Karl Kreutz's gunners were periodically diverted from training to sweep stretches of the countryside where there were reports of arms being parachuted to *maquisards*. Sometimes they found odd containers in the woods or fields, but more often than not the operation was in vain.

In the month of May 1944, according to Albert Stuckler, the division lost some twenty men and a hundred vehicles to terrorists. A soldier was shot with his wife who was visiting him in their hotel room in a village near Caussade. An NCO coming out of a cafe in Figeac was killed by a burst of Sten gun fire. Any vehicle travelling alone was liable to ambush.

In those last weeks before D-Day, the 2nd SS Panzer Division made the price of resistance very clear to the surrounding countryside. Reprisals were on a scale modest enough compared with those of Russia, but they seemed savage enough at the time. On 2 May, one of the tank battalions was training near the small town of Montpezat-de-Quercy when an SS patrol was fired upon a mile to the south-west. The SS swept through Montpezat, setting fire to several houses, looting extensively and assaulting several civilians who seemed slow to acquiesce. On 11 May men of the Der Führer Panzergrenadiers conducted a series of sweeps in the Lot. Twenty-four people, including four women, were seized for deportation in St. Céré, forty from Bagnac. In Cardaillac, two women were shot, of whom one died. In Lauze, fifty-year-old Mme. Moncoutre and her twenty-year-old daughter Berthe were shot among their sheep. Orniac was comprehensively looted. On 1 June, a tank unit moving north of Caylus machine-gunned six civilians in Limonge, one at Cadrieu and two at Frontenac. On 2 June, after a *maquis* attack in the countryside, twenty-nine farms were burned, along with the entire village of Terrou, whose 290 inhabitants became refugees. On 3 June, after an SS truck was attacked near Figeac, two men of seventy-two and seventy-four were shot on the spot, and six men and a woman from nearby Viazac were taken out and shot. The most massive action by the Das Reich before D-Day was a raid on Figeac, in which the Germans discovered a Resistance arms dump including sixty-four rifles, three Bren guns, thirty-one Stens and a bazooka. The town paid a terrible price: more than a thousand people were arrested and deported to Germany. Forty-one were killed.

Yet for all the thoroughness with which the Das Reich approached these operations when ordered to carry them out, they were a matter of exasperation to the divisional staff, anxious about its training program. Several protests were made to 58 Corps and Army Group G about this use of *Frontsoldaten* against communist bandits. "We were completely unsuited in character and mentality to this sort of warfare," said Major Stuckler. "There were specially trained units for this type of work." Training was also being hampered by the chronic shortage of fuel. Although they exercised intensively at company and battalion level, they lacked opportunity to maneuver as a division. Communication and liaison between units was poor. Many of the raw recruits who had joined them in February and March were scarcely past basic training. They were still acutely short of transport—above all trucks for the infantry units and tractors for the towed artillery. Deliveries of tanks were proceeding slowly. On 16 May, they had received thirty-seven Panzer Vs and fifty-five Panzer IVs toward their new reduced

establishment of sixty-two of each. But they possessed a full complement of thirty of the superb *Sturmgeschutzen*—assault guns that were
in effect turretless tanks, with a low silhouette that made them very
difficult targets for enemy fire. The two *Panzergrenadier* regiments—
each in British parlance a brigade—were at full strength, but under-
trained. Major Weidinger, casting a critical eye upon his men, believed
that they were capable of fighting a limited battle. His fear was that in a
prolonged action, under continuous strain for a period of weeks, their
inexperience and lack of training would tell against them.

Then Heinz Guderian, the godfather of all German armored forces,
arrived on an inspection tour. For three days he watched their exercises,
above all the night movements which they knew would be critical
against Allied air power, the "walking forest" heavily camouflaged
advances of the tank units who had been warned that there would be
none of the great sweeps across open plains that had been possible in
Russia. Guderian pronounced himself reasonably satisfied. On his last
evening, the officers arranged a dinner for him in their mess at a nearby
chateau. Silver candles and linen tablecloths were found, the black
market was swept for food, and that night a circle of dress-uniformed
young tankmen and gunners sat down to dinner with the general at the
head of the table. He was at his most affable and talkative. He told one
of his favorite stories:

> How long have infantry existed? Four thousand years! And in all
> that time, no one has been able to invent a useful pair of infantry
> boots. They are always too long or too short. How long have cavalry
> existed? More than four thousand years! And in all that time, they
> have never been able to invent a useful lance—they are always too
> long or too short! How long has artillery existed? Five hundred
> years. I suggested to our designers a revolutionary measure. They
> answered: "My dear Oberst Guderian, you may be a very good
> tankman, but you know nothing about artillery. Artillery has been
> pointing backwards for five hundred years! Now you say you want
> a gun that will go into action pointing forward!"

The officers of the *Sturmgeschutzabteilung* (battalion) laughed with the
rest at his version of the development of their self-propelled guns.

With the benefit of hindsight, the success of the Allied landings in Normandy, against indifferent and poorly directed German resistance, seems inevitable. It did not seem so to either side at the time. Even a skeptic such as Fritz Langangke said: "It did not seem impossible that we could defeat the invasion. We did not then realize that not all Germany was fighting as we were." It has sometimes been suggested that the Das Reich in June 1944 was so weakened by its large intake of recruits of doubtful enthusiasm that it could have played no important role in Normandy, even had it arrived much earlier on the battlefield. In reality, its deficiencies of training and equipment were no worse than those of most other Panzer divisions in France at that period. It was better equipped with tanks and assault guns than most of its counterparts. Lammerding reported to Army Group G that 2nd SS Panzer was "conditionally ready for battle."

Sadi Schneid, the young Alsatian recruit who wrote a fascinating personal memoir after the war for SS veterans' consumption, testifies that many of the Aslatians were indeed lukewarm in their enthusiasm for the war, but intensive training and the fierce spirit of the SS had imbued an astonishingly high proportion with a determination to do whatever was expected of them. He described an evening in their barracks, when his company of the reconnaissance battalion returned from an anti-terrorist sweep. Their senior NCO, Hauptscharführer "Hascha" Kurz, a formidable veteran of the Eastern Front, was relieved and delighted that not one of his motley crew of *Volksdeutsche*, former prisoners of war and green Alsatians had attempted to desert while they had the chance to do so, in open country. He made a speech to them:

> "Boys, if the Americans land one day, they won't be throwing potatoes, and I'm going to need all of you. That's why I keep emphasizing to you that I don't need dead heroes but live ones. Remember everything I've taught you in training. A fraction of a second's carelessness at the front, and it'll do for you. Once again, I urge you—trust me. If you do what I do, you've got a chance of coming out of it. Always obey my finger and my eye, and you'll thank yourselves later. I'll guarantee to do everything I can to keep your skins in one piece. Can I count on you?"

"JAWOHL, HAUPTSCHARFUHRER!" we shouted in chorus, from the bottom of our hearts. "SIEG HEIL! SIEG HEIL! SIEG HEIL!"

One might have imagined us at Munich, after an oration from Hitler himself.

CHAPTER 2

SOE: Baker Street

FOR THE MEN AND WOMEN of the French Resistance, D-Day was the decisive moment of the war. After years in which their potential power and enthusiasm had been doubted and disputed in London and Washington, now they were to be put to the test. Resistance did not wage a continuous four-year guerilla struggle against the Germans. Only late in 1941 and early in 1942 did a small number of French people begin to stir from the terrible lethargy and trauma of defeat. Clandestine opposition newspapers were printed. There were cautious meetings of handfuls of like-minded enemies of Vichy. Very many of these courageous pioneers were caught and shot, but others followed. The early handfuls began to grow into a hundred, a thousand independent Resistance groups and escape lines. Each began to develop its own links with one of many interested organizations in London—the British-run French Section of SOE, MI6, MI9, De Gaulle's BCRA and later the American OSS. These links, often forged by the chance of a brief encounter or an exchange of names, determined whether a circuit spent the remainder of the war gathering information, assisting escaping prisoners or preparing for open battle against the Germans. Despite the brief effective existence of a National Council for Resistance under the brilliant Jean Moulin in 1943, after his capture the quest for unity flagged, and in the interests of security this was probably fortunate. Until the end, Resistance remained a patchwork of overlapping and often mutually hostile independent networks. The British and French officers parachuted to provide arms and liaison with London could seldom do more than paper over the cracks of local rivalries, and try to steer the movement toward a broad common policy.

This policy was, quite simply, to direct every effort toward creating a clandestine army to rise on D-Day and cause the maximum difficulty for the Germans behind their lines. In 1942 and early 1943 the *Armée Secrète*—the AS as it was referred to—was composed of Frenchmen continuing their ordinary lives—*les légaux*—who had agreed that when the signal was given they would drop their cover and take up arms. The seizure of Unoccupied France by the Germans in November 1942 gave the AS an important boost. Many officers and men who had served with Pétain's Armistice Army, now disbanded, became *résistants* (members of the Resistance). Some, chiefly in the south, were able to bring arms with them. Then the German introduction of deportation for forced labor—the detested *Service de Travail Obligatoire*—gave Resistance a vast pool of recruits to which it could never otherwise have aspired. Hundreds of thousands of young men who would never have contemplated taking up arms against the Germans now found themselves compelled to do so. The only alternative to the STO was escape into the countryside, either to become a refugee in a remote community or to join a *maquis*. By the end of the war, the Germans had successfully carried away 17 percent of the youth of France to the factories of the Reich. But they paid for this by inflating Resistance in a matter of months from a slight faction into a mass movement of young men, with millions of their worker and peasant parents bitterly alienated from Vichy and the Occupiers.

The general instruction to all the men of the AS and those *maquis* under the influence of De Gaulle or of British officers—around two-thirds of all *résistants*—was that they should fight the Germans only when they were compelled to do so. There was a limited program of sabotage of vital industrial targets. But between 1942 and June 1944 most Resistance groups fought gun battles only when themselves attacked, or when a minor action seemed essential to maintain morale and stave off boredom.

The remaining one-third of *résistants*, the communists of the *Francs-Tireurs et Partisans* who scorned De Gaulle or any authority other than their own, pursued an entirely different policy. They were committed to an internal liberation of France by her own people—and of course to their own political glory in the process. From late 1942 onwards, they sought to damage the Germans wherever and whenever they could be attacked, at whatever cost in reprisals, and whatever the strategic futility of their actions. They captured or stole arms from Vichy, the Germans and noncommunist Resistance groups with equal energy. The attacks on the Das Reich Division's area around Montauban in the spring of 1944 were almost entirely the work of FTP groups. They despised the *Armée Secrète*'s policy of *attentisme, immobilisme* (wait and see). "The French know that a citadel is never so readily taken as from within," wrote their leader, Charles Tillon, "and that none has ever successfully resisted attack from without and within. This is why they are so astonished to be so poorly encouraged and assisted to play a decisive role. . . ."

Many FTP *maquis* achieved a terrible reputation in their regions as little better than bandits, murdering alleged collaborators with a ruthlessness that earned as much enmity from respectable Frenchmen as the reprisals of the Das Reich and the Gestapo. But there were also many non-communists who admired the energy with which the FTP inflicted violence on the Germans. "If there is no violence, how is France to know that there is a Resistance?" ran their argument. It possessed considerable force. The momentum that Resistance had attained by June 1944 owed more than its survivors may care to accept to the actions of the FTP—and to the hatred of the Germans which reprisals had inspired among workers and peasants who would otherwise have remained indifferent neutrals.

But London's policy was still single-mindedly directed toward D-Day. The success of Resistance, in the eyes of the Allied governments and the chiefs of staff, would be determined by the scale of difficulty that it then caused to the Germans—above all, the delay it could impose on the movement to Normandy of reinforcements. Among these, outside northern France the 2nd SS Panzer Division was the most formidable formation.

For the French Section of Special Operations Executive 6 June was the beginning of the end of four years of extraordinary labor. There was a rush to dispatch the last batch of agents to the field. A quarter of all the arms parachuted into France since 1941 were dropped in the single month of May 1944. For months, an acrimonious struggle for control of SOE operations in France had been approaching a crisis. It had been agreed that the Free French, in the person of General Koenig, should take command of French Section from the British once the Allies had landed. But to their bitter resentment neither Koenig nor De Gaulle himself was to be allowed more than a few hours' notice of the invasion. The private view at the top of SOE was that the vital work of French Section would be finished after D-Day. Once Resistance became an open rather than a secret army the alleged insecurity of the Free French could do no harm. Within "F," however, there was persistent bitterness about the new command structure. Vera Atkins flatly refused to leave Baker Street for the move to Koenig's headquarters in Bryanston Square, and indeed she never did so. This last unseemly wrangle somehow sullied their four years of passionate, dedicated struggle toward the great moment of the Allied return to France.

They held no celebration in the austere rooms at Norgeby House in Baker Street. They were too busy. Signals traffic and demands for supplies continued to pour into the office. In any event, throughout the war they had neither celebrated their secret triumphs, nor wept for their secret tragedies: "There was no place for emotional scenes. It would have seemed to cheapen what we were doing," said one of them. For four years they had worked to build an underground circulation system in France, to provide the lifeblood of arms, explosives and communications for the Resistance. Now, the body was coming to life. From D-Day onwards, French Section could do little to steer the battle—it could only report and support it.

Special Operations Executive had been created in the depths of Britain's strategic impotence in 1940 "to set Europe ablaze," in Churchill's memorable phrase. Ironically enough, it was that man of peace Neville Chamberlain who was responsible for drawing up its original charter for ". . . a new organization. . . . to co-ordinate all action by way of subversion and sabotage, against the enemy overseas." To understand SOE, and to judge what the French Resistance did and did not achieve in 1944, it is essential to remember that throughout its history the organization was dogged by controversy and skepticism in London. The Chiefs of Staff disliked and distrusted it. Beyond their instinctive distaste for irregular warfare, they considered it—like all "private armies"—a drain of resources from the main battlefields, above all a waste of precious aircraft. In 1942–3, much of the materiel parachuted to Resistance movements in Europe was from captured Italian stocks, simply because these were all that the War Office would release. Sten guns were unsuitable for guerilla operations in open country, because they were short-range weapons wasteful of ammunition in unskilled hands. But they were dropped into France in vast numbers because they were cheap and plentiful.

In February 1941, the Chief of Air Staff, Sir Charles Portal, one of the principal architects of area bombing, attempted to insist that one of the first SOE parties sent into France should be dropped in uniform: "I think that the dropping of men dressed in civilian clothes for the purpose of attempting to kill members of the opposing forces is not an operation with which the Royal Air Force should be associated. . . ." Portal never lost his skepticism about SOE, even when he was confronted with such achievements as the halting of tank production at the Peugeot factory in 1943, one of the great sabotage coups of the war. "I am not at all clear," he wrote acidly on 27 February 1944, "how far the promises and claims of SOE have been fulfilled or substantiated. I have in mind as a typical instance the Peugeot factory at Montbeliard. There must be many others. I believe SOE claims to have put this plant out of action by the sabotage of a single individual. . . . I should gravely doubt its being true."

MI6, the professional Secret Intelligence Service, had obvious cause to dislike its amateur rival because SOE's campaign to make conspicuous trouble for the Germans made the work of SIS agents, who were seeking to gather intelligence as unobtrusively as possible, substantially more difficult. There was also jealousy. All the evidence now available suggests that SIS achieved little through its agents in Occupied Europe in World War II, and certainly less than SOE. The prestige of SIS in 1945 stemmed almost entirely from the work of the Ultra decrypters at Bletchley Park, whom that skillful courtier Sir Stewart Menzies, head of SIS, had contrived to keep within his own empire. "C," as Menzies was known, together with his deputy Sir Claude Dansey, met the chiefs of SOE regularly throughout the war. But SIS was never better than a suspicious neutral in the Whitehall struggle for resources and support.

The fiercest battle of all, of course, was that fought by General De Gaulle, who claimed the right to control all agents and Resistance operations on French soil. To his bitter resentment, he was merely permitted to drop his own arms and agents through SOE's RF Section, created specifically to maintain control over Free French activities and communications. RF worked parallel to but with somewhat fewer resources than the British-run F Section. F's officers maintained regular contact with the Free French through meetings with "Colonel Passy," the austere young Captain André Dewavrin who commanded De Gaulle's *Bureau Central Renseignements et d'Action militaire* (Central Bureau for Intelligence and Action)—the BCRA—from Duke Street, behind Selfridge's department store. Although the British found little to like about Dewavrin, they respected his brains and did much informal business without friction. "But any time that Passy came to Baker Street in uniform, we knew that we were in for trouble," according to an SOE officer. When Passy spoke as the voice of De Gaulle, it was seldom without bitterness. It is a measure of the General's attitude that after the Liberation, on several occasions when he met a French Section officer in France he sought to have him immediately ejected from the country. It is a measure of British regular army feeling toward SOE that, after the war, General Sir Colin Gubbins—the Highland soldier who directed the organization with distinction from September 1943—found his career permanently blighted by his association with the "irregulars" and died a disappointed man.

But SOE also had powerful friends, above all the Prime Minister. Churchill seldom informed himself about the details of SOE operations in Europe, but his spirit was deeply moved by the ideal of Resistance. His support for Gubbins was strengthened by a number of meetings at Downing Street with British agents who had worked in France, above all Wing-Commander Yeo-Thomas of RF Section. When Lord Selborne became Minister of Economic Warfare in February 1942, with responsibility for SOE, he used his personal friendship with Churchill to some effect, especially in the struggle with Sir Arthur Harris and Bomber Command for supply-dropping aircraft. SOE's senior officers never felt much warmth for Major Desmond Morton, the former Secret Service officer who served as Churchill's personal aide and mediated when necessary between "C" and Gubbins. But one of the chiefs of SOE always believed that Morton made a decisive personal contribution in persuading Churchill that it was essential to support De Gaulle as the unchallenged leader of Free France. Had that decision not been taken, the course of events in France both before and after D-Day would have even more complex and possibly disastrous.

By June 1944, SOE had grown into an organization of almost 14,000 people, running a chain of agent schools in England and Scotland, dropping arms by sea and air almost nightly across Europe. Its formal title had also changed, to become SOE/SO. It was now officially a joint Anglo-American organization—the SO stood for Special Operations, an arm of General Donovan's Office of Strategic Services. An American officer had been placed alongside each of the senior British executives as part colleague, part understudy. To the American's chagrin, the British had largely excluded their men from an operational role in France until after D-Day. But they shared in the fierce debate about the role of Resistance that preceded the invasion, and which began with the establishment of a formal SOE/SO Planning Group on 30 August 1943.

Until the last weeks before the landings on 6 June, Yugoslavia was overwhelmingly the most important theatre of operations for SOE, where it was effectively sponsoring a full-scale war. More than twice as many weapons were being delivered to Yugoslavia as to France, chiefly because it was possible to land cargoes from the sea. But all over Europe, SOE's agents were becoming legends in the closed world of secret operations: Harry Rée, who organized the destruction of the Peugeot tank plant; Michael Lis, who pursued a charmed life through Hungary and Poland; Paddy Leigh-Fermor, who kidnapped the German general commanding in Crete; Alfgar Hesketh-Pritchard, who sent a last message from his doomed position in the mountains of Yugoslavia: "Give all my love to all at White's. This is no place for a gentleman. . . ."

Those with the best prospect of survival on SOE operations were the most ruthless and untrusting. But however strongly their instructors discouraged it, there was also a romantic, buccaneering streak about the organization that brought into its ranks many men and women who would never have become professional spies for SIS. Although reared as a regular gunner, General Gubbins himself had always been suspected of unorthodox tastes. He wrote an important pamphlet on guerilla warfare in the 1930s, and commanded the Independent Companies in

Norway in 1940, winning a DSO. But he incurred the lasting enmity of the Brigade of Guards in Scandinavia by sacking one of its battalion commanders on the battlefield. Animosity from some of the most senior soldiers in Whitehall dogged him for the rest of the war. "Gubbins had all the outward affectations of a regular Highland officer," said Selwyn Jepson, French Section's recruiting officer who later became his friend, "but underneath it all, there was great sensitivity."

After Yugoslavia, France was always Gubbins's overwhelming preoccupation, ". . . because the Allies were obviously going to have to land somewhere there in the end," in the words of Colonel Dick Barry, his chief of staff. From October 1941 until1945 the French Section of SOE was commanded by Colonel Maurice Buckmaster, with a staff of some thirty men and women in Baker Street, supported by hundreds of training instructors, signals and supply personnel at "the stations" all over England and Scotland. Like most of SOE, Buckmaster was not a professional soldier—indeed his only military experience had been gained as a cadet in the Eton Officers' Training Corps, on an Intelligence course in 1940, and as a liaison officer with the Free French on the Dakar expedition. Before the war, he had been a senior executive of Ford in France, and one of his staff said, not without respect, that "he brought the optimism of a sales director into Baker Street." His enthusiasm and energy made a great contribution to French Section's success, although the reverse of these qualities was a certain lack of skepticism: "He believed that all his geese were swans," according to a senior SOE officer. Buckmaster's deep respect and feeling for the agents whom he sent into France were shared by all his staff. They never achieved a battlefield commander's resigned detachment about losses. When mistakes were made, it was almost always because French Section had been too ready to believe that too much was being achieved in the field. Their greatest difficulty throughout the war was accurately to assess the achieve- ments and potential of networks in the field when there were no troops to inspect, no battlefields upon which to measure yards won or lost. Colonel Barry said: "One would hear that such-and-such a network was very efficient, but it was all hearsay. One never saw the bloody thing."

French Section has been the subject of some misunderstanding since the war. General Gubbins and the operational chief of the Western Europe department, Robin Brook, exercised rather more control of operations in France, and Colonel Buckmaster perhaps a little less, than has generally been recognized. F played the central role in sending officers to France to assess the capabilities of Resistance groups and to arrange arms deliveries to them. By June 1944 there were some forty French Section networks each operating with at least one British-trained agent. But throughout most of France, British officers did not control the Resistance or lead it into action. It was not their business to use a gun, except in self-defense. Their vital function was to act as a catalyst for Resistance, to make it possible for Frenchmen to translate their own will into action. They sought to teach, to encourage, and to convey the hopes and wishes of London. Most lacked the temperament or training to act as military commanders in the field, a function that former French regular soldiers undertook in most areas.

The operations of the Das Reich Division involved five of French Section's networks in southern and central France, and it will become apparent that in almost all their areas, as throughout the rest of France, the impetus for Resistance came from within. To the end, local commanders jealously guarded their right to command their own men. Some surrendered it latterly to De Gaulle's French nominees. Very occasionally, they accepted the direction of an Englishman of outstanding personal force, such as George Starr. But throughout the war, the most important function of the British staff in Baker Street was to search out, train and dispatch men and women of exceptional character, capable of moving others by sheer force of personality. In the early years of F Section, they were obliged to select agents who were capable of living a cover story, of acting as something close to the traditional image of the spy. By late 1943 and early 1944, as the para-military role of the Resistance developed, agents who could scarcely speak more than schoolboy French were being dispatched to the wilder rural regions. From beginning to end, the agents who failed were almost all those who lacked the inner strength, the lack of need to confide in others while themselves encouraging confidences, that was essential to their curious calling. Yet it is striking to notice that there was absolutely no common denominator between the men and women of SOE beyond their courage. There was no *genus* agent as there was a *genus* Guards officer, bomber pilot, even *résistant*. Each was entirely an individual, often whimsical and elusive.

Once these agents had gone to France, Baker Street could seldom give them useful tactical instructions about what to attack or where to go. The staff knew too little about conditions on the spot. Signals traffic was generally restricted to brief practical messages about the number of men an agent believed could be mobilized in a given area, and about rendezvous for the dropping of arms, explosives and money—the last always an essential lubricant in making local Resistance groups susceptible to reason. F Section knew a great deal about the conditions of life in France—ration cards, train times, German repressive measures—but very little about the detailed military situation. While SIS, through Ultra, was reading many German troop deployments and readiness states, virtually no military intelligence was passed on to French Section. Resistance was regarded as a strategic weapon. Baker Street was seldom brought into Allied planning debates, and Gubbins never achieved the place that he sought on the Chiefs of Staff Committee.

A perceptive SOE officer who served with distinction in France remarked that "there was no atmosphere of brilliance in Baker Street—just shrewd, sensible people working very hard indeed." Beyond Buckmaster, the most familiar figures were Gerry Morel, the Operations Officer—thought by some to be a trifle lightweight for his role; "BP"—Bourne-Paterson, a professional accountant who handled finance; Selwyn Jepson, a successful novelist who fulfilled the critical role of recruiting officer; and Vera Atkins, wryly pseudonymized by George Millar in his excellent book about his SOE experiences, *Maquis*, as "the intelligent gentlewoman." Coolly handsome, very tough, shrewd, quick, Miss Atkins (for she held no rank until she became a W AAF squadron-leader in August 1944 and seldom wore a uniform) was regarded by many people as the critical force in French Section. In Baker Street's years of almost chronic crisis, Vera was the woman never seen to lose her head.

Her father had been in the timber business. She was largely educated in France, and travelled widely in Europe before the war, learning to take shorthand in three languages. In 1940 she was living at home with her mother and working in Civil Defense when the superb British facility for word-of-mouth recruiting sought her out for French Section. She came to Baker Street as a secretary on a month's trial, and ended the war with an absolute grasp of every aspect of F's affairs. It was Vera who kept the signal log and card index that were almost the only written records. Much of the Section work seemed to be done at night, and again and again she, Buckmaster or Morel would find themselves catching two or three hours' sleep on a camp bed in the office before waking to read the latest signals brought by dispatch rider from the huge radio stations at Crendon and Poundon on the Oxfordshire-Buckinghamshire border. In a very English way, although they worked in conditions of such intimacy, they saw little of each other outside the office. Vera's mother was allowed to know nothing of the reasons for her endlessly absent lifestyle. One morning when she came home from Tempsford at breakfast time, Mrs. Atkins said with a sigh: "Well, I hope at the end of all this he makes an honest woman of you, dear." A Frenchman who was trained in England by F Section was among those who much admired Vera. He nerved himself to make a pass, but in the end could not go through with it—he was too frightened of her.

At the beginning of 1944, French Section faced a crisis: hundreds of thousands of Frenchmen were now believed to be ready to join an uprising when the Allies landed, but there were arms for only a tiny fraction of them. It required an average of twenty-five RAF bomber sorties to drop arms for 1,000 *résistants*. Each night, the RAF was dispatching enough bombers on a single raid to Germany to arm 30,000 *résistants*, but the Air Staff and Sir Arthur Harris resolutely refused to divert more than twenty-three Halifaxes to the needs of SOE throughout north-western Europe. The Chiefs of Staff showed little interest in the problem: they regarded General De Gaulle and the Resistance as a potential political liability, rather than an actual military asset. During the February moon period, against 1,500 tons of arms landed in Yugoslavia, France received only 700 tons. In desperation, the Free French and SOE for once made common cause in turning to the Prime Minister.

Churchill did not disappoint them. He had already been influenced by impressive pleas from leading Frenchmen, among them Emmanuel d'Astier de la Vigerie. At a meeting on 27 February attended by Selborne, Sinclair the Air Minister, and representatives of Gubbins and De Gaulle, Churchill over-rode the airmen, and decreed that supply-dropping to France should become the second priority of Bomber

Command, whenever aircraft could be spared from the Battle of Berlin. In the last quarter of 1943, the RAF had dropped 139 tons of arms into France. In the first quarter of 1944, this rose to 938 tons. In the second quarter, with American help, it reached 2,689 tons. Just over half of all these weapons went to F Section circuits, the remainder to those liaising with RF.

But the Allied invasion planners at SHAEF were less than delighted by the Prime Minister's intervention. "We cannot hope to equip all the Resistance bodies to the extent we wish to," said a SHAEF memorandum of 28 February. For the purposes of the invasion, all Allied Resistance and behind-the-lines commando operations were being co-ordinated by Special Forces headquarters, a specially created body answerable to Eisenhower, despite protests from Koenig. Throughout the winter of 1943 and the spring of 1944, the representatives of SFHQ debated plans for the participation of Resistance in Overlord. But to their increasing dismay, they found that the planners at SHAEF took little interest in the hopes and ambitions of guerillas and saboteurs. "It is unfortunate that Resistance only gets 'support by results,'" wrote SHAEF's G-3 Operations Department in answer to a protest from SFHQ, "and never ahead of results. The fact remains that owing to the nature of its indefinite contribution, Resistance has to prove itself before getting the support necessary. . . ."

After the initial Allied landing in Normandy, the decisive problem was to prevent the Germans from building up their counterattack against the beach-head more rapidly than the Allies could move reinforcements across the Channel to strengthen it. If the Germans could move unimpeded, predicted the Joint Planning Staff, by D+60 they could have a theoretical fifty-six divisions (with a strength equivalent to thirty-seven Allied units) deployed against thirty-six Allied divisions in France. SHAEF Intelligence staffs had created a mass of detailed projections of German troop movements in the first days after the Allied landings:

> . . . Assuming seventy trains are required to move a Panzer division; that it will take six hours to collect the trains; four hours to load; that forty-eight trains can move in twenty-four hours, given two main lines, ninety-six trains can move in twenty-four hours . . . one

and a half hours' minimum move-off time. . . . Assume two hours to pass a point . . . tracked vehicles are unlikely to move over 100 miles by road, or wheeled vehicles more than 150. . . .

Through Ultra, they were reading almost every German monthly equipment state. They knew, for instance, that "2 Sugar Sugar Panzer Div," as the decrypters incongruously recorded the Das Reich, was short of 257 trucks, had only two of a complement of seventeen tracked artillery tractors, and was 2,001 rifles and 546 machine pistols short of complement. But SHAEF consistently overestimated both the speed at which German units in the West would be ordered to Normandy, and the pace at which they would move once they had been set in motion.

They had to. It was their business to plan for a "worst case" situation. After much argument among the airmen and heart-searching by the Prime Minister about the cost in civilian life, it was agreed that Allied bombers should carry out an intensive bombardment of seventy-two critical railway junctions in France during the months before D-Day. To conceal the location of the landings, the attacks would be spread throughout the north and center of the country. Air Chief Marshal Tedder, Deputy Supreme Commander, rejected proposals for concentrating the attack on rail bridges, on the ground that these were too difficult to hit. The bombers would go for major rail centers, on the basis that even those which missed their aiming point would probably damage other rail installations.

The Free French, appalled by the prospective casualties, considered the possibility that the rail system could be immobilized by a general strike of SNCF workers from D-Day. But the idea was rejected not only because of the difficulty of carrying it out, but because it was essential to maintain some communication with the great cities of France in order to feed their populations: "It was unthinkable to compel 400,000 people to take to the *maquis* . . . and the total strangulation of the network would cause a famine." Contrary to the accounts of some Resistance historians, it was never intended that the entire rail network of France should come to a halt after D-Day.

But the other obvious course, keenly advocated by SOE, of attacking the railways by sabotage at minimal risk to civilian life, was politely brushed aside by the planners. "The weight of air effort necessary to produce results comparable to those achieved by the SOE/SO option would certainly be very considerable," wrote Kingston McLoughry, Air Commodore Plans and Operations at Allied Air Forces HQ, on 10 February. He went on:

> However, since these operations must necessarily involve a large measure of chance, it would be unwise to rely on their success to the extent of reducing the planned air effort. Furthermore, the cutting of railway tracks produces only a temporary effect which could not contribute materially to the general disruption of the enemy's rail communications. For these reasons the results of SOE/SO operations should be regarded only as a bonus, although this may admittedly be a valuable one.

General Morgan added a note to the same file: "I agree with you entirely that we must continue to do as we have in the past, and treat any dividend we may get out of SOE as a windfall. . . ."

Through all the debates that continued until the eve of D-Day about the role of the French Resistance, this was the unchanging view of the Allied planners. The Resistance should be encouraged to create whatever havoc it could for the Germans, but no part of the Overlord plan should be made dependent on Resistance success. This attitude must have been reinforced by a modest experiment carried out in southern France in December 1943. Local Resistance groups were allotted fifty rail targets, to be attacked on receipt of an "Action Message" from London, of the kind that would be transmitted across all France on D-Day. The message was duly sent. A few weeks later a full report reached London. Of the fifty targets specified, fourteen had been attacked, together with a further twelve chosen on local initiative by *résistants*. SHAEF was not greatly impressed. One of the officers who served in SHAEF's G-3 division in 1944, liaising with SOE and SFHQ, remarked:

> In the normal course of events, if one makes a military plan, provides the forces and avoids some Act of God, there is a good chance that the plan will be carried out. But in the case of guerillas, there is never any certainty whatever that the plan will be carried

out. It is unthinkable to make a major military operation dependent on irregular co-operation.

But to the Free French, the role of Resistance on D-Day was not a mere matter of military judgment: it was the critical moment in the resurrection of France. The overwhelming concern of De Gaulle's staff was to ensure the liberation of the largest possible area of their country as rapidly as possible. They were deeply dismayed by the great Allied transport bombing program. The lawyer Marcel Brault, alias Jérôme, who came to London from the Rhône Valley early in 1944 and played a leading role in persuading the Prime Minister to reinforce Resistance, wrote in February:

> The French population has become very discouraged by the postponement of the invasion which had been expected last autumn, by the Vichy propaganda which has called attention to the terrorism in the Resistance groups, and finally by the slow progress of the Allied armies in Italy. It could become absolutely apathetic if aerial bombing is intensified without a clear indication of its necessity.

Colonel Passy was among the pessimists about the real prospects of a mass uprising in France on D-Day. But many others among De Gaulle's men had a spectacular vision of open insurrection in southern and central France, where the Germans were thinly spread and great tracts of broken country lent themselves readily to guerilla warfare. There was discussion of possible Resistance "redoubts" in which great masses of *maquisards* might assemble, and to which they might withdraw if they were driven back on to the defensive by German counter-attacks. Although all these misconceived notions were finally quashed, one of the most serious errors of omission in the weeks before D-Day was that *résistants* were not discouraged with nearly sufficient force from concentrating in arms when the Action Messages came. Some groups were even left by London and Algiers with a clear idea that they were expected to gather *en masse*. This confusion in high places was caused by doubt about just what would happen when the Action Messages were sent. It was indirectly responsible for the tragedies of the Vercors, the Glieres and several lesser slaughters inflicted upon *résistants*.

On 7 May 1944 Churchill cabled President Roosevelt:

> Massigli handed me this morning a memorandum concerning Allied bombardments of French targets, expressing the serious psychological effect they are having on the French Resistance groups when the loss of human life obtained does not seem to correspond with the results obtained, notably in the case of stations and factories in occupied districts. It is suggested that sabotage operations would achieve a better result without risk of life.

The President disagreed, and the Allied military commanders almost unanimously followed him. A senior British staff officer scribbled upon the Free French blueprint for Resistance and D-Day:

> This plan gives the impression that the object of Overlord is to support the operations of the French Resistance, eg by drawing off enemy armour from freed zones, and not the other way round. . . .
>
>   The French at all times keep in mind the fact that they have the economy of their country to maintain during the period of military operations and after the war. They tend to put this consideration before military requirements.

The Allied air assault on the French transport system continued until and after D-Day on the "worst case" assumption, that Resistance could contribute nothing to the dislocation of communications. Between 9 February and 6 June 75,000 tons of bombs were dropped in 21,949 sorties by Bomber Command and the USAAF. The overwhelming consensus at SHAEF was that, when Resistance mobilized, its men should remain in small groups, and at all costs avoid concentrating in large bodies that invited German attack. However, the Allied commanders were obviously content to approve any Resistance plan that did not increase their commitment, and promised to cause difficulty to the Germans. The Free French had devoted enormous labor to compiling detailed plans for the destruction of key rail, road and telecommunications links on D-Day—Plans *Vert* (Green), *Tortue* (Tortoise) and *Violet*, in which both RF and F Sections had become deeply involved. SHAEF accepted these, on the basis that they cost nothing.

At a meeting at Special Forces headquarters on 20 May, Allied policy crystallized thus:

> The immediate offensive task of Resistance will be to give every assistance possible toward the build-up of the lodgement area:
> a) by the delaying of, and interference with, the movement of enemy reinforcements toward the area, and subsequently by attacks on his lines of supply.
> b) by creating, in areas remote from the lodgement area, diversionary threats that the enemy cannot afford to neglect, thereby tying down a proportion of his available forces.
> It must also be envisaged that, even in districts of vital importance to the enemy, the population may not remain inactive. Spontaneous popular activity may combine with the efforts of remaining Resistance to develop to a design of individually small but widespread guerilla activity.

An SFHQ memorandum of 4 June said: "It cannot be foreseen how Resistance will react to Overlord. It is clear that we must, generally speaking, reinforce where Resistance is most strong. Our policy will therefore be largely opportunist."

One critical dilemma was unresolved until the last moment: whether to attempt a selective mobilization of Resistance, sparing those areas most remote from and irrelevant to the Normandy battle from the inevitable consequences of German counter-attack. The overwhelming conclusion was that it was neither desirable nor possible to restrain whole areas of France from taking part at the great moment: "In view of the fact that the spirit of Resistance groups throughout France is keyed up to a high pitch, and that a wave of patriotic enthusiasm is likely to sweep the country on D-Day, it is considered that any restraint placed on certain areas of organized Resistance on D-Day would only meet with partial success."

Thus it was agreed that at the moment of the landings, all the *résistants* of France would be called to arms. Beyond the practical difficulties of restraining them, it was vital to keep the Germans in doubt for every possible day about the prospect of further Allied landings. Colonel Barry of SOE said: "We were, in an absolutely hard-headed way, sacrificing Frenchmen to that purpose." The Allied staffs expected that any benefits from Resistance would continue at best for a few days. "It is probable that action . . . will be taken for a few days, after which stores and enthusiasm will begin to run low unless further instructions, backed by supplies, are speedily issued," ran an SFHQ memorandum. By the end of May, there were believed to be around half a million active *résistants* in France. Of these, 10,000 were estimated to be already armed by RF Section in Region R5—comprising the Dordogne, Corrèze, Haute-Vienne and Creuse—the principal battleground of the Das Reich, and some 9,000 in R4, south-westwards from the Lot; 16,000 men in R4 and 2,500 men in R5 were believed to be already armed by F Section. According to SFHQ figures, 75,975 Sten guns, 27,025 pistols, 9,420 rifles, 2,538 Brens, anti-tank rifles and bazookas, 285,660 grenades and 183 tons of explosives and ammunition had been dropped to the Resistance, of which a significant but unknown proportion had been unrecovered by reception committees or lost to the Germans. There was a chronic shortage of ammunition of all types. Most *résistants* possessed two, three, sometimes only a single magazine for their arms, and there were few reserves. They had no heavy weapons beyond a few bazookas, despite constant pleading from the bigger groups in the field. But there were excellent reasons for this. Heavy weapons required training and transport, to neither of which most *maquisards* had access. To be effective, they required stocks of ammunition which it would have been immensely difficult to drop and handle on the ground. The other serious obstacle to any complex or co-ordinated maneuver by large group of *maquisards* was the complete absence of short-range radios.

Yet even with hindsight, it is difficult to fault the attitudes or the conduct of those in London who were responsible for organizing Resistance for D-Day. SOE and the Free French, concerned with supporting Resistance, had done everything possible with the resources they were granted. The Allied commanders charged with responsibility for Overlord were also eminently reasonable. Despite the claims of enthusiasts, a guerilla struggle in a major international war must always be a campaign on the margin. If the likely contribution of guerillas to victory is doubtful, then so also must be the resources expended upon them. General De Gaulle's preoccupation with restoring the soul of

France could only be courteously acknowledged at SHAEF. In the spring of 1944 it would have been unthinkable, indeed hopelessly irresponsible, to cancel or curtail the transport bombing offensive which cost 12,000 French and Belgian civilian lives, in favor of reliance on the Resistance.

If there was a failure, it was in frankness toward the networks in the field. Inevitably, *résistants* were given an exaggerated notion of the importance of their role in the attack on communications. But it was less necessary that most were allowed to believe that Liberation would inexorably follow invasion within weeks, if not days; and that the creation of Resistance armies would be rewarded from London by massive supplies of arms and ammunition, probably also by reinforcements of regular parachutists.

SHAEF confidently expected that the Germans would throw every man, tank and gun they could bring to bear into the struggle to defeat the Allied armies on the beaches of Normandy. To any commander with a clear grasp of strategy, this was the overwhelming priority. Fundamentally it could not matter to the Germans what Resistance achieved in the Vercors, the Dordogne, or other areas remote from the north coast. Any insurrection could be crushed at leisure once the Allies were thrown back into the sea. If they secured a lodgment, then the loss of southern France scarcely mattered. The simple truth was that French Resistance was strongest in areas that strategically mattered least to the Germans the Massif Central, the south-west, the Dordogne, the Corrèze and the Haute-Vienne. An important SHAEF paper of 28 February 1944 assumed that in their response to the Allied landings, ". . . the Germans will ignore local Resistance." This was a fundamental—albeit perfectly rational—misjudgment of German thinking. Hitler's obsession with retaining every foot of his empire once again betrayed him. The Germans would deploy resources to repress Resistance on a scale the Allies had never conceived possible. In the first, vital days after the Allied landings, the German struggle to hold France against Frenchmen employed forces—above all, the 2nd SS Panzer Division—that could have made a vital contribution on the battlefield in Normandy. There are many tales of tragedy, reckless error and even absurdity among *résistants* in the chapters that follow. It must never be forgotten that the Germans" response was absurd only in its cost to their battle for France.

CHAPTER 3

SOE: Southern France

FEW OF THE BRITISH and French agents parachuted into France fired a shot in anger during the battles of June 1944. Their names will seldom recur during the story of the Das Reich's march through their sectors. But to understand what Resistance was on D-Day, and how it came to be what it was, it is essential to know something of the men and women who made it possible. For thousands of *résistants* taking up their Sten guns and their gammon bombs and embarking upon open warfare, D-Day was a beginning. But for the agents of SOE and De Gaulle's BCRA, it was the flowering of four years' labor, the end of the most difficult and nerve-racking period of Resistance. The British agent George Hiller exulted in the sense of release that D-Day brought: "The beauty of life, the joys of spring, the stream of men and cars, the relief of being armed."

Hiller was French Section's officer in the Lot, the region dominated by high limestone plateaus thick with scrub oak and sheep grazing that lies between the Dordogne and the Tarn, on the Das Reich division's direct route north. With his twenty-one-year-old wireless operator, Cyril Watney, he had been parachuted into France in January 1944 to make contact with a socialist Resistance organization named the Groupes Vény. Its tentacles were reported to extend through southern France from Marseille and Toulouse to the Lot and Limoges. Hiller's business was first to assess their potential, then to organize and arm the *résaux*—the networks—in the Lot.

He was born in Paris, the son of an English father and French mother, educated at *lycées* (high schools) in Paris and London, then at Exeter College, Oxford. He had planned a career as a diplomat when the war intervened. Like a significant number of future French Section recruits, in 1939 he was a near-pacifist, and he joined the medical corps because he disliked the idea of killing people. Only in 1942 did he modify his opinions sufficiently to pass through Sandhurst and become an army officer. Then SOE's recruiters found him. He told his parents that he was being posted to the Middle East, but on the night of 7 January 1944, at the age of twenty-eight, this highly intelligent, sensitive, rather reserved young man landed near Quatre Routes high in the hills of the Lot to begin his career as a secret agent.

Like most F Section officers, Hiller and Watney suffered a severe shock of disorientation and bewilderment when they landed. Only moments after the reception committee had greeted them, the two Englishmen were appalled to see the headlights of a car approaching up the road. They flung themselves into a ditch as it passed, then were bemused to see the little group of *résistants* still standing nonchalantly by the roadside in its headlights, Sten guns under their arms. The two Englishmen agreed that there was a wide gulf between security as taught at their tradecraft school at Beaulieu and as practiced in France. From the dropping zone they were driven to Quatre Routes. They spent their first nights in a creamery at the edge of the little village, until Watney was moved to a safe house from which he could transmit, and Hiller began his travels among the *résistants* of the Lot.

Like many men who found themselves behind enemy lines in World War II, Hiller was profoundly moved by his experience in the spring and summer of 1944. In the timescale of those days, Liberation still seemed far away and the German command of France still appeared unshakable. Many Frenchmen and women especially among the business and official classes—had long since come to terms with their Occupiers, and feared and hated the Resistance as communist bandits who threatened the peace and stability of their communities. By no means all the girls who slept with the men of the Das Reich and others of the occupying army did so for money. Since the end of World War I, France had been a bitterly divided and fragmented society. "Her position," Sir Denis Brogan has written, "was unique. She was a victor, but she had in many ways the psychology of a defeated nation." Many, perhaps most, French bourgeois in the 1930s feared fascism far less than communism. Peasants were profoundly embittered by the ceaseless betrayals of their politicians. Their distaste for authority extended from contempt for Paris to hatred of their local landlords and parish priests. Religion was a waning influence in much of southern France by the 1940s. Most peasants, phlegmatically plowing the fields and driving the oxen on their meager farms, seemed to have set themselves apart from the war—indifferent both to the Allies and the Germans, concerned only with the crops and the seasons.

Yet beyond all these people, an utterly dedicated minority risked their lives, their families, everything they possessed to further the cause of Resistance. These were the men and women, whom he had never met before, to whom Hiller entrusted his own life. He was deeply moved by the strength of the bond created by the relationship between the hiders and the hidden. There was no common denominator among the *résistants* except perhaps that their leaders in the Lot and the Dordogne seemed to come chiefly from the professional and small business classes, and were politically of the Left.

Jean and Marie Verlhac, already in their forties during the Occupation, were legendary *résistants*. Of fifty *parachutages* (air-drops) in their region, Jean organized the reception of nineteen. His wife Marie, a teacher who had been active for years in the trade union movement, was one of the brains and principal driving forces behind the growth of Resistance in the Lot. It was at their house that within days of his arrival Hiller prepared the charges for a local *résistant* to lay at the Ratier airscrew factory in Figeac, one of F Section's most successful acts of sabotage of the war. In the weeks that followed, Hiller was passed on from the hands of the Verlhacs to those of other men and women who sheltered him as he travelled through the region, meeting contacts and assessing the prospect of building upon them.

He spent many nights at the home of Georges Bru, a teacher in the little town of St. Céré, a blunt, stocky figure with a genius for organizing and providing the unexpected. Late on those icy winter nights, Hiller would watch Bru come home blue with cold, his body wrapped with newspapers under his coat, after riding for hours around the region on his little moped on the business of the *réseau*. Despite an endless procession of clandestine visitors, his wife kept a spotless home, in which she seemed to be eternally cooking for her unexpected guests. Hiller watched fascinated as their two children did their homework at one end of the kitchen table, while the other was littered with explosives and Sten gun magazines. Sometimes the children cycled through the streets to look out for Germans or *miliciens* (members of the Vichy para-military forces). It was uncanny how young they learned the reflexes of secrecy. One night, at the home of another schoolteacher in Figeac, named Odette Bach, Hiller was sitting in the kitchen when there was a knock at the front door. Pierrette, the Bachs' five-year-old daughter, opened it to find a *gendarme* outside. He demanded whether anyone was at home. The child shook her head and replied unhesitatingly, "*Non, Monsieur.*" The *gendarme* departed. Hiller breathed again. Even thirty-five years later, Pierrette could not explain how she had known that she must lie except to shrug: "*Il y avait une ambiance. . . .*" ("It was a feeling. . . ."). And she was still enough of a child to enjoy herself immensely one day when Hiller took her to the circus.

He marveled at all these people, conscious of their fear, of all that they risked. The Bachs always seemed to him to be making a great effort to conceal their nervousness, yet their flat was known locally as "the stray dogs' home" because Odette would never turn away a fugitive from Vichy or the Germans. Odette and Hiller talked for hours about their common pacifist backgrounds. Then it would be time for her to leave to go to her class. It was difficult to come to terms with the relative normalcy of life: taxes were paid, people were married and baptized, the peasants continued their simple lives sleeping on mattresses filled with maize, working in the fields in their blue smocks and black hats, shaving once a week on Sunday, baking bread in great wheels two feet across. Yet amidst all this, for Hiller and the *résistants* there was unceasing danger, the extra layer of clandestinity to add to all the practical difficulties of finding enough food to eat, renewing the endless permits for every aspect of daily life, and queueing for the simplest commodities.

The Germans were seldom seen outside the big towns. Occasionally a black Citroën would race down the road, and the village postmistress would telephone her counterpart a few kilometers away to warn her that Germans were on the way. Only Germans or agents of Vichy or the local doctor had access to petrol-driven cars. Perhaps twice a year, a village might suffer the passage of one of the notorious German punitive columns sent into the countryside wherever Resistance activity became conspicuous. The Dordogne suffered terribly from the attentions of Division B in 1943, and the Corrèze and Creuse from those of the Jesser column. That year 40,000 French men and women were arrested under suspicion of Resistance activities, and many of them had been deported to Germany, never to return. The risks for a British agent in the Lot or the Dordogne were less great than in Paris or Lyon. But the tension and fear, the certain knowledge of the price of capture, never altogether faded even in the happiest and most romantic moments of their secret lives. In notes for an uncompleted memoir of his experience with Resistance, Hiller scribbled long afterwards: "Explain how very ordinary people can do it. . . . Many people were lifted out of their little lives, to be dropped down again afterwards. . . . Show the mixture of tension and light fantastic. . . . The extraordinary brotherhood, the immense enjoyment of being together, among ourselves, like children."

Hiller likened his first weeks in France to learning to ride a bicycle— there was "a quality of strangeness and uncertainty, everyone working in a fog." He was dismayed by the lack of force displayed by some of the senior leaders of Resistance in the region, but conscious of his own lack of authority. His only influence sprang from his ability to conjure up money and arms. "We were working on a number of uncertain variables: The weather. The amount available for the drop. The lack of information about what was going on around us. . . . The sense of isolation from London. The poor security." He found himself frustrated by the immense effort and time that had to be wasted upon petty personal logistics— finding safe houses for Watney and his transmitter; getting a *gazogène* charcoal-burning car for travel; passing messages and receiving answers even over short distances when he was constantly on the move. It took weeks to lose the screaming self-consciousness that afflicted him in a public place: "As I walked down the muddy high street with the debonair Jean at my side, I felt that everyone down to the dogs was staring at me. Loudspeakers were shouting: 'Look at the Englishman, freshly arrived, there in the grey check suit with the brand-new beret!'"

Soon after his arrival, one of the Groupes Vény's colonels took him northwards to Limoges, the great grey metropolis of china manufacture, to talk to its local supporters. It was the first of many such trips:

"Limoges was a dangerous town-small enough for most people to know each other, yet large enough for strangers to pass unobserved. And Limoges was plentifully supplied with Gestapo agents, not all of them natives of the town." Taillaux was the Groupes Vény's principal contact in Limoges,

> . . . a very cautious man, thoroughly drilled in clandestine work, he carried even into his discussions the habit of keeping negotiations on various subjects separate, and of telling no one mort: than they needed to know. . . .
>
> The Taillaux, like all people who continued to lead legal lives, were continually on the alert. If the German or French police wanted to arrest them, they had only to come and pick them up. They were well-known local figures leading busy working lives, yet somehow into these they had to fit in their clandestine work and meetings. And yet like many thousands of others, they carried on, because as normal citizens they were able to do things that would no longer be possible if they went underground.

Hiller and the colonel slept at the railway station, inconspicuous among hundreds of other stranded wartime travellers and the incessant clanking of rolling stock through the night. The Englishman dozed, gazing at the colonel asleep beside him: "This old man with his patched-up body could have chosen to live on his pension in his flat in Nice, yet here he was with his worn shoes and his battered overcoat, sleeping in railway waiting-rooms and dodging the Germans. Luckily, he looked a harmless enough figure as he slept with his head near the red rosette of the Legion of Honour. . . ."

As the weeks went by, Hiller's admiration for the *résistants* did not diminish, but he began to perceive that their networks were far less powerful than London had supposed: "I had been there long enough for my initial optimism to have worn off. The whole organization was much weaker than I had imagined." As they built up the clandestine arms dumps with the fruits of the *parachutages*, he became conscious that there was no precise plan as to how they were to be used: "It was all rather vague, but then so were our ideas of what would happen after D-Day."

Many of the *résistants* were simply not by temperament warlike people. They were men and women of great moral courage who sought to do whatever they could to oppose the Germans. But neither by background nor inclination were they killers. "It was not, on the whole, a heroic area," wrote Hiller. By this, of course, he did not seek to diminish the courage of local *résistants*, but to describe the difficulty of rousing the sleepy, rustic communities of the Lot to violent action. Hiller wrote later that he regretted wasting so much time on the movement's internal quarrels and jealousies. Perhaps he should have "started fewer schemes and followed them through; should have been more concrete; [adopted] a more aggressive policy, more firmness and ruthlessness." He was too hard on himself. He did not know that his were the fortunes and difficulties of most Allied agents all over France.

Hiller also encountered the universal difficulty in handling the *maquis*—the groups of young *résistants* who lived entirely outside the law in the woods and hills. Most were young evaders from the STO, and some were more enthusiastic about avoiding forced labor than about taking part in positive action against the Germans. In the Lot, the most active and numerous *maquis* were those of the communist FTP, to whom many of the wilder spirits defected, tiring of the AS policy of patience until D-Day. Hiller wrote:

> Organizing the *maquis* was difficult. Getting boys together in twos and threes; stealing camping equipment from government stocks; buying food. Getting a lorry made available for hasty flight. Large and regular supplies of tobacco were essential if morale was to remain good. The boys were often slovenly, and few had done military service. They wanted immediate raids. They had no amusements. Occasionally, on a very rare night, there might be an operation, yet every night in the moon period we were out on the dropping ground. The boys were pathetically grateful when they were given a small job in the outside world. Once a drunk and bored boy simply emptied his pistol into the air.
>
> After a while, we got used to it all. We lived with the moon and the weather. Hopelessly and impatiently waiting during the non-moon periods, then full of hope at the beginning of the new moon, when the weather prospects would be earnestly discussed.

The precious days would pass, and there would be no BBC messages for us. Sometimes the weather was obviously bad, sometimes it was fine and we had to tell everybody that the weather was bad over London. . . . At other times, there would be a great many messages, although none for us. We were envious of others, and wondered if we were not being forgotten. . . . We never managed to become indifferent to the moon periods, but we forgot all about hard and fast plans and just tackled things as they came. But I sometimes thought how nice it would be for a change to have to deal with a situation in which all the factors were readily ascertainable, and predictable in their development.

The Groupes Vény's strength in the Lot had grown from twelve in January 1941 to forty-eight in January 1942, 401 in July 1943 with eighty-five *maquis*, and 623 in January 1944 with 346 *maquisards*. It achieved a peak in July 1944 of 156 AS and 2,037 *maquisards* after the great D-Day mobilization. To the Frenchmen with whom he worked, Hiller was the very image of an English gentleman of *L'Intelligence Service*, to which all France was convinced that every British agent belonged. He became much liked and respected in his area. While many agents had no contact whatever with neighboring circuits, in the late spring of 1944 he began to work increasingly closely with his neighbors in the Dordogne and Corrèze. When he wrote of his assignment's extraordinary combination of tension and "the light fantastic," he must have been thinking of such moments as Soleil's banquet in the heart of the Dordogne.

Soleil was a ferocious, semi-literate, twenty-three-year-old communist, originally from Avignon and more recently from the darker corners of Marseille. His real name was René Cousteille. "Fearless and unscrupulous, a born leader, small, dark, twitching with energy," in Hiller's words, the little tough had formed a *maquis* on the south side of the Dordogne river, close to the marvelous golden hilltop village of Belvès. From his camps, he ruled a great swath of the region. He had forced every inhabitant of the neighboring hamlets to conceal some of his petrol and oil reserves, according to Hiller to ensure that all of them would suffer if any was indiscreet. In the spring of 1944, a young Englishman named Peter Lake "Jean-Pierre" of F Section—toured

Soleil's *maquis* in miserable discomfort on the pillion of a *"mota,"* holding weapon training classes for an eager audience. Jean-Pierre was not happy with the young bandits. He sensed that the slightest misplaced word could cause him to disappear rapidly and painfully. Soleil had already threatened to kill his SOE colleague, "Commandant Jack," if he cut off supplies of arms. His *maquis* was feared and detested throughout most of the surrounding countryside for the ruthless killing of any man suspected of collaboration, and Soleil's orders to his men to seize whatever they needed from whoever possessed it. But Commandant Jack respected Soleil's courage and toughness, and armed his men because he believed that they would excel where it mattered—in fighting the Germans. The *maquis* prospered, and one night Hiller found himself solemnly invited by the young killer to a formal banquet, with after-dinner entertainment in the form of a lecture on small arms by Jean-Pierre.

The castle chosen by Soleil's nineteen-year-old deputy, the Baron, was a fine example of late eighteenth-century Gothic, hidden away in a wood on the banks of the Dordogne. As we approached, we were repeatedly challenged, and we found that detachments of Spaniards armed with numerous Bren guns guarded all the approaches. Their French was poor, and they did their job so conscientiously that we were glad to get inside the castle. There we found the village leaders, some fifty fat, middle-aged men, dressed in their Sunday best. Jean Pierre fussed around like a good lecturer making sure that all the exhibits were ready. Against a background of tapestries and wrought iron stood a U-shaped table covered with linen and flowers and candelabra and fine porcelain. In front of each plate was a menu bearing the badge of the Groupe Soleil, a flaming sun and an inscription recording the occasion. The Baron, once he had been duly congratulated, explained that he had had great difficulty in finding a competent sign writer. For the rest, he merely told the butler and his wife, who lived there permanently, that the castle was requisitioned for the night, and there would be so many guests. They in turn prepared everything as if it were a formal peacetime dinner party. The service was perfect, and the butler and his staff impassive. But we could not help trying to guess from the fleeting expressions on his face what was going on in his mind as he leaned forward to pour the wine. He was probably scandalized at the way these ruffians had invaded the house, to which they would never have been invited before the war. He was probably frightened, too, that the dinner might end with a surprise raid by the Germans. Then, as the dinner went on, he seemed to thaw as he listened to the quiet conversation of these people who all appeared too young or too old to be terrorists. In the end, he was listening with interest to the panegyric on the Sten.

The inaugural lecture began very late. Some of us, in fact, thought that it would never take place after so many speeches and toasts. But we had counted without Jean-Pierre's determination, or the surprising resilience of the village's leaders, who had taken the banquet in their stride. Not only was the lecture a great success, but when we went off to bed in the small hours, Jean-Pierre and the fat men were still busy arguing about some of the finer points of the Bren gun.

Jean-Pierre—Peter Lake—was a twenty-nine-year-old diplomat's son who had been a merchant banker in West Africa when the war began, and took part in an early SOE operation in that area before being transferred to French Section and parachuted near Limeuil on Easter Sunday 1944. His French was very poor, but by that stage F was not dropping secret agents, but para-military instructors. A more serious deficiency in all F's training, however, was that in the interests of remaining apolitical they gave agents no briefing whatever on the intricacies of local Resistance politics, and many of them were confused and bewildered to discover the byzantine complications in the field. Lake was taken from his landing ground to the home of a carpenter named Charles Brouillet—"*Le bolshévik*," as he was known locally—in the enchanting village of Siorac-en-Perigord. It was a picaresque introduction to Resistance, eating a splendid 4 am breakfast with the recklessly confident *résistants*. "*Ha, ha, mon cher Jean-Pierre*," said Brouillet happily. "*Siorac a deux mille habitants, et sur ces deux mille habitants, il y a deux mille résistants!*" ("Ha, ha, my dear Jean-Pierre, Siorac has two thousand inhabitants, and of these two thousand inhabitants, there are two thousand *résistants*!") He confided that many of their arms were stored in the roof of the church: "*Tu vois, à l'église, c'est sous la protection du bon Dieu!*" ("You see, at the church, they're under the protection of the good Lord!")

Yet in catching the genuine, extraordinary romance of secret survival and the preparations for war in one of the most beautiful regions of all France, it is essential never to forget its darker face. Those whom Soleil's men threatened or robbed hated him as bitterly as the Germans. Each of those at that exotic banquet could never entirely erase from his mind the fear of betrayal, the knowledge that capture meant certain imprisonment and torture, concluded only by an appallingly lonely death. So much sentiment has been expended upon British agents and *résistants* killed by the Germans that it is sometimes forgotten that the Germans were perfectly entitled by the laws of war to shoot them. It was the fact that execution was invariably accompanied by such ghastly cruelty that made their fate seem so intolerable. Commandant Jack had only succeeded to responsibility for the eastern Dordogne and Corrèze in March, after the capture in Brive-la-Gaillarde and dispatch to Buchenwald of his commanding officer, one of SOE's greatest agents, Harry Peulevé.

Commandant Jack—officially Nestor—was a big, robust, handsome, compulsively adventurous twenty-two-year-old who was assumed by all the *maquis* to be a British officer. In reality, he was the Frenchman Jacques Poirier, who concealed his nationality until the moment of Liberation to safeguard the lives of his family. He was one of those fortunate spirits blessed with the ability to inspire laughter and affection wherever he went. It was Poirier who, with Peulevé, armed most of the *maquisards* of the Corrèze and Dordogne who met the Das Reich division after 6 June.

Poirier had reached SOE after an odyssey remarkable even by Baker Street standards. He had been destined for a career in the air force, following his father, until the war intervened and the family retreated into the Unoccupied Zone near Nice. Young Jacques was running small errands for the local Resistance when he encountered Harry Peulevé, making a painful escape to England after being badly injured parachuting into France as one of SOE's wireless operators. Poirier formed an immediate intense admiration for the Englishman, and offered to go with him across the Pyrenees. After many adventures, the two men reached Gibraltar and Peulevé was at once flown back to England.

Poirier had to wait rather longer for transport. When at last he arrived in Bristol, to his intense fury he was detained for five days for screening. He was then taken to London as a prisoner, before being handed over to SOE.

He never remembered asking to go back to France—he always took it for granted, just as he assumed and insisted that it would be with Peulevé. French Section put him through the usual training courses under the name of Peters. He had some cheerful evenings in London, some of them with Violette Szabo. Then, one night late in 1943, he found himself at Tempsford airfield, being handed the customary gold cigarette case as a parting present from Buckmaster, *en route* to join Peulevé in the Corrèze.

Poirier reached the soil of France to find that his dropping aircraft had ejected him more than 100 miles from the rendezvous. He walked for some hours to reach a station, survived asking for a ticket in English, and fell asleep on the train to wake up surrounded by a compartment full of Germans. They mercifully ignored him, and within a few hours he found himself in the substantial town of Brive-la-Gaillarde, deserted in Sunday silence. He could think of no less conspicuous refuge than a church, and sat through four masses before slipping discreetly out of the town to a nearby hillside for the night. The next morning, he found Peulevé.

In the months that followed, Poirier and his commanding officer travelled ceaselessly through the eastern Dordogne and the Corrèze, meeting the men of the AS and the FTP, arranging *parachutages* and holding weapon training classes. Roger Beauclerk—"Casimir"—was parachuted to act as Poirier's wireless operator, and settled down to the usual nerve-racking, monotonous existence. The operators suffered terribly from boredom between transmissions, unable to wander because of their schedules, moved constantly from safe house to safe house to avoid the risk of German direction-finding, and thus never able to relax amidst established relationships. They had too much time to think, and too few of the compensations of the agents. Many found the strain intolerable unless, like Cyril Watney, they were blessed with unshakeable patience and good nature.

In March 1944 Poirier slipped away for a few days to visit his mother, now living in the foothills of the Pyrenees. By the merest chance, one night he was sitting in the kitchen listening with half an ear to the BBC *messages personnels*—which it was wildly unlikely would bear any special signal for him—when he caught an electrifying phrase: "*Attention à Nestor! Message important pour Nestor! Ne retournez pas chez vous! Jean est très malade!*" ("Attention Nestor! Important message for Nestor! Do not return to your home! Jean is very sick!") Peulevé and his wireless operator Roland Malraux had been arrested—by terrible ill luck, denounced by a neighbor as suspected Jewish black marketeers. George Hiller heard the news, and with immense effort and ingenuity managed to have the warning broadcast to Poirier. Jacques took the train to Martel, high in the Lot, and sought out the Verlhacs who were astounded to see him, because they believed that he had already been taken by the Germans.

Contrary to popular belief, it is never expected that an agent will tell his captors nothing. The most critical achievement that is expected of him is silence for forty-eight hours, until warnings can be circulated and men take to hiding. Then he can begin to reveal small things, odd names and places. Eventually, under extreme duress, it is recognized that he may begin to talk of more vital matters. Peulevé revealed nothing important under torture in Fresnes prison, or later in Buchenwald. But the Germans had a description of Poirier. He vanished into hiding while they combed every possible contact point in Corrèze and east Dordogne for him.

Roland Malraux's brother André said that the region was obviously too hot to hold Poirier for the time being. He suggested a cooling-off period, in Paris. This young, still impressionable ex-student found himself hiding in the flat of André Gide, with its window looking out on the courtyard of Laval's Interior Ministry. He walked by the Seine between Malraux and Albert Camus. To his lifelong regret, he never remembered a word of what either man said.

Of all the extraordinary figures who held the stage in the Resistance of Dordogne and Corrèze in the summer of 1944, none surpassed André Malraux. Young men like Poirier, Hiller, Lakeso worldly about so much in their secret lives—found themselves awed and fascinated by this mountebank of genius who thrust himself upon them. He was already a legend—the author of *La Condition Humaine*, exotic traveller, film-maker, commander in Spain of the Republican fighter squadron he himself had raised, *Malraux-le-rouge* who had his uniforms tailored by Lanvin.

Yet his record as a *résistant* from 1940 to 1944 had not been impressive. After serving with a French tank unit in the debacle of 1940, he retired to the Cote d'Azur to work—though he wrote nothing of merit—and to reflect, in circumstances of sybaritic ease by the standards of the world in those days. In September 1941, Jean-Paul Sartre and Simone de Beauvoir cycled the length of France to appeal for his support in Resistance. "They lunched on chicken Maryland, exquisitely prepared and served. Malraux heard Sartre out very courteously, but said that for the time being at any rate, action of any sort would be quite useless. He was relying on Russian tanks and American planes to win the war." Later, when the *Combat résistants* also approached him, he asked simply: "Have you arms? No? Have you money? No? Then it's not serious. . . ." Towards the end of 1943, he moved with his mistress Clara to a comfortable little chateau on the Dordogne. Still he showed no urge to have any part of Resistance.

Yet when his brother Roland was captured—his other brother Claude was also working for SOE—Malraux presented himself to the Resistance of Dordogne and Corrèze, quite without humility, as a man ready to take command. He was forty-two. It is a remarkable tribute to his force of personality that "Colonel Berger," as he styled himself after the hero of one of his novels, quickly persuaded Poirier, Hiller and others to treat him as an equal in their counsels. He began to travel with them around the region, addressing *maquisards* and attending conferences. He created the notion of a joint Anglo-French (and later, with the coming of OSS agents, American) council to bring together the Resistance groups of the region, with himself at its head. Malraux had left behind the mood of 1941, when he wrote that "a German defeat would be a victory for the Anglo-Saxons, who will colonize the world and probably France. . . ." But he was still Red enough to give the clenched fist salute. Chain-smoking English cigarettes from *parachutages* (a status symbol among *maquisards*), he would talk off-handedly yet at breakneck speed about "old man Churchill," "that chap De Gaulle," Chinese art, the acoustics of a chateau dining-room, "occasionally interjecting 'Your turn now!', which it was as well not to take too literally as an invitation to reply." When later captured, he claimed to have declared himself to the Germans as "the military chief of this region. . . . I have nothing to confess. I have been your opponent since the day of the Armistice." He also convinced himself that his captors were of the notorious Das Reich Division, although by then they were a month gone from the department.

The FTP regarded Malraux with withering scorn and took no notice whatever of his opinions, and even the AS had their reservations about him. But Malraux visibly enjoyed the confidence of the F Section officers, and encouraged the *résistants* to believe that he himself was an SOE-trained officer with important influence on *parachutages* and weapons and money supplies. By the summer of 1944, he had become a familiar figure to the *résistants* of the region.

Asked many years later about the lack of substance in Malraux's claims and achievements as a *résistant*, Jacques Poirier paused for a moment. Then he said: "There are a few people born in every century who are important not for what they do, but for what they say. Malraux was one of those." All of them were mesmerized by his obsessive fluency, the torrent of ideas that flooded over their heads in conversation. Visiting the camps of bored young *maquisards* in the torrid heat of the summer woods, Poirier knew how to talk pragmatically to their leaders. But he watched fascinated as Malraux leaped on to the roof of a *gazogène* and harangued the guerillas about the glory of France, the dignity of struggle, the nobility of sacrifice. It was irresistible, and it brought tears to their eyes. Poirier quoted a favorite word of Malraux's—*un farfelu*, a compulsive activist who is also half-crazy. Malraux had for years been obsessed with the story of Lawrence of Arabia, and had himself always been a compulsive role-player. There is no doubt that while other Frenchmen in the woods of the Corrèze in 1944 thought of the next *parachutage*, the next cigarette, Malraux saw himself acting out a great heroic drama.

Some *maquisards* joked about his unsoldierly appearance—a certain physical clumsiness, one eye chronically weeping, Basque beret tilted, the constant sniffing. Poirier admitted that it was difficult to concentrate Malraux's attention on practical military problems. The SOE officer would urge: "André, we must discuss the blowing of that bridge." But Malraux would say: "No, tonight I think I would prefer to hear Casimir play the piano." And in the chateau that was now their headquarters, in the failing summer evening light Malraux would sit lost in thought, gazing at the ceiling, while their wireless operator played his brilliant repertoire of classical music surrounded by a little group of half-naked, half-literate *maquisards* lying beside their weapons.

But Malraux's personal courage was beyond question. One day, he and Poirier were driving together down a road when they were hailed by a *maquisard* who warned them of German vehicles ahead. Neither man wished to be the first to suggest turning back. Poirier drove nervously but defiantly onwards, until inevitably they rounded a bend to meet a German tank. Poirier desperately swung the car in a screaming turn. Malraux seized the small automatic pistol from his belt and absurdly—yet to Poirier, also nobly—stood up and emptied it at the tank. Miraculously they escaped to tell the tale, although later that summer Malraux was less fortunate. He was with George Hiller in a car that ran headlong into a German column. Malraux was slightly injured and captured. Hiller was terribly wounded and was rescued, close to death, by Cyril Watney and a group of *maquisards*. He was operated upon under the most primitive circumstances in an abandoned presbytery high in the hills of the Lot, and narrowly survived. Malraux was delivered unscathed from imprisonment at the liberation of Toulouse, not without incurring the skepticism of some *résistants* who inquired acidly how he had "conned" the Germans out of a firing squad.

That April with Poirier in Paris, Malraux had been as flamboyant as ever. He took him to dine at Prunier, relishing his immediate recognition by the head waiter. He introduced the young Frenchman to Camus as a British officer. Poirier began to be infected by the other man's style. One morning, walking up the Champs-Ely sees, he saw a huge German shepherd dog in the window of a pet shop, and knew instantly that he had to possess it. Ten minutes later and 10,000 francs of SOE's money the poorer, he was leading it past the Arc de Triomphe when he met Malraux. Even the *farfelu*'s sense of discretion was appalled: "Jack, you're crazy—you're in Paris to *hide*." But Poirier would not be parted from the dog. He arranged for it to be taken down to the Dordogne, and all through that wild summer of 1944, Dick the dog rode with him on the wing of his car, trotted behind him through the camps in the woods, and slept in his room at the chateaux where, with increasing confidence in their own power, the *maquisards* made their headquarters.

"I was always a chateau type at heart," said Poirier wryly. In the weeks before D-Day, he and a band of Soleil's *maquisards* took over the lovely Château le Poujade, set high on a hill above Urval, overlooking the great river and its irregular patchwork of fields and vineyards in the distance. Only once were they disturbed by the Germans. Early one morning, a *maquisard* guard burst in to report that a German column led by armored cars was crawling up the long, narrow road toward the chateau. Hastily they seized their weapons and took up position covering the approaches, conscious that their situation was desperate. But to their astonishment, halfway up the hill the Germans halted, paused, and then turned their vehicles and drove away. It seemed almost certain that they had seen the *maquisards'* movements. Yet by that phase, the Occupiers had become less than enthusiastic about meeting them head on, in battle. A large part of the contempt with which crack units such as the Das Reich regarded local garrison troops stemmed from the tacit enthusiasm of most security regiments for a policy of "live and let live" with the Resistance. To German fighting units and to the zealots of the Gestapo, local German commanders often appeared absurdly anxious to placate French opinion, and contemptibly preoccupied with shipping produce and loot back to the Reich.

Poirier survived a dozen narrow escapes that spring. *Maquisards* in their camps in the woods were comparatively safe except in action. It was organizers and couriers, who were compelled to travel, who constantly risked capture. Meetings of any kind were a deadly risk: in November 1943, eleven local Resistance chiefs had been captured at a single conference in Montpazier.

There was a delicate balance to be struck between the need for speed and that for security. To walk or cycle was safer, but much too slow for the huge area Poirier had to cover. He generally employed *gazogènes*, which were designed by a Brive engineer, Maurice Arnhouil, who was one of the *maquis'* most enthusiastic—although also least discreet—supporters. Even the *gazos* were maddeningly sluggish, often needing to be pushed uphill by the combined efforts of every passenger except the driver. Once, stopped at a German roadblock, Poirier fed all his incriminating papers into the charcoal burner under the pretext of filling it with fuel. Although the Germans seldom now ventured far from main roads and towns unless in punitive columns, as the aggressiveness of the Resistance increased, so did the enemy's nervousness and ferocity. "From February 1944 onwards," said Poirier, "it became highly dangerous for anyone to fall into the hands of the German Army." Racing through the sunlit hills, among the chickens scratching in the dust, the enchanting creeper-clad villages, it was easy to forget the terrible nature of their war. But when Poirier's friend and comrade Raymond Maréchal was seized by the Germans, they forced his hands into the charcoal furnace of a *gazogène* and held him against the burner until he died. They burned a hotel which they searched in vain for Poirier a few hours after he left it, on an inexplicable impulse, at 5 am one day.

The romantic aura surrounding Resistance, together with Poirier's gift for laughter, made it easy for him to attract girls but only very rarely did he sleep with those who were deeply involved in Resistance and utterly secure, "more or less for health reasons, you know." George Starr, his F Section counterpart further west, had no sexual relationship with any woman during his two years in Gascony, because he considered the security risk too great.

It is only human nature that, after the war, these men forgot the months of chronic tension, the habit that dogged Poirier for months after the Liberation of watching his back everywhere that he walked. They remembered the absurd moments. An excited *résistant* who had been a French air force pilot came to Poirier one day and reported that he had found an abandoned and forgotten Maubussin light aircraft at the nearby Belvès flying club. One extraordinary spring day, the two men took off in the aircraft and circled over Périgueux, hurling out propaganda leaflets. They returned to Belvès with the exulting pilot leapfrogging the Dordogne bridges. The terrified Poirier demanded to get out, and was duly landed. The pilot took off again and made a dramatic swoop upon the river bridge. Poirier heard the terrible noise of the crash, and raced miserably to the scene to drag out the pilot's body. Instead, he found the nonchalant young man sitting on the bridge, smoking a cigarette and surveying the ruins of the aircraft: "The Dordogne air force had made its first and last sortie."

All the months that he had been in England and with Peulevé, Poirier had assumed that his father Robert, another dashing spirit who became a racing driver for a time after leaving the air force, was somewhere working for Resistance. But the two had no contact until one day Poirier was informed that he was to meet a man at the *bloc-gazo* works in Brive whom local *résistants* thought could be helpful. To his utter astonishment, he walked into the room to find himself face to face with his father. His first thought was to mutter urgently: "Say nothing about our relationship!" He had concealed his real French identity very closely, even from Malraux. The two talked earnestly. Poirier's last words that night, before they went to bed, were: "Father, if you stay to work with me, you must accept that I am the boss." The next morning his father's first words were *"Bonjour, mon capitaine."* For the rest of the war Robert Poirier acted as secretary and administrative assistant to his son, without either man betraying a hint of the relationship to their colleagues.

As he toured the *maquis*, Poirier was indifferent to the political allegiances of each camp. Unlike some SOE officers, who would arm only those who would accept a measure of direction, and above all those who were not communist, Poirier cared only about how energetically they seemed likely to fight Germans. He overlooked the banditry by which some *maquis* existed, unless it appeared to threaten their security. Indeed, he was appalled one day to visit a *maquis* of Spaniards high in the hills—there were thousands of refugees from the Civil War all over southern France—and found them attempting literally to live off the land. They seemed to exist chiefly on nuts and wild plants. They were desperately hungry and passionately eager to fight fascists. At the end of the war, Poirier was deeply moved when their commander said to him: "And now, *mon commandant*, will you ask Baker Street to begin their *parachutages* to us in Spain?" He loved the Spaniards, and went so far as to relay their doomed request to London, deadpan.

"For a long time, those who had least were the best *résistants*," said Poirier. The poor and the radical, those whom respectable citizens dismissed as troublemakers and drifters, sowed the seeds of Resistance. If there was a hierarchy of courage, those who came to Resistance in 1942 or 1943—above all, before the great flood of recruits after D-Day—were at its summit. It may seem cynical or trite to remark that it is easier to abandon a workman's flat or a peasant cottage than a chateau, in order to become a *maquisard*, but it proved overwhelmingly true. Those who possessed most had most to lose from German revenge. Many of the aristocrats who owned the chateaux of the Dordogne detested and feared the Resistance. Many of the bourgeoisie, deeply frightened by the Popular Front government of 1936, the 1% million votes cast for the communists, the coming of such revolutionary specters as paid holidays for workers, feared the *maquisards* as the harbingers of revolution. And indeed many *maquisards* themselves—not all of them communists—regarded Resistance as a revolutionary act, the spur to radical change in their society: "After the war, it will all be different. . . ."

In French bourgeois terms, as Poirier remarked wryly, Robin Hood had been a dangerous bolshevik. Many small businessmen passionately believed that the experience of the 1930s had shown democracy to be a failure in France, a path to anarchy. German occupation was perfectly acceptable if it produced social and economic stability. Antisemitism had always been deeply rooted in French society. Hatred of the British remained very strong among a significant number of Frenchmen throughout World War II, especially in French naval circles after the destruction of their fleet at Mers-El-Kebir. Beyond even those who were ideologically sympathetic to the Germans—a significant minority—a much larger number profited financially from coming to terms with the Occupation—the contractors, the black marketeers. Great landowners with estates held in their families for generations were passionately committed to preserving them, even at some small moral cost. Unjust as it may seem, those among the aristocracy, the professionals, the bourgeois, the factory owners and the officials who supported Resistance must be awarded greater moral credit than their humbler countrymen, because they were few, and because they acted against the spirit and inclination of their class.

One of the most remarkable of these *résistants* was Poirier's professional neighbor in the Dordogne, known throughout the countryside as "Edgar," but in reality Baron Philippe de Gunzbourg. The de Gunzbourgs were a Russian Jewish family, bankers and landowners who acquired a Hessian title and moved to Paris in the early years of the century. Philippe's grandfather achieved an enormous coup by taking a founding interest along with the Rothschilds in the Dutch Shell company. His father consolidated the fortune by marrying an immensely rich bourgeois wife. Philippe himself, born in 1904, grew up rich, spoilt and essentially rootless, torn between his French and Jewish loyalties. There was a procession of family tragedies: his brother died, a sister was killed in a riding accident in England. Philippe was destined for Eton, but after a family change of heart went to a Paris *lycée*, and later spent a few terms at Oxford. In his early twenties he married a *demi-mondaine* (one of a class of women who relied on their wealthy lovers) twenty years older than himself, an absurd alliance which was quickly terminated. He explored all the traditional extravagances of rich, reckless young men, flying aircraft and racing cars between bursts of high living. He married a second time, more happily, a French Jewish girl with whom he went on a prolonged round-the-world honeymoon and had four children. Then he began to lead a more settled existence, with a Paris house and a large ugly mansion which he bought in the Lot-et-Garonne because he felt a growing sympathy for the countryside and its peasants.

But as he approached forty, he felt no closer to achieving an identity. The most consistent strand in his life was his feeling for England. He had been reared by an English nanny, taken constantly to England on visits, bought all his clothes in London, and had been taught by his father "to believe that England, and the British Empire, were the greatest institutions in the world." He was living in the Lot-et-Garonne—in the Unoccupied Zone—when the Germans swept across France, and the rest of his family prudently fled to America. One of their English nannies remained defiantly at their Paris house throughout the war on the grounds that she had to protect the family's possessions, and twice defied arrest and interrogation by the *milice*. In the south, the de Gunzbourgs listened reverently to the BBC each night, and shared the house with "the living embodiment of the British Empire," their own nanny Alice Joyce who regarded all Germans with withering scorn, and throughout the war declined to speak any tongue but her own.

As the months passed, de Gunzbourg reflected more and more deeply about his own position. He became convinced that he must play some active role in the struggle against the Germans and Vichy. He contacted like-minded friends in Toulouse, and one day in September 1942 one of them telephoned and asked him to come down: "There's somebody here that I think you should meet." In the back room of a scruffy little bar in Toulouse, he was introduced to an intensely English young man lolling back in his chair who asked him simply: "Why do you want to help?"

"Because for me, England is the only country in the world," said de Gunzbourg, "above all the only one fighting the Germans." He talked of his own horror of the French elite—the politicians, the magistrates, the generals. Two weeks later, he heard that he had been successfully "checked out" by the Englishman, one of SOE's early agents in the region, Maurice Pertschuk, "Eugene." De Gunzbourg entered the secret war, carrying messages and seeking out recruits. Eugene began to visit de Gunzbourg's home. He loved to eat Yorkshire pudding made by Nanny, and beyond this it became rapidly apparent that the young Englishman was obsessed with de Gunzbourg's beautiful wife, Antoinette. The Frenchman was less disturbed by this than by the agent's reckless lack of security. They began to hear stories of the leaders of the *réseau* sharing noisy tables at the best black market restaurants in Toulouse, of Pertschuk's wireless operator living with his girlfriend in a chateau outside the city. It was an operational style which could lead to only one conclusion: Pertschuk, his wireless operator and several of their key colleagues were betrayed, captured, and killed in a German concentration camp.

De Gunzbourg survived, but he was now a fugitive. He dispatched his wife and children to safety in Switzerland, and began a life that was to continue until the Liberation as a gypsy without a home, without possessions, whose only life was that of Resistance. This playboy who before the war had driven only the fastest cars that money could buy began to travel south-west France by bicycle, covering 15,000 miles before the war was over. In the first months of 1943, he could achieve little amidst the wreckage of Pertschuk's circuit. But one evening in May, in the house of a little railway worker in Agen, he met French Section's new agent in Gascony. This was a man of utterly different stamp from Pertschuk, the extraordinary George Starr, "Hilaire," who by the Liberation controlled a vast sweep of Gascony. A chunky former mining engineer from north Staffordshire whose false teeth gave him a permanent twisted grin, Starr inspired immediate confidence despite his atrocious French accent.

De Gunzbourg became his principal organizer in the Dordogne, while the Englishman concentrated his efforts on the Gers and the Landes. He learnt to assemble *plastique* charges, and arranged the first of many major sabotage operations against locomotives at Eymet,

Bergerac and other key rail centers on New Year's Eve 1943. He taught dozens of eager little groups of *résistants* the techniques of receiving *parachutages*, lighting bonfires to a prearranged pattern on receipt of a *message personnel* from the BBC (and by now each night scores of unarmed *résistants* the length of France lit bonfires whenever they heard an aircraft, in the hope of intercepting a silken bounty). Maurice Loupias, "Bergeret," a local official in Bergerac who became one of the key AS leaders of the region, has vividly described "a farmhouse with twenty silent peasants listening in religious silence to Philibert explaining *parachutage* drill, puffing their pipes by the fireplace as he described the method of folding the canopies." Bergeret called de Gunzbourg "the principal artisan of our victory."

De Gunzbourg also believed from what Starr had told him that they could expect parachute landings by Allied troops within days of the main invasion. Whether or not his understanding was correct, in his own mind the importance of seizing and holding a perimeter on D-Day became as dominant as among the *maquisards* of the Vercors. Like most Allied agents, de Gunzbourg found his recruits willing enough to listen to any man who could influence the coming of arms and money. Some were irked by his open devotion to the English—after the invasion, there were some sour jokes about his appearance in British boots. There were still many Frenchmen who wished to keep the British at arm's length. Despite his codename, de Gunzbourg was obviously an aristocrat and a Jew, and there were many *résistants* who loathed both. Some also felt that he was too assertive in giving orders. But it is a remarkable tribute to his dedication and personality that he was able to coordinate Resistance in the western Dordogne so effectively, without training or military experience.

Some regarded the latter as a positive merit: "We'll follow you because you're less of a '*con*' (bloody idiot) than the others," shrugged one group of peasant recruits, but they added—"if you start using the *naphtalinés*, we will never go with you!" One of the strongest prejudices among many French *résistants* was that against the "mothball brigade," former French officers who sought to take belated command of *maquis* now that the tide had turned decisively toward the Allies. The ORA, the Resistance movement founded by former officers, never achieved much support or success, and survived until the Liberation only because the Americans developed an unfounded faith in its future. It is also worth remembering that not all *résistants* in early 1944 were enthralled by De Gaulle, and many did not even know what he looked like. But some did. De Gunzbourg never forgot a *résistant's* wife declaring to him passionately one night, "*Oh M. Philibert, je suis amoureuse, je suis amoureuse de General De Gaulle!*" ("Oh Mr. Philibert, I am in love, I am in love with General De Gaulle!")

For all its discomforts and dangers, and the months spent in peasant cottages and workmen's flats without even a passing encounter with a man or woman with whom he might find enough in common to relax socially or mentally, de Gunzbourg enjoyed his war: "I had thought that I was incapable of doing anything with my life, and I discovered that there was something I could contribute. It gave me a purpose." He developed great respect for the peasants of south-west France, and above all for their wives, whose discretion and influence were so formidable. By the spring of 1944, de Gunzbourg was in touch with *réseaux* from Bergerac in the west to Sarlat in the east, and south toward Toulouse and Auch. It is a measure of the isolation in which most circuits worked that, although he was sometimes within a few miles of Jacques Poirier, neither man was aware of the other's legitimacy. Each simply heard reports of another alleged agent operating in what he considered his own territory. Starr told de Gunzbourg laconically that if the mysterious "agent" who was said to be causing difficulties over-reached himself, it might be simplest to have him killed. By the same token, Soleil was enraged to hear that de Gunzbourg was "poaching," and swore that he would shoot him if they met. The only relevance of these mildly silly exchanges is that they show the fog and confusion in which Resistance existed. Each group was an uncharted island upon an ocean. It was safer so, but it caused much bewilderment.

Over most of the south-west, George Starr had fewer such problems because he was unchallenged overlord, with half a dozen British-trained couriers and instructors, and a much greater degree of control over local Resistance than most of F's agents achieved. He was also an exceptional personality—"*un homme du métier*" ("a professional"), de Gunzbourg called him, "*un grand chef, de la classe de Lawrence*" ("a leader, the likes of Lawrence").

Starr was the son of an English mother and American father who owned a circus which travelled the length of Europe. He was educated at Ardingly public school, and studied mining at London University. He was a cosmopolitan, but he retained the accent and earthy hardiness of northern England. Through the 1930s he travelled Europe as a mining engineer, providing occasional reports to British Intelligence as a sideline. On 10 May 1940 he was down a mine near Liege when the Germans invaded Belgium. He beat a hasty retreat to England through Dunkirk, joined the army, and spent a year as a sergeant commanding the carrier pigeon section of Phantom, the GHQ Reconnaissance Unit based in St. James's Park in London. It was there that he received a summons to Selwyn Jepson of SOE, who asked if he would go to France. "Only if I choose where I go," said this dour little man. He refused to work in an area where he had friends, and might be recognized. After the usual training in the black arts, one night early in November 1942 he landed by felucca on the Mediterranean coast of France, near Marseille. On the beach to meet him he found his own brother, John, who was already an F Section agent, and who presented him with a ration card and other essential forged paperwork.

George Starr had been ordered to go to Lyon, ". . . but I didn't like the look of it. The whole situation had the wrong smell about it." His instincts were correct. The network to which he had been assigned was extensively penetrated by the Germans, and was crumbling rapidly. At the suggestion of Peter Churchill, Starr instead moved west, into the Lot-et-Garonne. These were still the most dangerous days of Resistance, when agents were compelled to feel their way through France "by guess and by God." Each man embarked on a process of exploring initial contacts, as sensitive and dangerous as dismantling an unexploded bomb. An agent's most priceless gift was luck, as again and again he exposed himself to men and women of unproven loyalty. To touch the wrong connection was usually fatal. There were occasional sabotage operations and spasmodic arms drops, but most of the work in 1942–3 was a long, unglamorous struggle to turn a thousand isolated groups of Frenchmen hostile to the Nazis into a coherent underground movement.

Starr's luck held. He reached Lot-et-Garonne with one contact address, which proved welcoming. He began to meet potential local helpers. His first priority was to gain radio contact with London—he had brought with him only an S-phone, by which he could establish short-range voice communication with an overhead aircraft. With some difficulty, he passed a message to London through another, distant agent, giving a rendezvous. Gerry Morel, F's operations officer, flew in person over the dropping zone and talked to Starr on the S-phone. When he asked for some evidence of identity, the blast of Staffordshire blasphemy satisfied him. Starr got his radio, and soon began to receive arms.

One of the key rules of clandestine life was "Keep moving." But Starr broke it successfully when he set up his headquarters in the little corner house by the church in the hamlet of Castelnau-sur-l'Auvignon, some twenty-five miles west of the Das Reich Division's cantonment area. Gascony had a deep-rooted tradition of resistance to authority, even from Paris. The peasant smallholders who farmed their tobacco among the gentle hills, living in villages without paved roads or piped water, were intensely hostile to the Germans. Starr's host, the taciturn, mustachioed Roger Laribeau, was mayor of Castelnau. He made Starr, in his cover as Gaston, a retired Belgian mining engineer, deputy mayor. This chiefly gave him access to the immense range of permits needed for the smallest action or movement in Occupied France. The Englishman began to travel the countryside by train, bicycle, and *"peut-peut"* motor bicycle, as far eastwards as Toulouse, west into the coastal forests of the Landes, north to Bergerac. When he met *résistants*, he tried to convey an impression that he merely bore orders from a senior officer, but they knew him always as *"Le Patron."* He had a strong streak of peasant cunning himself, and the maturity and judgment gained in twenty years of directing mining operations. "Building a network," said Starr, "is like making a ladder. You fix one rung. You stand on it. You jump on it. If it holds, you build the next one. It takes time. The people who wanted to do it in five minutes got caught. I was bloody lucky."

Baker Street soon recognized the quality of the circuit Starr was creating—Wheelwright, as they knew it. In August 1943 a thirty-four-year-old WAAF named Annette Cormeau was parachuted to join him as a wireless operator. She was the daughter of a British consular official who had been educated in Europe and was working as a secretary in Brussels in 1937 when she met and married a half-Belgian, half-English accountancy student. They had a daughter in 1938, and she was expecting another baby when a German bomb struck their flat in London in November 1940. Her husband, by then a British soldier, was killed. She herself was badly injured and miscarried. When she recovered, she joined the W AAF, and was serving in the operations room of a bomber station when she was called to London to see Selwyn Jepson.

She was troubled about leaving her daughter, but very eager to play a larger part in the war. She joined a training course with a group of F Section girls, most of whom were later killed by the Germans. They were worked hard. In their free time, "we used to discuss very feminine things—would we be able to carry off wearing high heels after so long in flat service shoes? We spent a lot of time talking to exiled Frenchmen on the course about conditions in France. We had our pub crawls, and sometimes everybody went haywire, but generally the atmosphere was very serious." There was a three-week wireless course at Thame Park—"Station 52"—then the tradecraft course in security at Beaulieu in Hampshire, which Annette found less exacting than she had expected—"They didn't want to frighten us off." Every few weeks, she took a train to Bristol to see her five-year-old daughter. One day the little girl came to London, to wave her mother goodbye as she got into a taxi. There were no tears, for no one told her that it would be more than a year before they met again, and that from the taxi Annette was to be transferred to a car for Tempsford, and then France.

Much has been written about the dangers of life as a secret agent—and it must be remembered that, statistically, F Section's men and women fared rather better for casualties in France than a front-line infantry battalion. But little has been said about the tedium and discomfort of living for months in humble surroundings, without personal friends, with only peasant hosts for company. Starr scorned any notion of finding romance in his work, and although it was part of their cover that Annette was his mistress, their relationship was entirely professional. Selwyn Jepson said that when he chose agents, he looked for people who had seen something of the world, discovered their own strengths and limitations, and learned self-reliance. Annette sometimes found the boredom of the tiny hamlet stifling. She helped with the cows and the babies and the housework, and dressed in the same simple peasant clothes. She and Starr were exasperated by a courier once sent from London, a very pretty girl who insisted on wearing high Paris fashion at every opportunity. The most important element in their security was inconspicuousness. Most nights Annette listened to the radio to stay awake until the time came for her own transmitting schedule.

She picked up South American stations, and sometimes RAF weather aircraft in the Bay of Biscay. "Air temperature L-Love," they reported cryptically. She never discovered whether this was hot or cold. Then, at the prearranged moment, she tapped out her own message of 100 or 150 words—fifteen or twenty minutes of transmission time. The set, hidden behind her bed, was powered by six-volt car batteries, because the Germans had an irksome habit of switching off power in rotation to every village when their direction-finders picked up a transmission. If there was a break in the morse, they had pinpointed their set.

Unlike Annette, Starr seemed to enjoy the long evenings at the kitchen table, sitting with his head in his hands while the soup pot simmered over the huge fireplace, talking about crops, beasts and wine. Sometime he lent a hand at the back-breaking business of tending the tobacco fields. He had a bottomless stock of anecdotes about England and earthy jokes that delighted the villagers. Sometimes, when there was urgent work to be done, he tugged insistently at his beret in tension and excitement. But never, even after the fiercest evening with the villagers and their formidable capacity for Armagnac, did he betray the slightest indiscretion. Starr was a natural secret agent.

There is just one other Englishman to be mentioned here—of them all, the agent closest to the heart of the Das Reich Division, indeed the only one who had walked and driven past the lagers and vehicle parks of 2nd SS Panzer Division in the months that they lay around Montauban. One night, Germans interrupted a *parachutage*, and he was compelled to spend hours taking refuge in a tree while they talked and searched beneath him. The troops were very probably of the Das Reich. The agent was a twenty-two-year-old veteran named Tony Brooks.

Brooks was an Englishman brought up in Switzerland and living in the Jura at the outbreak of war. Like Jacques Poirier, he became involved in an escape line, in his case in Marseille, and himself walked over the Pyrenees in the autumn of 1941, reached England and offered himself to SOE. In July 1942, just turned twenty, he was given a crash course in French trades unionism and parachuted into France with instructions to explore the creation of a *réseau* based on the railway workers of southern France. He spent the next two years—an extraordinary lifespan for an agent in Occupied territory—establishing a marvelously successful network among the *cheminots* (railway workers) who, all over the country, provided some of the most dedicated recruits for Resistance.

The Germans fought unceasingly and unsuccessfully to stop the railways being used for the transport of fugitives on engines and as centers of sabotage. Every rail yard in France bore signs: "AVERTISSE-MENT: PEINE DE MORT CONTRE LES SABOTEURS. POUR LE PAYS, POUR TA FAMILLE, POUR TON RAVITAILLEMENT, POUR TOI, CHEMINOT, IL FAUT ENGAGER ET GAGNER LA LUTTE CONTRE LA SABOTAGE." ("WARNING: PENALTY OF DEATH FOR SABOTEURS. FOR THE COUNTRY, FOR YOUR FAMILY, FOR YOUR SUPPLIES, FOR YOU, *CHEMINOT*, WE MUST ENGAGE AND WIN THE STRUGGLE AGAINST SABOTAGE.") The rail workers were the most valuable saboteurs of all, because they knew exactly what to hit to achieve most damage without permanently wrecking the railways of France, as opposed to the Allied bombings "which did more harm than good," as their official historian remarked acidly. They were also exasperated by the extravagant, irrelevant demolitions of the FTP, which destroyed viaducts and installations which would take literally years to rebuild. They believed there was a better way.

Brooks was blessed with a natural sense of security, working with small cells each of which remained unaware of each other's existence. He preserved one refuge for himself in Lyon of which he informed not a single soul. "So English, so careful," said a respectful French officer who met him in 1944. Weeks before D-Day, Brooks had established that the key to the movement of heavy armor from southern France by rail was the limited stock of flatcars capable of passing under the nation's bridges laden with tanks. He had pinpointed the whereabouts of most of them. In the days before 6 June, he and some of his enthusiastic *cheminots* spent many hours of many nights working on their axle bearings with abrasive paste supplied from London. They were now incapable of travelling more than a matter of miles before seizing. Like Starr and de Gunzbourg, Brooks had also briefed his saboteurs in great detail about *Plan Vert*. At his safe house in Toulouse in the first days of June 1944, Brooks felt tolerably confident that if German reinforcements were moving north in the wake of D-Day, it was most unlikely that they would be doing so by train.

CHAPTER 4

The Road

WITHIN HOURS OF THE Allied landings on the morning of 6 June across the Lot and Corrèze and Dordogne, as across the rest of France, men were streaming on foot and by car and truck and bicycle to collect their arms and take to the *maquis*. Odette Bach was in the hairdressers' in Souillac when she heard the news, and bicycled thirty miles home to Figeac, bursting with exhilaration. Her husband abandoned his job as a cashier at the local Credit Lyonnais with a doctor's certificate to enable him to continue to be paid—and joined his group. Jean Sennemaut, commanding the AS detachment at Bellac, north-west of Limoges, took his wife, Sten gun and grenades, left their nine-month-old daughter at her grandmother's, and abandoned their home for the farmhouse seven miles into the countryside which he had designated weeks before as the group's rendezvous on mobilization. In the Corrèze, especially, men began to flock to the various rendezvous of the *Armée Secrète*. Many of them had no previous connection with Resistance, and there were not remotely enough weapons to arm them. When Deschelette, De Gaulle's *Délégué Militaire Régional*, heard of the great concentrations moving to join Vaujour and Guedin's companies, he was deeply concerned, for he feared the consequences of massing more men than they could possibly arm and control. But it seemed unthinkable to turn them away, and their leaders were that day a little drunk with the exhilaration of the moment. Deschelette, whom some of his subordinates found an ineffectual figure, was soon much preoccupied with reports of a major FTP action around the town of Tulle, and an even more alarming AS concentration developing around Bergerac in the Dordogne. In the Corrèze, Marius Guedin's AS companies deployed as he and Vaujour had arranged weeks before, on the bridges across the Dordogne and the key junctions west of Brive.

The Resistance made no direct assault on the German garrison of Bergerac in the days following 6 June, but the entire countryside surrounding the town rose in open insurrection. De Gunzbourg took command of the *résistants* south of the Dordogne river, and Bergeret—Maurice Loupias—of those to the north. They reckoned that they had some 2,800 Stens, 450 rifles, 100 Brens and twenty anti-tank weapons. With these arms, they believed that they could cut off the Germans in Bergerac and control the eastern Dordogne until the expected Allied parachutists arrived. In the area he had chosen as a landing ground, de Gunzbourg was directing hundreds of men who had arrived in trucks from all over the department to distribute weapons, clear obstacles and cut down trees on the field, then set up an all-round defense to cover it. There was one predictable disappointment when the local FTP, whom they had armed, refused to have any part in the AS uprising. But Soleil arrived with sixty of his *maquisards* and took up position at Mouleydier, on the direct route between Bergerac and Brive-la-Gaillarde. "Barricades are a great tradition in France," said de Gunzbourg. Barricade fever seized the area, and he wrote:

> With immense enthusiasm the whole region put itself in a state of war. Bridges were blown, roads blocked with tree trunks, wagons and so on. The obstacles were mined at points I had chosen in advance. Some men were deployed for guerilla action. Others patrolled the roads and made all civilian movement impossible without papers being checked. Indeed, people overdid the roadblocking, and Jean and I had the greatest difficulty in dissuading them . . .

It was Bergeret's proudest hour—he himself publicly proclaimed the Fourth Republic. From a distance, Poirier at Belvès was horrified to hear of all these events. The *résistants* of western Dordogne had created a static threat to German control which it seemed impossible for them to ignore. The ingredients were assembled for a tragedy which could have been as horrific as that of the Vercors, where 2,000 *maquisards* died in the hopeless attempt to defend a "redoubt" against the Germans in July 1944. This was not at all what London had in mind.

As Starr's men assembled and armed in the Gers and the Landes, the first rail demolitions were taking place. Brooks' *cheminots* cut the vital line north from Montauban to Brive-la-Gaillarde. Starr and de Gunzbourg's teams hit the lines westwards to Bordeaux, and Peter Lake several of those in the eastern Dordogne. At Brive, a taciturn, soberly Catholic SNCF engineer named Jean Marsat directed his *cheminot* resisters in cutting the lines to Tulle and to the south and west. In the first week following D-Day, 960 of 1,055 rail cuts scheduled under *Plan Vert* were carried out.

It is essential, however, to keep a sense of perspective about rail sabotage. Even SNCF's official historian remarks that "in spite of the active help of the *cheminots*, the execution of *Plan Vert* was only partial on D-Day. . . ." The Allied commanders' objections to dependence on sabotage had partly stemmed from the knowledge that explosions on stretches of main line could be repaired within sixteen to forty-eight hours. More sophisticated attacks on points and turntables by *cheminots* could do much more damage, but these accounted for only a minority of D-Day targets. The greatest weakness in the execution of the sabotage plan was that it placed insufficient emphasis on repetition at almost daily intervals. Contrary to the assertions of many *résistants* and Resistance historians, the Germans continued to run some trains on the lines that they considered vital across most of France after D-Day. A group of Guedin's *maquisards* was in action against a German armored train which arrived to repair a line cut at Noailles, south of Brive, on 7 June. Two were killed and one was captured. He was burnt to death in the furnace of the locomotive.

But the evidence is overwhelming that, from 7 June, it was impossible to move the Das Reich Division at any speed by direct routes north or north-west from Montauban. A little of the credit for this undoubtedly belongs to the Allied air forces, as do all of the laurels for their difficulties north of the Loire, but it was principally the achievement of Brooks, Starr, de Gunzbourg and other SOE officers, together with the Frenchmen whom they had equipped and instructed. Without SOE, Resistance could have achieved nothing.

At 6 pm on 6 June, General De Gaulle broadcast to France from the BBC: "The supreme battle has begun. . . . For the sons of France wherever they may be, whatever they may be, the simple and sacred duty is to fight the enemy by every means at their command."

The first of scores of G-3 SHAEF daily bulletins on the development of Resistance reported that, despite heavy German short-wave jamming, the Action Messages had been generally well received on the medium wave: "General reports indicate that the *maquis* are increasing in strength earlier than anticipated, without much interference from the Germans."

The news of the Allied landing trickled erratically to the officers of the Das Reich. Many men heard it for the first time from exulting or nervous French civilians on the streets of Montauban or the villages in which they were quartered. Among most veterans, it inspired a sense of relief that at last the waiting and uncertainty were ended. The decisive battle had begun. But most unit commanders were acutely conscious of their shortages of equipment and transport, and the inadequate training of the new drafts. Ernst Krag, commanding the assault gun battalion, had been retraining an infantry company to make up his shortage of gunners. Heinrich Wulf's reconnaissance battalion was still awaiting an entire company's complement of heavy armored cars.

Karl Kreutz, commanding the artillery, heard of the landings at the little chateau where he had his headquarters from his adjutant Gerstenburger, a middle-aged reserve officer who had been a bank clerk before the war. Kreutz, a robust, jovial man unlike any stereotype of an SS officer, began urging his batteries into activity: "We knew that every single day was vital, every day lost was a day won for the Allies." His 105mm battalion's gunners were sadly under-trained. One entire unit lacked towing vehicles. In some of the division's dispersals, on their own initiative officers ordered drivers to begin requisitioning French civilian trucks and cars to make good the transport shortages. Some officers and men were absent on courses and on leave. Borkmann, adjutant of Otto Pohl's tank unit, was still on his way back from his own wedding in Silesia, and did not rejoin them until four days later, having hitch-hiked perilously in their wake. One entire tank company was absent in Germany, collecting new Panzer Vs.

As the news from Normandy filtered through the camps and parks around Montauban, there was little doubt in any man's mind that within hours they would be ordered to entrain for a move 450 miles north to support the counter-offensive in Normandy. Yet all through that critical day of 6 June no orders from Army Group G reached the Das Reich. One of the decisive factors in the triumph of the Allied landings was the hesitant, poorly co-ordinated German response in the first hours of D-Day, and for that matter in the days that followed. As wave after wave of British, American and Canadian forces advanced across the beaches, the four weak infantry and one armored division of Dallman's 7th Army were left alone to man the defenses. OKW* prevaricated, hypnotized by the specter of a second landing conjured up by the brilliant Allied deception operation.

The SD's** interception of the Resistance Action Messages was ignored. At 4 am, Von Rundstedt requested Berlin's assent to move the Panzer Lehr and 12th SS Armored Divisions against the beach-head, but received it only twelve hours later. At 6:30 am, 21st Panzer was only fifteen miles from the coast and ready to move, but at 10 am it was ordered to shore up the defense of Caen. That afternoon, 21 Pz launched the only armored counter-stroke of the day, without support. Its tanks reached the coast at one point before they were driven back, having lost a quarter of their strength. At 4:55 pm, Von Rundstedt telephoned 7th Army HQ, and

> . . . emphasized the desire of the Supreme Command to have the enemy in the bridgehead annihilated by the evening of 6 June, since there exists a danger of additional sea and airborne landings. In accordance with an order by General Jodl, all units will be diverted to the point of penetration in Calvados. The beach-head there must be cleaned up not later than tonight. The Chief of Staff answers that such action would be impossible. . . .

At 5 pm, Sepp Dietrich's 1st SS Panzer Corps was given its first orders since the landing—to prepare to counter-attack west of Caen at first

---

* Oberkommando der Wehrmacht—German Army High Command.

** The *Sicherheitsdienst*, or security service (the SD), an arm of the Gestapo.

light on 7 June. In the event, Allied air and artillery action, together with the fuel shortages that crippled every German troop movement, prevented the Panzer Corps from passing its start line on the seventh. Its first, belated assault was launched the following day, 8 June. All over northern France the destruction of the rail system, the Allied fighter bomber attacks and the chronic petrol problem left units straggling over hundreds of miles of road and track as they crawled forward to the battle zone.

Yet while the signals centers of Army Group B were swamped by ill tidings of Allied success in the north, so those of Army Group G at Toulouse were receiving a torrent of messages from isolated German garrisons all over south and central France, announcing the uprising of Resistance:

> Impression growing that the *maquis* are a strictly organized military force, and effective action against them possible only with mobile heavy weapons. . . .
>
> Tarbes infested with guerillas. . . .
>
> OKW to C-in-C West: vital importance to protect wolfram mines east of Limoges. . . .
>
> Two trucks of 2nd SS Pz pioneer battalion attacked by guerillas in lorry with machine gun at approaches to Figeac. Enemy lorry destroyed by gunfire. 5 enemy killed, 2 SS killed, driver taken prisoner. . . .
>
> First Army signaled from Bordeaux: "The departments of Dordogne and Corrèze are held by terrorists. Part of the department of the Indre and the town of Tulle are dominated by gangs.* The town of Limoges is besieged. Perigueux and Brive are expecting attacks by gangs. Tulle has been under attack with mortars and artillery since last night (information from the SO)."

It had been obvious for many months to the abler German commanders—above all Rommel and Von Rundstedt—that an attempt to hold every yard of Occupied France once the invasion began would be militarily disastrous, and would merely cause weakness everywhere. Yet as late as

---

* *Banden*—the customary Wehrmacht term for Resistance groups.

16 June, when Von Rundstedt urged OKW to abandon all France south of the Loire and bring the sixteen infantry divisions then in southern France to join the line in Normandy, this idea was rejected as "politically impossible" by Berlin.

If OKW and Army Group G had kept their heads, withdrawn their weak, and obviously panicky, local garrisons and abandoned large tracts of southern France to the Resistance, it would have avoided immense problems. The *résistants* posed no military threat to major formations, and could be disposed of at leisure once the vital battle in Normandy had been won. Instead, Army Group G now deployed piecemeal every man, gun and vehicle that could be scraped together to counter-attack *résistants* wherever they had massed. Not even the most optimistic Allied planner before the invasion had anticipated that the German High Command would be so foolish as to commit major fighting formations against *maquisards*. Perhaps the greatest contribution that Resistance made to D-Day was now to goad the Germans into deploying against the *maquis* forces out of all proportion to the real threat that they represented.

General Heinz Lammerding had argued even before D-Day that it was essential to retain control of south central France, and to suppress the *maquis*. On 5 June 1944 he drafted a memorandum to 58th Corps which bears heavily on much that followed:

> SUBJECT: Anti-terrorist measures.
>
> The development of the *maquis* situation in the zone Cahors-Aurillac-Tulle represents a threat which, in the event of a landing, could adversely influence operations. The majority of the terrorists are pursuing the objectives of communism and destruction. The population only assists them under duress (especially the moneyed and official classes). The measures taken so far against the terrorists have not had much success. . . .

Lammerding suggested a forceful propaganda offensive to drive home to the population that the miseries of repression were brought upon them by the actions of the terrorists. He proposed a wholesale seizure of vehicles and petrol stocks throughout the terrorist area, intensive sweeps and checks on movement, and the occupation of Cahors, Figeac and Brive by powerful units. Then, most formidably:

> On 15 June, I propose that we should round up 5,000 male suspects in the Cahors-Aurillac-Tulle area and deport them to Germany. The terrorists, according to local reports, have enlisted the classes of 1945 and 1946 in this region. If one removes that number of men, the terrorist organization will lose the elements to make any major expansion of their strength possible.
>
> [I propose] the freeing of a member of a family or a friend taken prisoner, in return for information about arms dumps or *maquis* leaders; to make it known that for every German wounded, three terrorists will be hanged (and not shot), and for every German killed, ten terrorists will be hanged. . . .
>
> The division is convinced that if these steps are taken, the area will be pacified, and there will be no further problems for operations in the event of an invasion. . . .

Lammerding's memorandum was forwarded to Army Group G by 58th Corps endorsed by its commander: "With reference to the punitive and reprisal measures proposed by 2nd SS Pz, the general commanding heartily concurs."

Early on 7 June, Army Group G dispatched a long signal to 58th Corps which began:

> The development of the gang situation in the Massif Central demands immediate and unhesitating action by major formations. To this effect, on the orders of OB West and with the agreement of Führer headquarters, the 189th Infantry Division and the 2nd SS Panzer Division are immediately placed under the orders of 66th Reserve Corps. The 2nd SS Armoured Division thus reassigned is to deploy in the Tulle-Limoges area, where substantial formations of gangs appear to be gathered. . . .

In other words, despite the onset of invasion, a version of Lammerding's own plan was to be put into immediate effect. It was an extraordinary decision, and one which OKW would quickly regret.

At 11:15 on the morning of 7 June, signals were at last dispatched to all elements of the Das Reich warning that a move was imminent. Unit commanders were summoned to the villa on the edge of Montauban where Lammerding's headquarters stood festooned with its aerials, busy with scurrying clerks and signalers. All that day and far into the night, around the divisional area men labored filling tanks, assembling fuel and ammunition, checking guns and vehicles. Most of the local population were heartily glad to see them preparing to go. But there were also partings with girlfriends and sincere expressions of good wishes. A few girls tied flowers to the radiators of trucks and half-tracks. One gave Private Schneid a paper bag full of biscuits for the march: "Did her compatriots later cut off her hair for that gesture?" he mused afterwards. Some of the SS gave the civilians with whom they had been billeted their unused ration books. Ernst Krag was saddened that he would no longer hear the elderly doctor with whom he had been billeted play the piano so beautifully. Whatever hatred the German Occupiers inspired as a mass, it is absurd to imagine that there were not moments of private sympathy, even warmth. Several German officers found that the families with whom they lodged apologized in private for being unable to greet them in public. Marguerite Rollet, one of the Frenchwomen who had a group of troopers billeted in her house, was struck by the irony that they would bring her food to supplement the rations and behaved with perfect courtesy in the house. Meanwhile, they returned from anti-partisan sweeps laden with booty from bicycle parts to the ducks and chickens of the hapless households through which they had passed.

For the divisional staff, the movement order created immense problems. Every armored formation takes it for granted that its tracked vehicles move between battlefields by rail or transporter, for they are chronically prone to breakdown if driven for long distances on their caterpillars. On receipt of the warning order from 58th Corps, Major Stuckler at once signaled a routine request to the Corps for rail space for his tanks and assault guns, which could be of no possible value to anti-terrorist operations. To his utter astonishment it was peremptorily refused, without explanation. A heated exchange of signals followed as he remonstrated with Corps about the consequences to the tank units of a long road movement. But the order stood. The tanks and assault guns were to drive north via Figeac and Tulle. This was the first important, direct achievement of the Resistance rail-cutting operations, of the havoc wreaked by Brooks and his men with the precious flatcars.

Next came a further furious message from the division to 58th Corps about wheeled transport. Weeks earlier they had been assured that, when the day came, they could count upon the provision of a pool of requisitioned French vehicles, sufficient to move an entire battalion. The staff had repeatedly warned Corps that unless pre-emptive action was taken, these vehicles would mysteriously disappear when they were needed. Now, indeed, their fears were fulfilled. The vehicles were gone, and every local Frenchman denied knowledge of them. Worse still, to the fury of the unit transport officers who had requisitioned vehicles on their own initiative, they were now ordered to return these. The local commander, desperate to maintain some *modus vivendi* with the local population after the Panzers had gone, insisted that no transport was to be arbitrarily commandeered. To the SS, it was another example of the feeble attitudes of local garrisons. They complied sullenly, and divisional headquarters began the difficult struggle to reorganize its formations for movement.

Stuckler, the division's 1a or senior staff officer, was an effective administrator. A thin, somber man of thirty-one, the son of a works manager who had been an air force NCO in World War I, he had yearned to be a pilot himself, but the family had lacked the money. Instead he had joined the Bavarian police, and three years later, in 1935, the new Wehrmacht. After five years as a gunner, he was put through the superb General Staff course and was serving as a Corps staff officer in January 1944 when he found himself transferred to 2nd SS Panzer.

His first problems now were the two Panzergrenadier brigades. Both were desperately short of transport and contained too many under-trained recruits. A drastic solution was decided upon. The Deutschland regiment would hand over its best battalion—the 1st— and all regimental transport to the Der Führer. The Der Führer would transfer its least effective battalion—the 2nd—to the Deutschland. The weaker Deutschland brigade would remain at Montauban, together with the least equipped artillery battalion and a rag-tag of support units until their training and transport position improved. After a further exchange of signals with 58th Corps, the Deutschland under Major Wisliceny was ordered to form a 600-man battle group from its better-trained elements to operate in a local security role under the orders of Toulouse. This force achieved its own terrible notoriety in south-west France in the weeks that followed, but its operations in Gascony have no part in the story that follows.

At dawn on 8 June, the great columns of vehicles and armor began to roar into life in lagers for thirty miles around Montauban. Lurching forward with their great clatter and screeching of tracks, they started to swerve out on to the roads, tearing up the asphalt behind them as they moved north through the sharp early morning light. It was an immensely complex maneuver to organize some 15,000 men and over 1,400 vehicles in order of march. Wulf's reconnaissance unit, the *Aufklärungsabteilung*, was a few minutes late. The headquarters group of the Der Führer, led by the inevitable motor cyclists, impatiently rolled away up the Cahors road without waiting for them. Behind, throwing a long, pursuing dust cloud into the sky, came the trucks and half-tracks and field cars.

In the heavily armed armored cars and gun-mounted half-tracks of the reconnaissance group, the men ate cherries and sausages purchased with the last of their ready money from the fat, blackhaired grocer's wife in Beaumont-de-Lomagne where they had been billeted. Every vehicle had been ordered to maintain 100-meter spacing in case of air attack. Karl Kreutz, the artillery commander, sat beside his driver with a Sten gun between his knees, souvenir of an Allied container drop captured by his men. It was a tradition that, on anti-terrorist sweeps, they kept what they found. While any Allied officer would have willingly thrown away his Sten in exchange for the much superior German Schmeisser, in the way of soldiers it pleased Kreutz to carry a captured weapon. Behind him and his elderly driver, Feldwebel Lehmann, sat their "looky-looky," the man nominated in every vehicle in the division to search the sky for enemy aircraft. From the moment that they crossed the Loire, the "looky-lookies" would have plenty to do.

Far behind the towed artillery and the assault gun battalion, divisional headquarters and the flak units, came the two tank battalions, which were to swing eastwards at Cahors, taking the 0940 north to Tulle. On exercises, engineer squads followed the armored columns, repairing the havoc that they had wrought with the road surfaces. Today there were no such refinements. The tank squadrons were not expecting action. Two forty-gallon petrol drums were lashed to each hull—an essential measure when fuel supplies were uncertain, but unthinkable if there was a risk of gunfire. Within a few hours, as the sun came up, the heat and dirt and stink within the tanks were becoming intolerable. They moved far more slowly than the lighter elements, and halted every two hours to rest and make running repairs. Within a few miles of leaving Montauban, the maintenance crews were under pressure: the pins connecting the tracks snapped with heart-breaking regularity. Corth, the *Schirrmeister* or maintenance king of Pohl's company, raced up and down the column with his men, sweat pouring down their bodies as they labored over the roasting steel. They were grateful that Corth had wangled MAN engines for their entire company's Panthers. Other, less fortunate units, equipped with the notoriously unreliable Daimler-Benz engine, suffered ceaseless problems. Major Tyschen, with his bullet head and the appalling scar on his chin, moved from company to company in his Volkswagen, checking tanks and driving their commanders. Already it was apparent that for the tank crews the road march would be a nightmare.

The division rolled without incident down the long, straight road beside the railway from Montauban to Caussade, and began the winding climb into the hills. It was open country here, unsuited to ambushes or sniping. The men relaxed and sang as they lay against the guns or clung to the supports of their trucks. They breasted the ridge and saw the road fall away to Cahors, down a long avenue of plane trees, past the great rail viaduct, and then across the river into the medieval town. A number of isolated civilians were already dead, killed by fire from one or other of the columns on pretexts that will never be known. It may have been enough that they were under orders that this was to be a *ratissage*—a clearance and demonstration of dominance of the countryside which would not be complete without a heavy blood price. The reconnaissance battalion, the Der Führer regiment, the towed artillery and divisional headquarters followed by the support units of the division—pressed straight on northwards, toward Souillac and Brive.

The heavy armor branched east, to Figeac and St. Céré. An hour up the road, Major Dickmann and his 1st battalion of the DF turned west at Gourdon. They were to swing through the eastern Dordogne, taking up their final position on the flank of the division in the Limousin. Ten miles up the road, at the tiny hamlet of Groslejac, the Das Reich Division began to fight.

Local Resistance histories record formally an action by "3rd Section, Company Remy, Ace of Hearts *maquis*." One of the survivors saw the day more simply. At 7 am on the morning of 8 June, Marcel Vidal, a stonemason who was also mayor of Groslejac, received a visitor. It was a woodseller named Victor, who was also an enthusiastic *résistant*, one of Guedin's men. Germans were expected to pass through the village, said Victor, on their way north to fight in Normandy, and the order was that everybody must do everything possible to delay or to stop them. Vidal and Victor left the house, and began hastily knocking on doors up and down the village. There was a sharp difference of opinion among the men. Was it really worth it? What reprisals would the Germans take? How many of them would come, and was Victor sure that they would only be in lorries? . . . But one by one they dug out their weapons and walked, still arguing heatedly, toward the old bridge across the Dordogne that lay at the north end of the village. Marcel Malatrait, the butcher who was also a radical socialist like so many of the people of the Lot, took command. There were two men from one of Soleil's *maquis* who had come down from nearby woods where they were camped. One of them took his post on a rock overlooking the road, to fire a warning shot as the signal that the Germans were approaching. Ironically enough, Vidal had been given a revolver by the Germans as a mark of his status as mayor. Like most of the others there that day, he also possessed a 1914 vintage French Army rifle and bayonet. Each man held two grenades, from Resistance supplies. Almost all of them had served their time in the French Army—Vidal in the Alpine Infantry. But before that day, not one of them had seen action. The *maquisards* brought with them a single Bren gun. Fifteen men in all, they crouched and lay around the short, narrow bridge, and began the long wait in the sunshine. A few wore the brownish tunics affected by some AS men. Most were in everyday peasant blue with berets. None really possessed the slightest hint of what was about to happen to them.

At around 8:30 am, they heard the warning shot from the rock. Up the single village street, round the curve toward the bridge swept the leading armored half-tracks of Major Dickmann's battalion of Panzergrenadiers. The little cluster of Frenchmen began to fire. The German vehicles slammed to a halt. Helmeted, camouflage-smocked infantry spilled out, racing for the cover of houses and trees, working swiftly round to outflank the defenders clustered at the bridge. A devastating hail of automatic fire poured on to the French position, answering the single shot, bolt-action rifles. René Lacombe, thirty-one, was mending his car outside his house, absurdly seeking to ignore the intruders, when German fire killed him as he stood. The Hôtel Jardel, just short of the bridge, was hit by cannon fire and began to billow flames. A gaggle of civilians fled hopelessly through the front door and were shot down as they ran. Louis Cauquil, one of the men on the bridge, tried to bolt across it as the Germans advanced, and was blown dead into the roadway. The remainder of the Frenchmen, without lingering to try conclusions with their hand grenades, scrambled hastily down the river bank and fled toward the woods. The gunfire ceased. The Germans remounted their vehicles, leaving the French dead where they lay. The convoy rolled on over the Dordogne, with slight loss. Groslejac lay in silence again. Only the flames rising from the hotel and the bodies beside the road showed that there had been a battle. This mad, absurdly courageous act of defiance had lasted perhaps twenty minutes, and cost the lives of five of the defenders and five non-combatants. Today, a plaque beside the bridge records their names above the inscription: "It was here, on 8 June 1944, that a German column suffered an appreciable delay due to the sacrifice of these patriots."

North of the river, the column approached the hamlet of Carsac. As they crossed a little bridge, they met a truck bearing five astonished *résistants*. One fled, pursued by fire. The other four were shot down at point-blank range. Dickmann had now intended to turn right, and move along the river to rejoin the main road at Souillac. Here, on 6 June, Guedin's men had attacked a German outpost just after an armored train had arrived to resupply it. The French had lost three wounded, and the region was duly marked down on the German maps as a hotbed of Resistance.

On 8 June, at Carsac, the SS briefly took the wrong road, and moved through the village toward Sarlat, firing as they went. Thirteen people died in as many minutes, including a Jewish refugee doctor, the eighty-year-old blacksmith Pierre Trefail, and a man driving oxen in the fields. Several houses were set on fire. The Germans then turned their vehicles, and disappeared down that most beautiful riverside road toward the east.

At Rouffilac, *maquisards* enthusiastically assisted by local civilians had erected a huge barricade across the road. The French later claimed to have killed the motorcyclist leading the column and hit an armored car with a bazooka rocket before the Germans broke through, killing one *maquisard* and wounding two who were later taken to the hospital at Sarlat. Fifteen civilians also died. Little more than a mile further on, at Carlux, the Germans shot two women at the approach to the village. They then rejoined the main road at Souillac, rather later than they had intended, without further incident. The Occupying army had reminded the eastern Dordogne of the cost of rebellion.*

It should be noted that all the active *résistants* mobilized in the Lot that day were either directed by the Corrèze *Armée Secrète*, or belonged to the FTP *maquis*. The Groupes Vény were simply unaware that the German forces were upon them until it was too late. George Hiller wrote:

> The first we knew of the movement of the Das Reich was when its advance columns rattled up the roads in the Lot. They met with little opposition except at Bretenoux. The Germans were quickly able to open themselves a passage. For a couple of days after, one heard the rattle of armoured vehicles on the road, and at night saw farmhouses set alight in reprisals. In the Dordogne the *maquis* were

---

* Many historians of Resistance have mentioned a battle between local *résistants* and the Das Reich at Souillac during its advance. There was certainly a clash on 6 June. I have been unable to trace a further action on the eighth in German records, or from the information that I received from local Resistance sources. However, because of the uncertainty of evidence, it remains just possible that there was a minor brush that I have failed to discover.

During all the actions described in this chapter, the Germans suffered a total of around a dozen killed according to their casualty reports, which will be discussed below. It is impossible to determine which were caused in which battles on the road.

much more successful, partly owing to their greater determination, and partly to more favourable terrain.

The most pathetic tragedy of the day was at the little hamlet of Gabaudet, a few miles south of Gramat in the heart of the Lot. Among hundreds of local young men who were streaming into the countryside from their homes to join the *maquis* after D-Day, a large party gathered in a farm at Gabaudet—it is thought *en route* to join the FTP group led by Robert Noireau, "Colonel Georges." That evening, Noireau heard of their coming, and drove to join them. He and his colleagues were half a mile away when they heard heavy automatic fire, and prudently halted. Later, when silence fell and they could see only the smoke from the burning hamlet, they went into Gabaudet. An unknown unit from the right flank column of Das Reich had chanced upon the gathering of would-be *résistants*—which included a number of *gendarmes*—while patrolling up a side road. Ten boys and men, together with one girl, were shot on the spot. Eighty others were seized and driven off for deportation to Germany. To their overwhelming relief and astonishment, they were later released on the road to Tulle. Noireau's men subsequently executed a French *gendarme* who was said to have informed the Germans of the gathering at Gabaudet.

The Ace of Hearts *maquis*, under Guedin's command, was deployed across the southern Corrèze and northern Lot. Most were somewhat better armed than the little band at Groslejac, but like them they lacked the vital discipline and confidence that can only come with long training and experience as a unit. Very few *résistants* understood fire discipline—wasting ammunition is a chronic vice of guerillas. It is worth quoting the report of Maurice Parisot, commander of the Armagnac battalion, the most effective Resistance fighting group operating with George Starr, after their first action:

> The men shoot too much, without sighting and often without a target. This is unacceptable—we are short of ammunition. Even if one is surprised, it is essential to fire from the shoulder and not to shoot beyond the range of your weapon (Sten 75 or 80 metres, rifle 300 metres, Bren 1,000 metres, revolver 15 metres). Men don't

know how to use shelter or cover; they expose themselves and don't understand fire and movement. Instructors must immediately drum into them these basic rules of tactics. . . . Men must "keep their cool" in action. It is essential for them to keep in closer touch with their commanders.

These injunctions and failings applied to almost every Resistance group in France. On the N20, up which the Der Führer and reconnaissance battalion were advancing, Guedin's men had wasted hours felling trees and placing carts across the road, ignoring the vital precept of roadblocks—that to be effective they must be covered by fire, since otherwise any convoy with heavy vehicles can sweep them aside with contemptuous ease. So it was with the Das Reich, that long afternoon of 8 June. The Germans were irritated, even outraged. But they were not seriously hampered. The headquarters group of the Der Führer, including its commander Colonel Stadler in his staff car, were still cruising at the head of the division when they reached the little village of Cressenac, ten miles north of the Dordogne river.

It is a pretty, creeper-clad place with a single wide main street dusty in the June sun. It had been the scene of a minor action on 31 March, in which two *résistants* had been killed by the detested Vichyite *Garde Mobile de Réserve*—the GMR. On the afternoon of 8 June, the first vehicles of the Der Führer suddenly found themselves swept by a long burst of fire at the approaches of the village, which hit several men and caused the Germans to leap in confusion from their soft-skinned vehicles. The trucks laden with infantry pulled in beside the road, and for a few minutes both sides exchanged fire without effect. But the infantry, to their considerable fury, found themselves pinned down. Then the huge armored vehicles of the reconnaissance battalion roared up the road, past the trucks and the headquarters group. Wulf and his men enjoyed the spectacle of the infantry officers crouching in the ditch as the price of their impatience in driving ahead of them. They moved into the village, spraying cannon and machine gun fire into the *maquisard* positions. A 7 5mm Pak gun started to blast the houses from which fire was being directed, and blew a hole in the church spire. The *résistants* began to break east and westwards into the countryside, leaving four dead behind them. The Germans mounted their vehicles again, and prepared to move on, this time with Wulf's half-tracks undisputed in the lead. It was around 4 pm.

Eight miles further north, at Noailles, on the crest of the hill that guards the approach to Brive-la-Gaillarde, a little group of men of the 1st section, 6th company of the Ace of Hearts covered the crossroads, listening to the gunfire. Their leader, Commandant Romain, had been talking to them when he heard the shooting at Cressensac. He hurried away down the road on his little *mota*, just too late for the action, and narrowly avoided encountering the Das Reich. The Noailles party had just been reinforced by a group of nine defectors from the GMR, whose men had been hastening to join the Resistance in large numbers since D-Day. Several of these *Gardes*, including their leader, a man named Lelorrain, were still beside their vehicle when they heard "*un bruit infernal*" ("an infernal noise"), in the words of one of the survivors. The first of Wulf's vehicles ground over the crest and instantly opened fire, hitting Lel6rrain and several others with the first burst. Some of the *résistants* fired a few shots, but most scattered among the houses and gardens by the road. After just three hours' service to the Allied cause, the GMR leader lay dying by the roadside, along with several other dead or mortally wounded Frenchman. The long hill into Brive lay open to the Germans. Through the evening and far into the night their vehicles crawled onwards through the little villages, each successive unit speculating idly about the source of the flames that still played through the ruins of houses fired in the little skirmishes, and the wreckage of bullock carts and fallen trees from barricades swept aside by the half-tracks as they advanced up the road. Guedin's *maquisards* could consider it their principal achievement that it had taken the Das Reich Division six hours, rather than perhaps three, to cover the last forty miles to Brive-la-Gaillarde. A young Swiss girl from the Château de Noailles and a grocer's daughter named Denise Neymarie ran out into the gardens to do what they could for the *maquis* wounded, bleeding behind the trees on the hilltop.

The small town of Bretenoux, a medieval *bastide* (walled town) founded in 1277, stands beside the upper Dordogne at a point where the great river has dwindled to resemble a mellow Hampshire chalk stream, with a race and a graceful weeping willow below its ridge. The old timbered, shuttered houses slope to a walled quay on the southern bank, from which generations of townspeople have nursed their fishing rods.

On the morning of 9 June, the 1st Section of the 3rd Company of the Ace of Hearts *maquis* guarded the bridge under the command, ironically enough, of a young Alsatian named Sergeant Frédéric Holtzmann—"Fred" to most of his men. He was twenty, tall and fair, the sort of young man who might have been drafted into the SS had he remained at his home on the German border. In the early hours of the morning, word reached the village—probably by telephone from the St. Céré area where the Das Reich armored column had lagered for the night—that a German convoy was approaching. Many of the townspeople, roused from their beds, prudently departed into the woods and fields for safety. One young *résistant*, seeing a friend on his way to join them, embraced him emotionally in farewell. Then the twenty-six Frenchmen under Holtzmann, armed with rifles and a scattering of Brens and Stens, deployed around the bridge and on the roofs of the houses covering its approaches.

At about 6:30 am the first German vehicles approached the bridge down the main street of Bretenoux. Two *maquisards* who had ridden their *mota* toward St. Céré to reconnoiter were fired upon, and hastily fled. The *maquisards* around the bridge began to use their own weapons, and a stubborn little battle began. For the next three hours the Germans fought for possession of the road, while the *résistants* clung to their river bank. At his headquarters at Montplaisir, Marius Guedin heard the gunfire, and sent a *sous-officier* (NCO) and a party of men to investigate. They reached the outskirts of Bretenoux to find that there was no means of reaching the bridge. They lay watching and listening as the Germans began to use mortars. Guedin himself arrived to join them. There was nothing to be done. The SS had at last forded the river and worked around the flanks of the *résistants*. Holtzmann himself was badly wounded and could not move had he wished to. Most of the others had left it too late to withdraw. Several houses and three German vehicles were in flames. Eighteen of the twenty-five defenders of the bridge were dead. After the Liberation, Sergeant Holtzmann was awarded a posthumous Medaille Militaire.

Five miles further north, at the village of Beaulieu, another group of Guedin's men exchanged fire briefly, and lost three killed. One last section, at the crossroads of la Grafouillère still further up the road, saw the armor approaching and decided that discretion demanded that they hold their fire. The right flank of the Das Reich reached the summit of the hills, and began the long descent into Tulle without further interruption.

Resistance estimates of the casualties they had inflicted upon the Das Reich between Montauban and Brive/Tulle on 8 and 9 June ran into hundreds, and as such were written into many regional histories. In addition to the actions reported above, Colonel Kreutz was dismayed to discover that a small maintenance party who were left behind the main body of the column to repair a disabled vehicle had been fallen upon and killed by a Resistance group. There is room for doubt about an additional one or two German casualties. The armored column was engaged in a further battle, which will be described in the account of the Allied Jedburgh operations. But there seems no reason to doubt the overall German casualty report to 66th Reserve Corps for the fighting on that first march—some fifteen men killed and more than thirty wounded. French dead, as we have seen, were already over a hundred.

A signal was drafted that day from OKW's Operations Department, concerning the situation in Corrèze, Dordogne and Lot:

> Reports coming in on the secret army and acts of terrorism in the area show that *maquis* actions are reaching considerable proportions. The 66th Reserve Corps with the 2nd SS Panzer Division which are placed under the orders of the military command in France must immediately pass to the counter-offensive, to strike with the utmost power and rigour, without hesitation. The outcome of these operations is of the utmost importance to other operations in the West.
>
> In those areas partly infested, it is necessary to use intimidatory measures against the inhabitants. It is necessary to break the spirit of the population by making examples. It is essential to deprive them of all will to assist the *maquis* and meet their needs. . . .

From the high plateaus of the Lot, the road falls steeply into the spacious town of Brive-la-Gaillarde—"Brive the Bold," named for its many gallant defenses during the wars of the Middle Ages. In 1944 it possessed some 30,000 inhabitants, better fed than much of France at the period thanks to the fruit-growing and market-gardening of the area. Its central streets and squares suggest respectability and prosperity rather than beauty, but Brive has always enjoyed a reputation as a cheerful, welcoming place. Here, on the evening of 8 June, the first vehicles of the Das Reich swept down the road from Noailles and the south. "Brive was like a beehive," said Heinrich Wulf. Civilians crowding the street corners to exchange rumors and fears fled into their houses when they saw the column approach. As the most powerful German formation the town had ever seen roared up the road to the *Ortslwmmandantur*, (District Commander) they peered bleakly through the shutters. Some vehicles showed scars of battle. All of them were caked in dust and crowded with grim, camouflage-smocked troopers. A grisly souvenir was draped across the bonnet of the half-tracks—the body of a *maquisard*, Maurice Vergne, picked from the roadside in Cressensac.

The local German headquarters received them as an American western fort beleaguered by Indians might have greeted the coming of the cavalry. For two days they had clung to the safety of the *Kommandantur* building, protected by sandbagged emplacements, convinced that an attack by several thousand *maquisards* was imminent. They had received word of an attack on Tulle on 7 June, but there had been silence from the town all day on the eighth. Most of the Brive garrison and administrative staff were reservists ten, twenty, even thirty years older than the SS troopers. Beneath the universal coalscuttle helmets and detested uniforms of the Occupiers, had the inhabitants of Brive known it, there were several hundred very frightened and unenthusiastic enemies.

Major Wulf, Major Stuckler, Colonel Stadler and Major Weidinger strode into the Brive headquarters at the Hôtel de Bordeaux less than impressed by what they saw. They had always regarded the terrorists with contempt, and been convinced that aggressive, decisive military action could drive them headlong back into their woods. Nothing that they had seen that day at Cressensac or Noailles altered that view. The *maquis* were an infernal nuisance to regular military operations, but it was absurd that they had been allowed to achieve such psychological dominance over local German garrisons. The SS forcefully suggested to Colonel Luyken and the Brive command staff that a more active policy, with intensive sweeps and patrolling, would have prevented the partisans from achieving the concentrations that now threatened Tulle, Brive, and even—it was being reported from the Haute-Vienne— Limoges. In the view of the officers of the Das Reich, all this was the fruit of infirmity of policy and weakness of execution.

There was a brief discussion of how best to deploy the division's teeth elements to meet the situation. Divisional headquarters under Stuckler— more than a hundred men and thirty vehicles—were already intending to pass the night in Tulle, and Stuckler himself was supposed to pay a liaison visit to 66th Reserve Corps at Clermont-Ferrand the following day. If there was trouble in Tulle—and panic-stricken messages from the garrison had talked of encirclement and crisis—then Wulf's recon- naissance battalion with its armored vehicles and 75 mm guns should be more than competent to dispose of any *maquis* force. The artillery, flak and interminable tail units would lager along the Brive-Limoges road as they arrived, and General Lammerding proposed to supervise their disposal personally. The Der Führer regiment, as planned, would continue immediately to Limoges and deploy around the town in support of the local garrison. The heavy armor, of course, was still far to the south-east, making sluggish progress up the road south of St. Céré.

While the officers of the Das Reich were making their dispositions in the *Ortslwmmandantur*, among the little crowd of French civilians gazing stonily at the ranks of German vehicles in the Grand' Place was a young man named René Jugie, who had been following their progress with the keenest interest since the first word of their coming reached him early that morning of 8 June. Jugie was a member of the Corrèze committee of MUR—the *Mouvement Uni de Résistance* (United Resistance Movement), intended to co-ordinate the activities of all the department's fragmented *réseaux* and *maquis*. He was himself the founder of one of them, which bore his codename, "Gao"; he was also a great admirer of De Gaulle and a close associate of the SOE officers in the area—first Peulevé and now Poirier and Hiller.

Jugie took his codename from that of the air squadron to which he had been attached in 1940. He himself was thirty, a voluble, compul- sively energetic Brive businessman of more prosperous bourgeois origins than the general run of *résistants*. He became involved in Resistance as early as 1942, when they were gathering such weapons as they could collect or steal from private and Armistice army sources, and assisting young men to escape from forced labor for Vichy. At that time, some communists worked with him despite the party's official refusal to have anything to do with Gaullist Resistance. Jugie took part in a few early sabotage operations of 1942–3, killing collaborators and organizing *parachutages*, while continuing to live publicly as a respectable citizen of Brive. He was one of many AS men who throughout the war had to overcome the emotional misgivings of his wife about the risks that he was taking. On one occasion when he was questioned by the *milice*, he escaped only because his appearance was so shrunken by the consequences of a stomach ulcer that he bore little resemblance to the description of the fleshier figure whom they sought.

One night a team of which Jugie was a member shot a local *milicien* and informer in a Brive bar. They were horrified to discover that the ambulance had removed him to hospital still breathing, possibly able to identify them. It was Jugie who had to snatch an excuse to visit the clinic, where he exchanged condolences with the chief local *milicien*, with whom he had played rugger before the war. It was appalling, this "terror on the streets." Yes, tragically the young man had died without regaining consciousness.

Some of their efforts, however, verged on farce. A two-man "hit team" dispatched to the office of a prominent local industrialist and collaborator emptied an entire pistol magazine at him and bolted, only to discover later that not a single shot had struck the target.

By the summer of 1944 the efforts of Peulevé, Poirier and the BCRA had brought thousands of weapons to the Corrèze, and the enthusiasm of the local Resistance had created one of the most numerous departmental movements in France. The British and Malraux had devoted great efforts to persuading the disparate groups to work with each other, and the existence of MUR meant that they were at least aware of each other's major plans. But the division between the Gaullists and the FTP was beyond bridging. Guedin was among those who bitterly attacked the British agents for arming the FTP, furthering their own entirely selfish ends. Some 5,000 *maquisards* in the hills of the upper Corrèze accepted the direction of the French communist party, and had no interest whatever in the wishes or instructions of London.

In the weeks before D-Day, the split became decisive. On Sunday 28 May, Jugie—as the representative of MUR—met "Laurent," a cool, dark teacher from Marseilles who was a dedicated communist and the FTP's delegate to MUR. "Laurent declared that he had given orders to his men to attack [the main centers of Vichy and German activity] in Brive on the night of 30 May," the horrified Jugie reported to Emile Baillely, departmental chief of the *Combat* Resistance movement, and of MUR. He continued:

> I told him that we had received formal instructions from Algiers and from London to launch attacks only in open country and at the Dordogne bridges, while carrying out the prearranged rail cuts according to *Plan Vert*, on receipt of the "action messages." Laurent rep lied that the Allies would never land in France, and that only by taking an independent initiative ourselves could we drive them to parachute us arms and material. Laurent said that he had received no orders from London or Algiers, but that he obeyed the orders of his superior party chiefs. He insistently demanded that I cause the units of my group, both the *légaux* and the *maquis*, to join his troops' attack on Monday. Naturally I refused. . . . I believe it is a matter of urgency to make Laurent's chiefs see reason. . . .

In the days that followed, there was intensive secret discussion between the two factions. The AS leaders made it clear that they would have no part of an attack on Brive, which could provoke horrific reprisals, and contravened London's repeated injunctions to make no attempt to seize towns at such risk. At another meeting, on 30 May, the FTP renounced the attempt to organize an attack on Brive, but made it apparent that they would be proceeding with their own attack on Tulle, with or without AS support. Amidst considerable rancor on both sides, the factions went their way to prepare for action.

On 7 June, Jugie passed a report from Tulle to Baillely:

> FTP forces have attacked the German garrison in Tulle. Losses are heavy on both sides. The École Normale where the enemy was billeted has been destroyed. Edith* and Maes,* on missions to Tulle during the attack, met Laurent at the head of his men. Laurent told Maes that an attack on Brive had been scheduled for the next day, 8 June. I think it is *urgent* to get the *Comité départementale* to intervene,

because Guy I* and Pointer* say that armoured units are moving northwestwards, and threaten to pass through our region. . . .

Further frenzied activity by the MUR committee members ensured that no AS units made any move to take part in an attack on Brive, although it was learnt that a few groups in the north-east had joined the FTP attack on Tulle. By the morning of 8 June it was apparent that the FTP were too heavily committed in that town to have any chance of moving on to Brive. But the German garrison had heard enough from its own informers to be in the state of acute alarm that the SS found on their arrival.

At 9:30 am on 8 June, as Guedin's *maquisards* lay in their positions covering the Dordogne bridges, a prominent Vichy official who was one of the most vital sources of Resistance intelligence reported to Jugie that German armored elements were moving north toward Corrèze to conduct a *ratissage*. He had heard directly from Colonel Bohmer, commanding the German 95th Security Regiment, that the first units were expected in Brive around 2 pm. A prominent Brive *milicien* named Thomine had also remarked briefly to another Resistance informant that "Tulle will pay very dearly for the town terrorists' little joke."

At 5 pm that afternoon, Jugie passed a further message:

Pierre has just told me that companies Remy, Desire, Bernard and Gilbert are in action in the south of the sector against armoured elements of the Das Reich Division. It seems that this column will reach Brive toward 6 pm, because our men cannot hold for long against heavy tanks. I hope you will make Laurent and his friends see reason before it is too late.

The Corrèze committee held a secret rendezvous early that evening at the monastery of St. Antoine on the edge of Brive, under Emile Baillely's chairmanship. Jugie noted:

Some of *Laurent*'s friends insist that the plan for an uprising in Brive be immediately and vigorously implemented, so that it may

---

* *Noms de guerre* for AS agents.

be liberated like Tulle, and as Limoges may be this evening. . . .
Baillely, armed with the latest information on the imminent arrival
of the Das Reich—delayed on its march by the heroism of the AS
MUR Corrèze brigade—succeeded in dissuading Laurent's friends
from any further folly. Some minutes after the meeting, the first
elements of the Das Reich arrived in Brive.

Jugie's notes give an indication of the bitterness with which the argument
raged through those days, with mutual charges of betrayal and cowardice
flung and contradicted, when the AS refused to fight in Brive to relieve
the pressure on the FTP in Tulle. It is an interesting aside on the nature
of Resistance in the days after the Allied landing that none of the local
SOE officers was invited to take any part in the debate. These decisive
questions were fought out entirely between Frenchmen. Before the event
and subsequently, French Section's agents discussed, advised, persuaded
and argued, but neither here nor in any but a handful of departments of
France did the British or Americans have a chance to exercise executive
authority. In the Corrèze, indeed, they firmly resisted the efforts of De
Gaulle's BCRA to take a hand in directing their operations.

Reading Jugie's report, it is also essential never to lose sight of the
chasm between his impressive references to companies and brigades
and the reality on the ground of clusters of half-trained, half-armed
boys among whom it was intensely difficult to maintain discipline in
camp, far less in action. Rather than diminishing their achievements,
these difficulties only serve to enhance them.

Early that evening of 8 June, at the Cafe des Sports in the center of
Brive a courier from Marius Guedin reached Jugie. He reported that
the AS officer was furious to hear that trains were still running on the
line north of the town, toward Uzerche. Would "Gao" act immediately
to halt them? Jugie fetched his bicycle and began a long ride around the
town. First, he briefly visited three men of his circuit—Lescure, Briat
and Chauty. They would meet him outside the town. Then he rode a
mile or two to the farm of a man named Levet. Levet was one of many
thousands of Frenchmen who did nothing spectacular or worthy of
decoration during the Occupation, yet took terrible risks to support
Resistance. Under the straw in his barn was a dump of explosives and

detonators. Jugie rapidly assembled four "loaves" of around a quarter of pound of *plastique* apiece, and took a bunch of the deadly little grey detonators. Strapping his cargo in the bag on the carrier of his bicycle, he rode briskly to the rendezvous with the others. Well-distanced to avoid suspicion, they hastened onwards through the soft evening sunshine to a point where the railway dropped into a wood.

They passed a squad of French workmen working under German guard to repair the last section of line they had attacked. A mile or so beyond, they reached their target. Briat and Chauty held the bicycles and kept watch while Lescure and Jugie worked the charges under the track, one set to each of the north—and southbound lines. They pushed the detonators into the soft lumps of explosive, connected them with bickford cord, and scrambled hastily into the wood, trailing cable to the electric detonator. Suddenly, to their consternation, they saw a peasant leading an ox cart across the line only yards away. He had resolutely resisted the pleas of Briat and Chauty to halt, insisting dourly that he was only going about his business. Moments passed, and a girl rode up on a bicycle. She was the daughter of the railway-crossing keeper, and Jugie had known her brother in the army. She said that she could hear gunfire in the distance. Jugie waited a few moments for her to disappear from sight, then twisted the exploder. One charge detonated hurling a twisted section of line into the air, but the other failed to go off. They ran to it, fumbled hastily to replace the cord, and fell back. They were careless. Jugie was slow to take cover as he fired the charge, and the blast, together with a deluge of stones from the permanent way, caught him where he crouched. He lost his hearing in one ear for life. But the line was blown, and there was still no sign of any Germans. The four men slipped swiftly back into Brive.

The forward elements of the Das Reich had moved on. The Der Führer regiment was rolling up the long hill that led the way to Limoges, where its tired troopers arrived at last in the early hours of 9 June. The guns and miles of supporting vehicles were still moving steadily through Brive, toward their lagers on the Uzerche road. Major Heinrich Wulf's reconnaissance battalion, the *Aufklärungsabteilung*, followed by Colonel Stuckler and divisional headquarters, was closing rapidly upon Tulle.

CHAPTER 5

Tulle: The "Liberation"

THE TOWN OF TULLE clings to the steep hills of the Corrèze like a precarious alpinist, the shops and houses of its 21,000 inhabitants perched wherever nature will allow them a foothold. The bustling river Vézèré falls through its midst, banked on each side by walled quays and the main streets. On the hillsides above rise three large schools, the barracks, the prefecture and the town hall. On the plateau at the southern end of the town are clustered the station, the big arms factory which is the town's main employer, and a knot of shops, houses and small hotels. Tulle is a grey, architecturally undistinguished place, though some think well of its cathedral. It has suffered its share of historical misfortune: twice sacked by the English in the Hundred Years War, and stormed by Turenne when it was held for the Catholics in 1585.

The department of Corrèze was a pre-war radical stronghold. Of its four deputies elected in 1936, three were socialist and one was a communist. Communism in France does not mean quite what it does in Moscow. Many of its supporters see no inconsistency in being energetic businessmen, proud *propriétaires* who are married in church and have their children baptized. In the country, French communists have always been "leaders of a local faction rather than agents of Moscow," in Brogan's words. But the communists of the upper Corrèze were always well organized, and it was not surprising that when Russia entered the war and the French party reversed its policy of accommodation with the Occupiers, a strongly based communist Resistance developed around Tulle.

96

The steep, thickly wooded countryside made it a natural haven for *maquisards*. In 1943, as the German grip on France tightened and the flight of STO evaders began, the Corrèze was an obvious gathering place. Many of those who came—Jews from Paris, Spanish fugitives from Franco's rule, Russian deserters from the German Army, teenagers from half the departments of France, were not themselves communists, but they were willing to accept the energetic leadership of the local FTP. Among the Spaniards especially, it became common to find the absurd ideological rag-bag that Robert Noireau noted among one of his groups in the Lot: "orthodox communists of PCE, anarchists of FAI, anarchosyndicalists of CNT, Trotskyites of POUM and Catalan socialists. . . ." Few of them troubled much about politics in the *maquis*, and the zealots soon learned to hold their meetings unobtrusively. Only the jargon and the utter ruthlessness with which the FTP removed anyone—including a number of world-be defectors to the AS—whom they considered a threat made life for a rank-and-file FTP *maquisard* any different from that of a Gaul list. By the winter of 1943, perhaps 2,000 *maquisards* were grouped under FTP control in the Corrèze. The number had more than doubled by D-Day.

The communists' reputation for action appealed to enthusiastic spirits. They set up roadblocks and wrecked trains (George Hiller once found himself exchanging expressions of outrage with other, German passengers on a train which the FTP hijacked from under them). Between 27 April and 25 May 1944, the Tulle *gendarmerie* recorded seventy-eight terrorist outrages, almost all the work of the communists: fourteen were against railways, eight road attacks, seventeen against police, one factory sabotage, nineteen phone line cuts, seven attacks on *milice* and two on Germans, the remaining ten being thefts of food and material. The local population paid a terrible price in reprisals: after one minor FTP attack on a patrol near Camburet, the Germans burnt twenty-nine farms. Civilian hostages of all ages and both sexes were routinely seized and shot on the sites of ambushes. It is not surprising that Resistance only became a source of general national enthusiasm in France after the Liberation.

But the Germans were compelled to recognize that they no longer controlled large areas of the countryside. In March 1944, the Prefect of Corrèze estimated that seventeen cantons of the department were in the hands of the *maquis*, against nine held by the Germans and Vichy. The German garrison of elderly reservists in Tulle and Brive was supported by a *Sicherheitsdienst* security police and intelligence team and a detested following of several hundred armed Vichyites of the GMR and the Bony-Lafont gang—recruited chiefly from Parisian and North African criminals. The Hôtel St. Martin, in which they were based, became notorious for the torture sessions customarily conducted in its baths. From time to time punitive columns took to the country, distributing violence with or without provocation. But for weeks on end *maquisards* on foot or in their *gazogène* trucks possessed unchallenged passage through the villages and countryside. Hundreds more secret FTP members awaited the call to mobilize from their jobs in the shops and factories of Tulle. There was even a 300-strong Young Communist group, led by a fifteen-year-old cadre.

Until the winter of 1943 the FTP was receiving only a trickle of arms, organized either by SOE's Harry Peulevé, or by a BCRA agent who was transmitting for a time from the church spire of Tulle. But in the six months before D-Day, a deluge of weapons began to reach the *maquisards*: Stens, Brens, gammon grenades, rifles and a handful of mortars and bazookas. For a time these were stockpiled in secret caches in the forests, but the frustration and insistent demands of the *maquisards* persuaded their leaders to issue them directly to the groups. They had no London-trained instructors, and were compelled to teach themselves by laborious study of the pamphlets supplied with the containers, and sometimes at bitter cost in accidents. One man made himself horribly ill by eating off a knife that he had last used for cutting *plastique*. Two *maquisards* named Pagat and Rozier made their first essay in throwing a gammon bomb, only to find that it refused to detonate. They threw stones at it until it exploded, slashing their faces with pebbles and debris. More serious, however, was the shortage of ammunition which made it impossible for most men to have live firing practice until they did so against the Germans. Contrary to popular belief, using a Sten or Bren gun effectively is not a knack as naturally acquired as riding a bicycle.

Food and boredom were the greatest problems of the *maquis*. The Corrèze had none of the natural abundance of Gascony or the great truffle region of the Périgord. Local sympathizers gave what they could, and the *maquis* stole everything they could lay their hands on from Vichy and the Germans. Noireau's group in the Lot once captured an entire lorryload of *foie gras*, and declared cheerfully every time they opened a tin: "Here's one the Boche won't enjoy!" In the Corrèze there were seldom such extravagances. The *maquis* relied heavily upon raids on farms and villages which made some groups as detested as the Germans, whether or not they left promissory notes behind them. The borderline between Resistance and banditry was often thin. It was widely crossed all over France that winter of 1943–4. London, conscious of the problem, contributed what little it could by filling every spare corner of parachute containers with small blue tins of vitamin pills. But tobacco remained the greatest difficulty. A *maquis* with cigarettes retained some cohesion and morale. A *maquis* without them often came close to collapse. Very few FTP groups were led by men with any experience of command. It was hard to teach hungry, frustrated teenagers sleeping under parachute silk in a muddy clearing in the woods the need to wash, to dig latrines, to make route marches to maintain fitness, to post efficient sentries. Again and again, *maquis* were surprised by German patrols, sometimes undoubtedly tipped off by disgruntled peasants. A party of twenty-two was caught asleep at dawn one April morning in a wood near Roux. Only four escaped. On 5 May, two men were killed in another surprise attack, and the nearby village of Bordes was burned.

The drops from England or Algeria were the outstanding highlights of *maquis* life. "Those *séances de parachutage* remain for me the finest memories of the *maquis*," wrote Robert Noireau. "Feats of patience and dreaming, of exhilaration at the idea of this contact between those in the interior and those who had chosen exile, the better to fight. Ah! Those February nights when one had to remain motionless on the landing ground, swept by the icy winds from the Massif Central!"

With the coming of spring and warmer weather, conditions improved in the *maquis*. Leaf on the trees increased their protection from observation, above all from the air. Throughout south central France, the FTP made increasingly daring demonstrations, holding parades through villages with flags and arms. The leader of the Lot FTP, a teacher named Jean-Jacques Chapou, achieved an immensely admired coup when he occupied the small town of Carjac on 10 April, the day of its fair, executed three alleged local collaborators, and tele-phoned the Cahors Gestapo in the name of the mayor, demanding urgent help. When the Germans approached, the *maquisards* shot up their convoy before retiring. He attempted to lay the same trap in Gramat on May Day, but the Germans failed to respond. "The first of May was a success throughout the region," reported the Corrèze party chief, Louis Godefroy, who had organized other demonstrations like that of Carjac and Gramat. "The departmental headquarters showed a spirit of initiative and enthusiasm which surpassed all our hopes. The prospects for this month of May are rich with promise for the success of the continuing offensive." Early in May, the Corrèze FTP received a directive from Limoges, reporting the communist national military committee's commitment to preparation for "a national insurrection. . . . The uprising was forcefully advocated as the only means of self-defence. When the Allied landed, how else could the Nazi armies be prevented from carrying out massive internments and massacring millions of Frenchmen? Best not to take that risk. The national uprising is 'the supreme wisdom.'"

The communist leadership in the Corrèze considered itself uniquely well-placed to liberate its own territory. "Our forces, our weapons, the intelligence we possess about the enemy forces stationed in the area, the very favourable mood of the population" all gave confidence to André Odru, a twenty-two-year-old teacher who was their "commissar for the fighters." He wrote:

We also know the strength of armed Resistance in the neighbouring departments. In the north, the forces of Guingouin and the *maquis* of the Creuse; in the south, the FTP activists of the Lot; in the west the Dordogne, which will assist a mass uprising of fighters; in the east, the highlands of the Massif Central and their *maquis*. We cannot believe that the Nazi forces are stronger than our own. It is in these conditions that the inter-regional military committee decided a long time ago to strike a major blow, when conditions became favourable, against Tulle—the very heart of the area.

Louis Godefroy, the short, stocky, thirty-year-old sanitary worker codenamed "Riviere," who was their party chief, argued that it would be easy to cut off Tulle by isolating its road and rail links; that enemy morale was low; the garrison weak; and popular support for the *maquis* overwhelming. Much impressed by Jean Jacques Chapou's achievements in the Lot, they now persuaded him to move to the Corrèze as the FTP's military commander. "Kléber," as he was known, was a slim, austere figure of considerable personal force but limited military understanding. With some 5,000 men in the department, he and the others believed that they could easily dispose of the garrison of Tulle, whose strength they estimated at 250 Germans and 400 GMR. In reality, there were 700 Germans of the 3rd battalion of the 95th Security Regiment, 500 *miliciens* and a substantial number of SD, field police and German civilian and military administrators.

On 26 May Godefroy, the dynamic prime mover among them, made a discreet reconnaissance trip to Tulle with Albert Faucher, their quartermaster commissar. He claimed later that in the back room of a cafe full of local people, they were goaded and incited to act decisively. Both then and subsequently, Godefroy sought to escape acknowledging that he knew at the end of May that the FTP of the Limousin had decided not to attack Limoges. One of their most flamboyant leaders, the formidable and murderous Georges Guingouin, had shown surprising moderation when the Limoges project was being discussed. Perhaps, like some other FTP leaders, he had already determined to hold back the bulk of his strength for the moment when the Germans retreated from the city, and the communists could seize undisputed power. In any event, he declined to have any part in a *coup de main* against Limoges. Although rumors of its imminence panicked the German garrison, the Haute-Vienne Resistance continued to confine themselves to local attacks.

The Germans were correctly informed, however, that a crisis was imminent at Tulle. On the morning of 6 June, Pétain's detested deputy Pierre Laval personally telephoned Prefect Pierre Trouillé to discuss the threat. On the afternoon of the sixth, the schools closed early and remained shut through the days that followed. The same day, among the street posters inciting young Frenchmen to "Join the Waffen SS," a new Vichy notice appeared: "In the event of fighting or shooting in the street, shutters must be closed and civilians must remain in their own houses."

The FTP organized their attack before the Allied landings, as soon as they knew from the *messages personnels* that D-Day was imminent. They believed that Liberation would follow invasion within weeks, if not days. If they did not seize their opportunity, communism in the Corrèze might be swamped by the tide of history. In defiance of every order they had received through London, every protest of the *Armée Secrète*, every rule of guerilla warfare and common prudence, they attempted to seize and hold the town of Tulle.

A few minutes after 5 am on the morning of 7 June, the flat crump of a bazooka rocket explosion echoed through the sleeping streets of Tulle. A thin plume of smoke rose from the Champs de Mars barracks where it had detonated. It was the signal for the attack. Threading their way down the hills and into the streets came the first columns of guerillas clad in blue tunics and berets, draped in haversacks and bandoliers, clutching their Stens and Brens, carrying bazooka rounds and mortar bombs in makeshift harnesses, exultantly conscious that they had reached a turning point of their war. The Germans and *miliciens* in their barracks and the schools in which they were billeted dragged on their clothes and equipment and began returning the *maquis* fire from windows and rooftops. Street by street and house by house, Chapou's men advanced into Tulle.

Assaulting a strongly held city without artillery or air support is one of the most difficult operations of modern war. It calls for surprise, close co-ordination, resolution and highly trained men. Not one of these advantages did the FTP possess. In the first hour, they threw away surprise. The signal bazooka was fired forty-five minutes before the main attack was launched. It had already been postponed by twenty-four hours at the request of some units who had many miles to cover on foot to the rendezvous. Many of those in the assault force knew neither the town nor the way to it, and had to be led by local guides. Two hours after the first shot, barely half the guerilla army was engaged. All that day, little columns were trickling belatedly into Tulle to join the attack. Without radio or telephone links, each company fighting in the dense streets had no means of judging the progress of others, of summoning help or ammunition or medical aid.

The first hours gave the *maquisards* a terrible lesson in war. Among the Germans and the *miliciens*, even the reservists were trained soldiers with plentiful ammunition, firing from solidly constructed buildings. The *maquisards* had been led to suppose that when the enemy saw the forces deployed against them, they would quickly surrender or flee. But when a young man named Marcel Chrétien leaped upon the *Monument aux Morts* and called to the *miliciens* in the billets opposite to surrender, he received only a fierce burst of fire. Few of the attackers had any experience of using firearms in action, far less of accurate marksmanship. From their street corners and doorways they blazed at the German positions 100, perhaps 200 yards distant. They lacked the cohesion to get to close quarters and mount a determined assault. After some painful early casualties, most preferred to hold their positions and exchange fire. In the first hours, ammunition began to run short in many companies. Many wounded men lay where they had fallen. From their first, dashing descent on Tulle, the *maquisards* found themselves pinned down in a deadly street fight. One of them, Roger Simonot, described an experience that morning.

> We are cut off. The *feldgendarmes*, firing from the Hôtel La Tremoliere and its gardens, bar our escape route. The situation is difficult. From my doorway, I can clearly hear a Nazi working the bolt of his rifle after each shot. I decide to break out toward the top of the Rue d'Epierre. The section leader motions me to move and covers me with his Thompson. A rush, then in the exchange of fire, I get through. A few seconds later Jean Bordas follows me. Alas, he is hit and falls in the midst of the road. My other companions abandon the initiative, and remain trapped. . . .

Jean-Jacques Chapou and Louis Godefroy had moved swiftly to the town hall when the attack began and established their headquarters in the council chamber. It was there that Constant Magnac, a twenty-nine-year-old teacher among the attackers, came to report:

> I find a perplexed Kléber. Things are not going as well as he thought. I have seen Alfred and Luc in the Rue Louis-Mie, and they are no longer in dashing spirits. Albert Faucher is dead. Communications

are very bad, and there is an almost total blackout of news from the north and north-east of the town. Have the units of Sub-Sector B arrived, and are they in place? Is Sub-Sector A here and in position? I learn that the GMR stationed at the Champs de Mars barracks are still holding out. . . . Kléber cannot satisfy my request for reinforcements for the south and south-east of the town. . . .

"Towards 8 am," wrote Chapou himself, "after two hours of heavy fighting, none of the runners whom I had sent to the battalion commanders had returned. . . . The enemy maintained a heavy fire." Francesco Molinari, a young Italian communist who had won a Croix de Guerre fighting with the French Army in 1940 and was now an STO evader, shot his way into the Hôtel Moderne in the midst of the quays at the head of a group of *maquisards*, to be met by fierce resistance from the opposite end of the bar and the stairs. The attackers hurled themselves behind overturned marble tables to return the fire. Table by table they worked across the bar, one man crawling behind them, feverishly refilling Sten magazines from loose rounds in his haversack. At last the Germans retreated up the stairs. Molinari seized a bottle from the bar and raised it to his throat, only to have a bullet smash it from his grasp. Furiously he dashed for the stairs, firing as he ran. The Germans had escaped through the back door. He caught a glimpse of himself and his men reflected in a huge mirror on the landing, and they laughed at the image: filthy, exhausted, bearded, their clothes torn and their arms scratched and bleeding. They moved warily out of the hotel, and on down the street.

At about 11 am, a civilian approached a *maquisard* company commander in the street. He brought a message from the GMR and the gendarmes beleaguered in the Champs de Mars barracks. They had had enough. Could they withdraw up the road to Limoges under a flag of truce? Grudgingly the *maquisard* assented. Not long after, one by one a cautious procession of trucks emerged from the barracks yard, each one bearing a white flag. They were not fired upon. In haste and intense relief, the Vichyites retreated northwards toward the hills and Limoges. Some of the *maquisards* who saw them depart were infuriated, above all that the enemy had been allowed to take their weapons. But by now the FTP's leaders were under no illusions. The GMR would never have handed over their arms, given the *maquis*'s disposition to "*bouziller les gars*"—eliminate Vichy's agents out of hand. Chapou's difficulties were more than great enough that day. Any diminution of the number of defenders must be welcomed on any terms.

When the first euphoria of the battle had receded, fatigue came quickly to the *maquisards*. Many had marched on foot for hours to reach the rendezvous, before they began to fight. They lacked the mutual confidence that supports trained units. Their clumsiness with their weapons caused repeated accidents. "Fanny," a boy loading one of the bazookas, was horribly burned on the face as he lay carelessly in the path of its back blast when the gunner fired. A few moments later, a well-timed stick grenade from a window above a florist's caught the injured boy again, agonizingly, together with two other men beside him. A few hundred yards away, another group was attempting to drive the Germans off the roof of the École Superieure with smoke and shrapnel rifle grenades. Two men were terribly wounded by premature explosions as they pressed their triggers. The others abandoned using rifle grenades.

The only German sally of the day took place at the bottom of the town at about 1:30 pm, when a party broke out of the buildings they were holding opposite the station, and took up positions on the platforms. In a waiting-room they burst in on eighteen nervous young French line guards who had taken refuge out of the line of fire. The Germans shot three immediately. When they withdrew to the hotel, they herded the other Frenchmen with them. One managed to break away and escape. The other fourteen were killed at once.

The afternoon wore on without decision. The *maquisards* now occupied most of the town, but the Germans were still holding out in the École Normale, the arms factory and a school just in front of it. Two reconnaissance aircraft droned overhead, inspecting the town and raking the *maquisards* with desultory machine gun fire as they scuttled beneath. As evening approached, it was still impossible to move freely along the quays, because of the Germans' commanding positions on the heights above. The attackers were tired, hungry, and depressed by their losses. Kléber and the others in the council chamber weighed the events of the day: "Positive—the Germans are reduced to a cautious defensive (if one excludes their determined counter-attack on the station); negative—disastrous communications. Obvious lack of training among the men. Insufficient caution, lack of heavy weapons and shortage of ammunition. . . ." The *maquisards*' best chance against the arms factory would probably have been a forceful night attack, but as darkness fell they had no spirit for such adventures. Most men slept where they stood, or slipped into the bedrooms of houses from which they had been firing, in some of which the terrified inhabitants still lingered amidst their possessions.

That evening, a car bearing couriers from Godefroy slipped out of Tulle and raced north to the chateau in the forests south-east of Limoges where Georges Guingouin had his headquarters. Like so many Resistance leaders, he had awarded himself colonel's rank and shoulder pips on his uniform, and hugely enjoyed playing the part of military commander. The FTP visitors from Tulle were exasperated by the patronizing, bombastic reception they received from "this great devil of a man, brandishing his pistol at intervals to emphasize his remarks." They heard a lecture on the folly of their action, and the flat rejection of their request for arms, ammunition or men.

At first light on the morning of 8 June, the firing resumed in Tulle sporadically at first, then with more purpose as each side reawakened to its role in the drama. It continued hour after hour, with occasional casualties among attackers and defenders. The *maquis* had learned more caution, and showed no urge to storm the remaining enemy positions. The Germans appeared content to stand the siege until help came. But by early afternoon the *maquisards* had worked close enough to the École Normale to use smoke grenades and incendiaries. After repeated efforts they succeeded in setting fire to one corner of the building, and soon the blaze was out of control. Smoke was pouring from the windows, and the *maquisards* perceived the enemy's fire slackening.

At 4 pm, to the delight of the exultant besiegers, a white flag appeared at the door. It was carried by Louise Boucheteil, a girl courier for the FTP who had been captured ten days earlier and held prisoner in the cellars of the building with some twenty other *maquisard* captives, expecting death at any time. Now, behind her from the school, unarmed and withtheir hands on their heads, came some forty Germans in uniform and civilian clothes. They had had enough. The jubilant *maquisards* seized their weapons and equipment and herded away the prisoners. One of those in civilian clothes was spotted by a *maquisard* who shouted, "I've seen you before—in the Hôtel St. Martin!" It was a Gestapo agent, who instantly broke from the column and ran for his life. A hail of fire belatedly pursued him. A *maquisard* ran down the hill in his wake, at last overtook the agent and shot him.

Now the only German garrison left in Tulle was pinned in the arms factory and the school in front of it. The Germans' fire effectively covered only a few streets, and they showed no desire to assert themselves. Through the rest of Tulle, as silence overtook the town, one by one frightened and exhausted families began to emerge from their homes, nervously to congratulate the victors, bring out what little food and drink they had, tend the wounded and carry away the dead. One of the *maquis* leaders, a twenty-one-year-old farmworker named Elie Dupuy, told Prefect Trouillé defiantly: "If the Germans counter-attack, we shall ambush and beat them just as we have done in the past two days. In any case, we are perfectly certain that the armed struggle will bring about the liberation of our department—and of France!"

The cost had been high, but the great objective was all but gained. Excepting only the impotent huddle of Germans in the arms factory, the communist *Francs-Tireurs et Partisans* had by their own efforts liberated the town of Tulle and brought its Occupiers to naught. Kléber, Godefroy, Dupuy and their men exulted in their triumph as they counted the dead and began to clear the wreckage, discussing how best to quell the fires that were still burning around the École Normale. André Odru drove a few miles out of town on the road eastwards to visit his outlying pickets, puttering triumphantly up the hill in a borrowed *gazogène*.

He returned shortly after 9 pm. As his car approached the station, a knot of frightened townspeople flagged him down in the street. "The Germans are there!" they shouted, gesturing toward the town center. "Run for it!" Odru hastily reversed the car. A few moments later the first flares began to burst over Tulle. Once again, the hammer of machine gun fire and the crump of heavier shells and mortars began to echo through the town. The Das Reich Division had entered the reckoning.

CHAPTER 6

Tulle: The Price

WHEN MAJOR HEINRICH WULF'S reconnaissance battalion—some hundred half-tracks and trucks bearing more than 500 men, even without their armored car squadron—clattered out of Brive-la-Gaillarde at around 7 pm on the evening of 8 June, its officers were not in the best of tempers. They were irritated, almost affronted by the division's losses during the afternoon, doubly so because some of them had heard General Eisenhower's broadcast demanding full combatant status for *résistants* in arms. They were irked by the panic-stricken behavior of the local garrison in Brive. So feeble was the German Empire's grasp on the Corrèze, it seemed, that an SS Panzer *Aufklärungsabteilung* (reconnaissance detachment) had now to be deployed to rescue the Tulle garrison from a band of half-armed communist terrorists. Neither they nor their men had much hint of what to expect when they reached the town.

The road from Brive to Tulle winds steeply upwards, overlooked by cliffs and woods for much of its course. Had the FTP possessed the smallest sense of self-preservation or tactical judgment a small force of *maquisards* posted to cover it could have felled trees across the road and delayed the advance of any German force for hours with Brens and gammon grenades. Yet the watchful Germans in the leading half-tracks observed nothing for mile after mile except a hint of smoke from the hills masking Tulle. When Wulf saw from his map that they were within two or three miles of the town, he raised his arm to signal the convoy to halt. With unknown assail ants ahead, it was time to close up, and take the opportunity to refuel the vehicles from their jerrycans. They could still hear no sound of firing, but it seemed possible that the noise of battle was being muffled by the hills which encircled the town.

The evening light was softening now, as they mounted the half-tracks again, and swept round the last bends and past the first houses of Tulle. Every man crouched with his weapon raised and cocked, mutely cursing the clatter of the tracks that made it impossible to hear shooting. They reached the approaches to the station, and still they did not see a soul. Every door and shutter was closed. The column swerved contemptuously around a single felled tree trunk in the road. There was a brief burst of fire in their direction which died within seconds. Wulf motioned his driver to halt. He jumped down from the half-track. Seeing nothing, he ordered the man to switch off the engine. There was still silence. Cautiously, with an NCO and his runner behind him, he moved on foot down the street, searching for signs of life and seeing none. He walked perhaps a hundred yards, then turned back to order his adjutant to deploy the companies around the town. He was still a street's width from the column, when, as if at a signal, a barrage of gunfire burst around them. Brens, Stens and the crash of grenades echoed through the houses. The Germans in the half-tracks began to pour back fire. Wulf and his two men crouched for a moment against a bus shelter, then dashed back to cover behind their own armor. He was rapidly briefing his company commanders for the advance through the town when a single elderly, obviously terrified German NCO scuttled across the street toward him. He had been sent from the be leaguered garrison in the school in front of the arms factory 200 yards away. When they heard the approaching vehicles, they had guessed that it must be a relief column. With three of his own men behind him, Wulf and the NCO zigzagged from cover to cover down the street and into the shelter of the school.

Wulf could scarcely credit the picture he saw before him inside: fifty or more elderly reservists, blazing nervously at shadows from their windows; a handful of wounded on the floor; the men so shaken that they could not dispose of a *maquis* sniper firing from a position thirty yards away. Wulf curtly ordered his men to silence the enemy weapon, which ceased fire after a few moments. Then he turned to the cluster of delighted old men gathering around him, all talking at once. They were members of the 95th Security Regiment, and were commanded by Captain Reichmann, a fifty-five-year-old dentist from Baden-Wiirttemberg. Wulf said:

> They were sitting there like mice in a trap. They all started stammering at me, so that it was impossible to get any description of the situation. They said that they had heard nothing from the garrison in the other school for two days, yet they had made no attempt to make contact. I couldn't understand how they had allowed this situation to happen. It was a sad place, with these frightened old men who had had no sleep for two nights. I stayed only two minutes, then ran back to my adjutant at the vehicles. I felt outraged that we had been diverted from the battle in Normandy to deal with this nonsense. My immediate aim was simply to sort out the town before it became completely dark. . . .

Wulf reached his half-track to find Albert Stuckler arrived beside it at the head of the divisional headquarters column. They could plainly see *maquisards* moving on the hillsides above the town, and hear firing from the other end of Tulle. The first priority, clearly, was simply to sweep them from the streets.

The *maquisards* scattered through Tulle never organized a coherent defense against Wulf's companies. Many were at the limit of exhaustion and had no more ammunition. At the sound of heavy firing, they began to trickle away into the hills. One party was counting the German dead at the École Normale when someone shouted that enemy vehicles were approaching. They gave their only bazooka to a young Parisian watchmaker renowned as a marksman, and watched the German convoy crawl toward them. A motor cycle and sidecar passed, then the watchmaker fired at the half-track behind. The rocket exploded against it, and the column stopped abruptly. The partisans began a hasty retreat from the town, leaving only a handful of bolder spirits who stayed long enough to fire off the last of their ammunition at the Das Reich.

Private Sadi Schneid, one of the young Alsatians who had been posted to the battalion anti-tank company at Bordeaux, crouched nervously with his fellow-recruits in their half-track as they moved into the streets of Tulle amid sporadic gunflashes. Their senior NCO, their almost worshipped Hauptscharführer—"Hascha"—Kurz was the only man in the vehicle who knew his business perfectly. "We've got to make that machine gun shut up!" he shouted, slamming the driver on the shoulder to make him halt. As the engine cut, for the first time they heard the gunfire. The men leaped down, unlimbered their towed Pak 75, and swung it toward the hillside from which a *maquisard* was using a Bren. The gunlayer, another raw recruit, was still peering intently through the eyepiece when, in a moment of black comedy, the gun fired and he was hurled bodily from his seat. On the asphalt road, the spades that stemmed the recoil could not grip. The "Hascha" swore violently, the team pulled itself together and fired again. There was no sign of an explosion from the hill. The "Hascha" cursed again: "That clumsy hippopotamus"—this to the loader—"is feeding us solid anti-tank rounds instead of shrapnel!" When the Pak crew fired again, the *maquisard* ceased fire.

Another of the company's vehicles roared up to them, bearing two dejected prisoners with FTP arm brassards. An NCO stood up in the back and shouted a question to the "Hascha" about what was to be done with them. Nobody knew. The half-track clattered away. Another followed with a shaken crew. A *maquisard* bullet had caught one of the young Alsatians in the eye, killing him instantly as he crouched covering their rear. The "Sani"—the company medical orderly—confided to Schneid that he was feeling unhappy because he had killed a woman as they drove up the street. He saw a curtain move, fired at the window, and saw a middle-aged Tulle housewife topple forward over the sill. Another half-track returned with a man dead and another wounded. A *maquisard* had lain poised above it to lob a gammon grenade into the interior as it passed.

But Wulf's companies suffered very few casualties that night. There was no serious resistance to the reoccupation of Tulle. Within twenty minutes of the Das Reich beginning to deploy around the town, their dominance was complete. Dejected files of evicted *maquisards* were trudging away into the hills, bearing such wounded as they could carry off. "It was a Dante-esque spectacle," wrote one of them, Elie Dupuy. "Flares being fired from all directions, bursts of machine gun fire, cannon and mortar explosions overwhelming every other sound. Tired, beaten, our units and our men see all their efforts, their sacrifices and their hopes evaporate in a matter of minutes. . . ."

The Germans, now unchallenged, deployed around the town for the night. Every wall in the center was hacked and pockmarked by gunshots; windows stood shattered, shutters hanging torn and loose, glass strewn in the street. The townspeople remained closely hidden behind their doors, many already terrified by the prospect of German vengeance. Private Schneid slipped into a garage close to his platoon position, in search of some tools to repair a panel on the half-track damaged when the Pak gun recoiled into it. Suddenly he found himself overshadowed by an enormous, menacing figure—a *"Kettenhunde,"* a "chained dog," one of the *Feldgendarmes* so called because of the chains of office around their necks. "And what are you doing here?" demanded the man fiercely, and led Schneid, protesting, to his company commander to report a suspected looter. The officer sent the *Feldgendarme* on his way. It is an odd aside on the events of Tulle that such a matter at such a moment attracted the attention of German authority.

Hungry—for they had no more rations—and exhausted by the first encounter with live ammunition for many of them, the SS lay by their weapons, dozing and standing guard through the brief summer night of 8 June.

Shortly after midnight, Wulf was called to divisional headquarters, temporarily established in a hotel at the foot of the town. Stuckler was furious. While the division had suffered only three killed and nine wounded in retaking the town, the body count among the German garrison showed that 139 men had been killed and forty wounded by the *maquis*. At first light, Wulf was to send one company to a point some twelve miles from Tulle which was reported to harbor the French headquarters and arms dump. The other two companies, less those men essential to control the perimeter, were to sweep the entire town, house by house. They were to seize any hidden weapons, and bring every male Frenchman in Tulle to the courtyard of the arms factory for an identity check. As a convenient starting point, any man without papers could be assumed to be a terrorist.

It was the beginning of the day that Tulle would never forget. From first light, files of SS troopers marched rapidly through the streets, hammering on doors, ordering out their terrified inhabitants, forming the first pitiful huddles of civilians to be herded toward the arms factory. The Prefect, Pierre Trouillé, had come close to summary execution himself when a case of grenades was found in his office, but he convinced the Germans that he had been an innocent spectator of the FTP takeover. Now, he asked Major Kowatsch, the divisional 1c or third-ranking staff officer, if there were to be any reprisals. He pointed out with perfect justice that the citizens of Tulle had been totally uninvolved in the events of the past two days. Kowatsch told both Trouillé and the German-speaking secretary-general, Maurice Roche, that no punitive action would be taken. This assurance was echoed at more junior levels. Private Schneid was summoned to interpret for one of his company officers who was commandeering a schoolteacher's house for quarters. In answer to her frightened question, the officer said that reprisals had indeed been considered, but had now been decided against. Kowatsch told Trouillé that a decisive factor in the decision to show mercy was the care with which German wounded had been treated in the town hospital.

Yet at 10 am, with some 3,000 Frenchmen of every age standing bewildered in the yard of the arms factory under the guns of the SS, a new order was given. There would, after all, be reprisals. Schneid and an SS detail were ordered to escort the town fire engine as its crew drove through Tulle reading a terrible proclamation at the street corners. Clinging to the back of "this antediluvian machine" as it rang its bell to seize the attention of the citizens, they set off through the streets. The chief fireman—in tears according to Schneid declaimed a brief German announcement which the soldier recalled as follows: "Because of the indescribable murder of forty German soldiers by communist *maquisards*, the German authorities have decided that three Frenchmen will pay for each German killed, as an example to all France." Within the hour, a formal proclamation copied by a local printer, hauled from his home, was being posted on the walls of Tulle:

CITIZENS OF TULLE!
Forty German soldiers have been murdered in the most abominable fashion by the communist gangs. The peaceful population has submitted to terror. The military authorities wish only for order and tranquillity. The loyal population wishes this equally. The

appalling and cowardly fashion in which the German soldiers have been killed proves that the instruments of communist destruction are at work. It is most regrettable that there were also policemen and French *gendarmes* who, abandoning their posts, did not follow their orders and made common cause with the communists.

For the *maquis* and those that help them, there is only one penalty, the hangman's noose. They do not recognize open combat, they have no feelings of honour. Forty German soldiers have been murdered by the *maquis*. 120 *maquis* or their accomplices will be hanged. Their bodies will be thrown in the river.

As a warning, for every German soldier wounded, three *maquis* will in future be hanged. For every German soldier killed, ten *maquisards* or an equal number of their accomplices will be hanged. I expect the loyal co-operation of the civil population in fighting the common enemy, the communist bands.

Tulle, 9 June 1944

The General Commanding the German troops

It was now that the most dreadful drama of Tulle began, which to this day remains shrouded in controversy. The precise truth is beyond discovery. It is only possible to report the accounts given by the surviving participants.

Heinrich Wulf and his SS colleagues say that, early on the morning of 9 June, the senior divisional doctor who had been collecting the German dead from the battle arrived at headquarters to report that a single group of forty bodies had been discovered, horribly mutilated. Their faces had been stove in, and their testicles cut off and stuffed in their mouths. It was for this act, the Germans alleged, rather than for the Resistance attack, that reprisals were to be taken. Private Schneid claims to have heard the same story from his friend the "Sani," the company medical orderly. He and his platoon went to the cemetery to bury their two men killed the previous night:

> We arranged ourselves in front of the grave, each avoiding the eye of his neighbour because we were all crying silently. Our eighteen-year-old (minus three months) hearts could not restrain the emotion welling in our throats. I don't know if my comrades

were praying, but for my part, I saw myself at the bottom of that grave, and if I recited a prayer, I don't know whether it was for the comrades at my feet, or for myself. . . .

As soon as they had fired their ceremonial volley over the grave, he and the others were ordered to form a burial detail to carry away the corpses of the forty dead Germans:

> We refused to look closely at these bloody corpses. Was it fear of death, or did we refuse to admit to ourselves that Frenchmen could do such a barbaric thing? The German soldiers had always behaved correctly to the French population—why then this fury, to massacre Germans in this fashion? Couldn't they wait for the chance to join the regular liberation army . . . which would permit them to join a decent war of revenge, with prisoners protected by the Geneva Convention?"

One of the prime movers among the Germans for wholesale reprisals was Lieutenant Walter Schmald of the Tulle SO, the security police. Schmald had been in the École Normale throughout its siege. He was a mechanic's son from St. Vith, in Belgian territory that had shuttled between German and Belgian possession since before World War I. A former chemistry student, he had served with the SS on the Russian front, transferred to the SO, and had been based in Tulle for five months. He and his colleague, Lieutenant Beck, knew that they had no hope of mercy from the FTP. When fire overtook the school and the garrison prepared to surrender, Beck put a pistol to his head and shot himself. Schmald found a hiding place in the kitchens, and far into the night of 8 June he lay suffocating amidst the smoke and ruins of the school, barely clinging to life. When he staggered from his refuge to meet the relief column, he was consumed with bitterness. He claimed that most of those who had surrendered were now among the mutilated bodies found by the SS. But for the persuasion of Maurice Roche, pleading urgently with the German divisional staff, if Schmald had had his way the Germans would have been preparing to hang several hundred Frenchmen.

When the war crimes tribunals were examining the "*affaire de Tulle*" years afterwards, the SS witnesses concocted various alibis to excuse or conceal their own role. French historians have always assumed that the supposed murder of German prisoners was a Nazi fabrication, and indeed it may have been. The FTP insisted that when they evacuated the town, they released several large groups of prisoners, having no means of holding them.

Nothing can excuse what the Das Reich did in Tulle, but it is important at least to consider the motives that the Germans advanced. Both in the past and the future, *maquisards*—above all those of the FTP—frequently shot German prisoners out of hand. The author, during his researches for this book, never credited the possibility of the truth of the German allegations until the subject was raised in conversation with a former leading member of the *Armée Secrète* in the Corrèze, who since the war has done much research on local Resistance history. He told me:

> Ah, yes, the business of the mutilated and executed prisoners. I have written and said many times since the war that it is unthink-able that *résistants* could have behaved in this fashion. However, I have spoken to many of those who were in Tulle during the battle, and there is no doubt that it was true. The Spaniards among them, you know. . . . I tell you this because I, as a Frenchman, can never say it. For you, as an Englishman, it may be of interest. But should you ever suggest that I was the source of this assertion, of course I shall deny it absolutely. . . .

It would be absurd to accept the truth of the SS allegations on the unsupported private testimony of one man who was not an eyewit-ness. There was intense bitterness and ill will between the AS and FTP in the Corrèze, as we have seen, and it is possible that this colored the willingness of an AS veteran to believe the worst of the commu-nists. But I am impressed by another, admittedly circumstantial piece of evidence. The FTP claim to have lost seventeen killed and twenty-one badly wounded in the original Tulle attack. Yet there were 139 German corpses. Is it really possible to believe that the garrison, fighting from strong defensive positions, in a battle which the FTP themselves admitted did not go as they had planned it, suffered such disproportionate loss in action? The balance of suspicion must be that the FTP indeed executed a substantial number of Germans who had surrendered to them.

The second significant controversy concerns the source of the order for mass reprisals in Tulle. Throughout the long post-war struggle to indict Lammerding for war crimes, from his secret refuge in Germany the general asserted repeatedly that he did not even arrive in Tulle until the late afternoon of 9 June, when the reprisals were already ended: "I am still ignorant of the source of the order for executions in Tulle," he said, "but I do not think that it was given by a higher authority." The hangings were, therefore, entirely the responsibility of his senior staff officer, Major Albert Stuckler. General Lammerding's alibi rested upon the interesting claim that at the time of the hangings in Tulle, he himself was in Uzerche, conducting an entirely separate hanging of his own.

Uzerche is a small town on the Limoges road twenty-five miles north of Brive-la-Gaillarde. After many hours visiting the scattered lagers of his units, up and down the main road, Lammerding passed the night of 8 June in the flat above the shop of a tanner named Laporte. Early on the morning of the ninth, one of his officers reported to him with three *maquis* prisoners. When the Das Reich advanced into Tulle the previous evening, the Frenchmen had escaped north-westwards in a Citroën van. At the outskirts of the town, they were flagged down by two frightened girls, who begged a lift. Uzerche is only fifteen miles distant by the direct road, and they were approaching the town when an SS patrol surrounded and seized them. The two girls, it transpired, were the mistresses respectively of Lieutenant Schmald and the late Lieutenant Beck of the SO, and they immediately denounced the young Frenchmen. Then, damningly, it was discovered that one of them was carrying three *Feldgendannes* neck shields, which in a moment of madness he had retained as souvenirs.

The young men were brought before Lammerding himself. The Laporte family were bewildered by the courtesy with which he received them. He offered one, Raymond Monteil, a cigarette. The boy declined, saying that he was too hungry to smoke. Lammerding ordered food to be brought. There was no debate about the future of the *maquisard* who had been found in possession of the *Kettenhunden* chains. A rope was tossed over an electric pylon, and he was hanged. The two women pushed and twisted the body as it swung, joking with the SS executioners. Raymond Monteil and the other *maquisard* were spared, for deportation to Dachau where they died, not yet twenty.

According to Lammerding's later testimony, he had had no radio communication with his headquarters in Tulle since the previous evening because of the steep hills intervening. Only late in the afternoon of the ninth did he leave for the town, travelling because of the security situation, via Brive in a slow-moving armored vehicle rather than taking the direct route in a staff car. Lammerding also drew particular attention to the fact that the proclamation of Tuite's doom was signed by "The General Commanding the German Troops." If it had been his own signature, he said, he would have naturally have signed himself "Lammerding."

Colonel Stuckler and Major Wulf—not surprisingly, whatever the truth of the matter—testify emphatically that Lammerding reached Tulle about 1 pm, and personally ordered the executions. The balance of probability favors this version. It is difficult to imagine a conscientious staff officer like Stuckler giving such an order entirely on his own initiative without consulting his commanding general. It is also significant that Stuckler testifies that "there was no specific order to carry out hangings from 66th Reserve Corps." Had he wished to shift responsibility from himself, the least difficult means of doing so would have been to cite the order of a higher formation. There was ample encouragement from OKW and Army Group G to carry out ruthless reprisals. Finally, however, the printed proclamation bears the authentic odor of Lammerding, as witnessed by his memorandum to 58th Corps of 5 June. If anyone still doubts that the reprisals in Tulle were a cold-blooded act of divisional policy, for which Lammerding bore full moral and military responsibility, it only remains to read the text of the division's memorandum on anti-guerilla operations, issued to all units that day of 9 June, and published here as Appendix A. It is extraordinary that a senior SS officer who had commanded anti-partisan operations in Russia could have attempted to persuade a post-war generation that he did not authorize a divisional mass execution.

It is at this point in the narrative that a sullen, grudging tone enters the voices of the surviving SS witnesses. Major Wulf claims to have been affronted when he was ordered to assemble an execution squad: "I protested that this sort of thing was the responsibility of the *Feldgendarmerie*." But the battalion found the men anyway. Private Schneid reported:

"Hascha" Kurz took me with him to the headquarters of the adjutant who was talking to the company NCOs. It was a matter of finding volunteers to act as hangmen. . . . Execution was to be by hanging, because it was more humiliating than a firing squad. . . . Executioners were chosen from among the pioneer company, composed principally of native Germans, with the balance from men of our company who had recently joined us from the Russian front when their units were disbanded. It proved difficult to find enough volunteers. . . . But they were reminded what these *maqui-sards*, these communists had done to their fellow-countrymen.

Schneid claims to have seen a fellow-Alsatian named Pierre walk away in tears "saying that he could not do 'that.'" He himself was told by an NCO who despised "*Franzenlopfe*" like himself "that if I did not have the courage to do some hanging, I could at least act as an escort." So Schneid and some twenty of his fellow-troopers took up position on the street at the lower end of Tulle, close to the courtyard of the arms factory, for the odious tragedy that now unfolded.

All that morning, Lieutenant Schmald and his colleagues had been screening the great crowd of Frenchmen in the courtyard of the arms factory. Many had been allowed to depart. By early afternoon something over 400 remained, and they were becoming increasingly apprehensive. Schmald strode among them, asking acid questions: "Why are your shoes so dirty? If you were a decent citizen, they would be clean. You must be a *maquisard*." He did not conceal his personal craving for revenge for the days of terror that the *maquis* had inflicted upon him: "I am one of the few survivors of yesterday's battle," he told the Abbé Espinasse, the tall, slender almoner of the *lycée* who had been allowed to remain with the captives. "We were almost all Rhine Catholics. We would very much have liked a priest to comfort us." As soon as it became known that many of the prisoners were to die, Herr Brenner, the German director of the arms factory, intervened. Some of the men in the courtyard were key workers, almost irreplaceable. Surely they could be excluded? His interpreter, a thirty-two-year-old Ulm woman named Paulette Geissler, moved busily through the ranks, selecting a man here and another there, and gesturing to the SS to release him. Twenty-seven in all were allowed to go. Then Fraulein Geissler joined Schmald and a little group of other Germans at a table outside the Cafe Tivoli, where they could watch the balance of the afternoon's activity in comfort—some witnesses later claimed to the music of a gramophone.

The essential difficulty facing the Germans was that among all the men in the courtyard, only two were indeed *maquisards*. Among all the remainder, there was not even a shred of evidence to implicate them as accomplices of the FTP. Schmald was compelled to resort to methods arbitrary even by SD standards. One by one, the young, the dirty and the unshaven were ordered to join a group at the side of the courtyard. They were men like Louis Chieze, twenty-six, hairdresser; Marcel Demaux, thirty, a teacher married to another teacher, with a child of four; Georges Gloria, forty, fitter in a bicycle works; Raymond Le Souef, forty, manager of a *gazogène* works; Guy Peuch, twenty, a worker in the arms factory; and his brother André, twenty-three, a restaurant-owner; Jean-Marius-Joseph Rochedix, nineteen, a tramway employee compulsorily transfered to the Tulle armament factory. . . . And so on, 120 men in all, of whom the youngest was seventeen and the oldest forty-two.

The first group of some fifty victims was marshaled in the courtyard. The Abbé Espinasse was permitted to address them: "My friends, you are going to appear before God. There are Catholics among you, believers. Now is the time to commend your souls to the Father who will receive you. Make an act of contrition for all your sins, and I will give you absolution." An SS officer read the order for their execution in German, incomprehensible to most of them. At a gesture from the officer, the guards began to move the group out of the yard, round the corner into the street that passes over the river Vézèré at the southern end of the town. Schneid, watching them come with their hands tied behind their backs, was struck by the absurdity that some still carried loaves of bread or coats tucked under their arms, because when they left home that morning, they had not known whither they were to go. A squad of young Vichyite *chantiers de la jeunesse* (recruits of the regime's compulsory youth camps) had been recruited by the Germans to help with the arrangements—gathering ladders and ropes from the town when it was found that the cables on the SS vehicles were too heavy for the purpose. "Hascha" Kurz nudged Schneid and pointed to the tall, blond French teenager at the head of the *chantiers* squad: "You see this boy, Schneid? These are the sort of men we need—I'd make a fine Waffen SS of him!"

The operation was commanded by Major Kowatsch, a big man of around thirty who had been in the police for some years before joining the SS. Several witnesses claimed that Kowatsch taunted the condemned men before their execution. The hangings themselves were carried out by a pioneer NCO of thirty-one from the Saar, named Otto Hoff. "Because our wounded were so well-treated," Kowatsch told Prefect Trouillé, "we shall be merciful and not burn the town."

The captives were halted by the first lamp post in the street, from which a noose already dangled, and against which two ladders stood, one for the victim and one for the hangman. The first Frenchman mounted, Hoff adjusted the noose and pushed him off. He moved on to the next lamp post and repeated the process. A routine was established. Some of the pioneers laughed as they worked, but even among the SS most found silence less disturbing. As the lamp posts filled, they began to tie nooses a yard or two apart on the first-floor balconies overhanging the street. A few prisoners sobbed as they waited, but most mounted the ladder submissively enough. Some died instantly. Others twisted and twitched convulsively for several minutes, occasionally irritating a German into delivering a brief burst as a *coup de grâce*. There were brief moments of drama. A man suddenly broke free from his group and sprang over the bridge into the rock-strewn river below. An NCO emptied his Schmeisser from the parapet, and the Frenchman's body drifted down to lodge against the foot of the bridge. Some men leaped from their ladders with deliberate force, to end their suffering instantly. One of these caused his own rope to snap. He fell heavily on to the road. His neck was broken, and the Germans saw him twist and shake as he staggered to breathe. After a pause that seemed to Schneid interminable as he gazed on the man's "terrible look of mute supplication," one of them shot him. He lay still. Then a prisoner fell from his ladder, apparently accidentally, and dropped into the river. He was dispatched with two pistol shots. Another suddenly sprang from his waiting group and darted to a body already swinging from a balcony, to shake it by the hand. Was it his brother, mused Schneid? He was instantly shot down.

The hangings had begun at around four in the afternoon. At about 7 pm, Schneid was dispatched to the arms factory courtyard to report that if there were many more to come, there would not be enough rope. He looked about him, at the score or so of condemned men remaining, and the 300 almost equally terrified captives still under guard. Ninety-nine men had been hanged. The Germans decided that enough was enough.

It has never become clear why the Germans suddenly decided to halt the executions and reprieve the remaining twenty-one condemned men. Some witnesses have claimed that the pleas of the Abbé Espinasse for the Germans to show mercy were granted. Others suggest that the secretary-general of Corrèze, Maurice Roche—who possessed the priceless asset of fluent German—persuaded the divisional staff to desist. In any event, the last twenty-one men were sent to join the 300 captives now incarcerated in the arms factory. Later that evening, they were all loaded on to trucks and taken away. They were told that they were merely being driven to the Hôtel Moderne for further identity checks.

The *chantiers de la jeunesse* were ordered to cut down the bodies of the ninety-nine hanged men and load them on to lorries. French officials persuaded Major Kowatsch that if the SS carried out their promise to throw the bodies into the river, they would pose a threat to hygiene that might ultimately affect the garrison as well. Instead, they were tossed on to the town rubbish dump on the Brive road, and later buried there. Thirty-six years later, Major Wulf said that "French officials expressed their satisfaction that the business had been correctly and cleanly carried out."

It is interesting that every single officer of the Das Reich interviewed in the researching of this book, including several who had no part in the extravagances of the division if only because of technical responsibilities, approved the action at Tulle as a correct and proper response to the FTP's actions. Major Wulf was mystified by the energy with which war crimes charges were later pursued against himself and others for that day's work. "We let them have a priest," he said. "Where else have you heard of people being hanged in the war who were allowed a priest before they died?" It was Himmler who had given them their cue. "One basic principle must be the absolute rule for the SS man," he said. "We must be honest, decent, loyal and comradely to members of our own blood and to nobody else. What happens to a Russian, to a Czech, doesn't interest me in the slightest."

Lammerding transferred divisional headquarters to a villa on the road out of Tulle toward Clermont-Ferrand. A series of urgent conferences began, to discuss the division's next movement. Stuckler was still scheduled to drive himself to Clermont-Ferrand to hold a liaison meeting with 66th Reserve Corps, but with the road threatened by *maquisards* it was unthinkable to proceed without a strong escort. Perhaps they should conduct a major operation to clear the route to Clermont-Ferrand? Wulf was sent for. He was instructed to prepare his companies to advance eastwards at first light on 10 June.

Half an hour later, the order was canceled. OKW and Army Group B had come to their senses. As the battle in Normandy consumed its appalling daily toll of tanks, guns and men, it had at last dawned upon their commanders that it was madness to deploy an SS Panzer division to pursue terrorists across the Corrèze. The OKW War Diary reported:

> The third day was again distinguished by the continuous activity of the enemy air forces which swept the forward area and deep into the support areas, suffocating our tank attacks. . . . Reinforcements were brought in from the west and from the Reich. . . . But it was evident that these forces would not be sufficient to drive the enemy back into the sea. So the Führer ordered the following units to be moved in: 2 Pz Div, I Pz Regt of the 116 Pz Regt, 2 SS Pz Div (which had been on clearance operations in southern France). . . .

The signals hastened from OKW to Army Group G, from Toulouse to 58th Panzer Corps, even as the hangman in Tulle was doing his business:

> 2nd SS Pz Div will temporarily be tactically subordinated to Army Group B. General commanding 66th Reserve Corps has received orders to remove the parts of the division under its control from present operations by 1200 on 11 June, and to send its wheeled

elements overland direct to Army Group B in Normandy. Tracked vehicles of the division are to be entrained *immediately*, regardless of present operations. The planned entraining areas are: for full tracks—the Perigueux area; for half-tracks—the Limoges area.

In other words, Von Rundstedt was in desperate need of the Das Reich's heavy armor. But his orders were much more easily issued than executed.

CHAPTER 7

The Jeds

BEFORE FOLLOWING the Das Reich Division onwards north and west, there is one further piece of unfinished business concerning the movement of the armored columns on the eastern axis from Cahors, which did not bring even the leading elements into Tulle until late on the evening of 9 June. At almost exactly the moment that the first companies of the Der Führer regiment were crawling wearily into Limoges on the night of 8 June, above a dropping zone in south Corrèze a few miles from Aurillac three parachutes blossomed from a Liberator bomber. They began to drift slowly earthwards, to add modestly to the difficulties of 2nd SS Panzer Division.

A few moments later, an excited *maquisard* ran across the field proudly leading his newly arrived charges, and shouting to the rest of the reception committee: "We've got a French officer and he's brought his wife with him!" The officer was introduced as "Aristide" Aspirant Maurice Bourdon of the French Army. His real name—which none of them learned until after the war—was Prince Michel de Bourbon, nephew of the Pretender to the French throne. His "wife," however, was the commanding officer of the team, the splendidly kilted Highland officer Major Tommy Macpherson, among the most single-minded warriors that the war can have produced. They were accompanied by a British wireless operator, Sergeant Brown, and a load of arms and explosives with which to equip the local *maquis*. Their orders were "to assist Resistance teams in the Lot, to stimulate guerilla action along the lines of communication between Montauban and Brive, and to cut the

RN20," along which the Das Reich had been pouring all day. Two nights later another team, led by Captain Macdonald Austin of the American Army, parachuted into the Dordogne 100 miles further west, with orders to carry out the same mission from the opposite flank. Unlike French Section's agents, Austin had been specifically informed of the presence of the Das Reich and instructed to do everything possible to impede it.

These were the first of the inter-Allied "Jedburgh" teams, of which ninety-three were to be parachuted into France before the Liberation. Their arrival acknowledged the new phase of Resistance, open guerilla war. They were dispatched in uniform, and while they had been trained in some of the skills of clandestine war, they were sent to serve as commando officers in the field, not as secret agents. Their arrival in uniform was intended—as indeed it succeeded—to boost the morale of the *maquis*.

The origins of the Jedburghs were, however, overwhelmingly political rather than military. The Free French and above all the Americans were seeking a larger share in behind-the-lines operations in Europe. General Donovan and his American OSS had been disappointed, and indeed infuriated, by the reluctance of the British to see its men dropped into France.

SOE in their turn pointed out that while OSS had sent a handful of American-controlled Frenchmen into France, the prospective agents of American nationality all spoke French with an instantly recognizable accent, and few showed much aptitude for living a cover story successfully. Although most of the British liked and admired Colonel David Bruce, the elegant OSS chief in London, they were unimpressed by General Donovan, whom they judged an ambitious empire-builder. "The British kept tactfully reminding us that they had been in the intelligence business since Queen Elizabeth's day," said the British-educated American Henry Hyde, who joined the intelligence branch of OSS in April 1942. "'Those naive Americans,' they said, and by and large we were a naive lot. Americans are naive. But I felt that the American Army was entitled to its own sources of information. We said: 'We're not that much stupider than you. If we're taught properly, we can do it.'"

After much discussion and argument, a compromise was agreed. On the intelligence side, OSS would continue to build up its modest network of French agents reporting to SI—there were twenty-seven of them by D-Day. At the suggestion of the British SIS—frankly desperate for joint Allied projects which would not interfere with their existing networks in France—a project codenamed Sussex was created, to drop fifty two-man SIS/OSS teams into northern France from May onwards, to provide tactical intelligence for the Allied armies. But once again, the OSS agents would have to be Frenchmen.

Americans could only take their part in France, the British insisted, after the transition from secret to open guerilla war, when they would no longer be compelled to live a cover story. The Jedburgh training program would be established under the auspices of SOE. A mixed group of 250 American, French and British trainees was assembled, to be parachuted to support Resistance in rural areas that lent themselves to guerilla war. "The Jeds," said one of their British recruits, "plainly represented the enormous power and interest of America in the European war."

Tommy Macpherson reached the organization after a war that would already have sated most men. He was the youngest of seven children of a judge. In May 1939, at the age of eighteen and before he had even technically finished at Fettes public school, he took a commission in the Cameron Highlanders. In June 1940 he joined the Scottish Commando, and after training went to the Middle East with Layforce. He took part in two raids on Crete, and was then detailed to reconnoiter the landing area for Major Geoffrey Keyes on his famous mission to kill Rommel at his headquarters in North Africa. Macpherson had already developed a low opinion of the staff work for commando raids of the period, ". . . and it stuck out a mile that this was an absolute disaster." Rommel was not even at the headquarters, Keyes was killed in the attack, and Macpherson was captured soon afterwards, attempting to walk back to the British lines through the desert.

He was sent to Italy, to one of the "naughty boys'" establishments, Camp 5, which he found "quite an enjoyable place to be, because there was so much going on." He escaped, was recaptured and sent to a camp in Austria. He escaped again with two New Zealanders, and made his way to northern Italy before being recaptured. This time he was sent to "a very nasty sort of interrogation center" in East Prussia, and thence to the Polish-Silesian border. He and a New Zealander exchanged identities with two private soldiers in order to be able to join an outside working party, and crawled away under the wire of the commandant's rabbit farm. They caught a train to Danzig, where they arrived in the middle of an air raid one night in October 1943. They hitched a lift to Gdynia from a sympathetic Pole, and hid up all day until they were smuggled aboard a Swedish ship carrying coal dust. They lay deep in the cargo while German guards and dogs searched the ship, and surfaced when they were safely at sea. The Swedes briefly detained them, but they were finally allowed to catch a Liberator to England. On 4 November, two years to the day after his capture, Macpherson landed home. At his debriefing, he was asked if he would like to join SOE. It seemed that General Gubbins, a family friend, had suggested him. He toyed briefly with the idea of a quiet holiday in a staff job, then took the SOE job. Early in December 1943, a captain with the Military Cross, he reported to the Jedburgh training center at Milton Hall, the Fitzwilliam stately home in Northamptonshire.

Many of the Frenchmen who joined the Jedburghs were also veterans, or had escaped from France after desperate adventures. But Prince Michel de Bourbon had been taken to America in 1940, and was still there in 1943 when he ran away from school to enlist at the age of sixteen and a half. The French Military Mission in New York had an arrangement by which their nationals could be trained by the US Army, and de Bourbon (or Bourdon, as he should henceforth be called) was sent to an officer training school at Fort Benning, Georgia. From there he was plucked out by OSS recruiters, who sent him to their spy schools for three months to learn the usual routines of shooting, sabotage, unarmed combat and morse. After so many changes of environment, he found that he had ceased to think as a Frenchman, and identified more easily with Americans or Englishmen, although he was disconcerted by those American trainees who admired the Germans and were naive enough to say so. They seemed to possess an engaging, innocent enthusiasm for adventure ahead, rather more so than the other Frenchmen on the course, most of whom had been recruited from exiles in North and South America and seemed happy to remain as far as possible from the war.

On 23 December 1943, Bourdon landed in Glasgow from the *Queen Elizabeth*, and was promptly assigned to spend Christmas with a local suburban family who owned a circus. They found this obscure French teenager somewhat uncouth, and gave him stern advice about the proper use of a knife and fork. Early in the New Year, he was sent on a British-run selection course to assess his suitability for commando or clandestine operations. To his utter dismay, he was rejected as too young, and had to launch a furious campaign to change the authorities' minds. At last he succeeded, and was one of only two Frenchmen from his course in the US who were accepted for operations. The rest of the French Jedburghs were recruited from Free French officers in England.

Macdonald Austin, universally known as "Mac," was a quiet spoken southerner who failed to win a regular West Point cadetship before the war, and was studying accountancy at the University of Florida with a reserve commission when he was suddenly summoned to active duty. One day in 1943, at the age of twenty-six, he was instructing parachute infantry at a vast tented camp of 100,000 men in Georgia when a mysterious civilian from Washington arrived. The man interviewed Austin and several other jump-qualified officers. His file showed that he had some high school French; was he interested in volunteering for a dangerous mission that involved being dropped deep behind enemy lines in France? He was. The volunteers were shipped to Washington, where an extraordinary selection process took place. A French-speaking captain announced in French: "All those who can understand what I'm saying go to the end of the room." Austin and about half the others moved smartly. They were considered sufficiently proficient to train as guerillas for France. The failures were sent on language courses.

In the weeks that followed, about half Austin's companions were weeded out in training. Those who were left were amused and bemused by the OSS passion for melodramatics. Their school was situated at the Congressional Country Club outside Washington, and whenever they went into the city, the students were given strict orders not to move publicly in groups. The notion of secrecy, of unobtrusiveness, seemed alien and funny to the young officers. Even as they plunged through the two-week commando course at Arisaig in Scotland, and afterwards during initial Jedburgh training at Hatherop Castle in Gloucestershire, they could not escape a sense of fantasy, even absurdity.

At Milton Hall, where they came together and began their training in earnest, the British and French with their seriousness about the war—and in many cases experience of battle—found the Americans touchingly gauche. After years of stringent rationing, Macpherson and the others "were shattered to see bacon, waffles, marmalade, scrambled eggs provided because we had an American contingent. And they had this mania for surrounding themselves with weapons." The Americans, with their easy conversation and high poker games, found most of the Frenchmen tense and uncommunicative. Experienced British officers like Tommy Macpherson were effectively honorary instructors. Harry Coombe-Tennant had also escaped from Germany. Geoffrey Hallowes had survived ten days in a rowing boat, adrift off Sumatra. One elderly trainee who was thought to be too well known to be allowed to drop into France had his face altered by plastic surgery while on leave, and returned claiming that he had been in a car smash.

These men were bemused by such exotic American recruits as René Dusacq, who had been a Hollywood stuntman; Prince Serge Obolensky, a former New York socialite; "Baz" Bazata, a red-haired adventurer who addressed all colonels as "sugar"; and several near-gangsters. There were some good ex-West Point regulars, and serious students such as William Colby, future head of the CIA, who spent much of his spare time at Milton Hall pouring over *Seven Pillars of Wisdom*. But while the British admired American organization and equipment, they doubted whether they possessed the instinct for improvisation in the field. Many seemed to be acting out a role. "The great thing in this game is that you may have a letter in your pocket signed personally by De Gaulle—as we all did when we landed in France," said Tommy Macpherson, "but you are in fact, in yourself, nothing. Success depends on the moral hold you can establish upon the people you are working with."

Brigadier Modder-Ferryman, commanding Special Forces HQ, came down to address them. Denis Rake, a wonderfully courageous and unashamedly high camp F Section wireless operator, delivered a brilliant and witty talk about life in Occupied France. The French treated all their training with desperate earnestness. "They were very conscious of the debacle of 1940," said Geoffrey Hallowes. "The idea that France should be liberated without their help was intolerable to them."

Towards the end of the spring, the "mating period" began. The students were told to sort themselves into pairs, and to choose an NCO wireless operator. Macpherson took Bourdon, whom he liked

Vera Atkins, regarded by many as the critical force in French Section.

"Soleil," René Cousteille, leader of the Groupe Soleil.

George Hiller, French Section's officer in the Lot.

Violette Szabo

Marius Guedin (*right*), Jacques Poirier (*left*) and other *résistants* of the Corrèze.

Jacques Poirier—"Nestor"—who, with Harry Peulevé, armed most of the *maquisards* of the Corrèze and Dordogne who met the Das Reich division after 6 June.

Odette Bache, who kept the "stray dogs home" in Figeac.

André Malraux, author of *La Condition Humaine* and one of the most extraordinary figures who held the stage in the Resistance of the Dordogne and Corrèze in 1944.

Major Otto Weidinger of the Der
Führer regiment of which he assume
command on 16 June 1944.

Baron Philippe de Gunzbourg on the
bicycle on which he travelled more
than 15,000 miles on his missions for
Wheelwright in the Dordogne, often
with *plastique* on the carrier.

General Heinz Lammerding with one of the division's Panzers in the background.

One of the most famous *parachutages* of the war—a vast daylight drop near Loubressac on 14 July—Bastille Day—1944, which provided huge supplies of arms for the *maquis* of the Corrèze, Lot and Dordogne.

Jean-Jacques Chapou, known as "Philippe" in the Lot and "Kléber" in the Corrèze.

A unique unpublished photograph from the private album of an SS officer: as the march north from Montauban began, (*left to right*) Major Helmut Kampfe, Major Ernst Krag, Colonel Albert Stuckler and General Heinz Lammerding.

A *maquisard* sabotages a railway line.

René Jugie, of the Corrèze AS, who blew the Uzerche line on the night of 8 June 1944.

An SS officer's impression of the hangings at Tulle, sketched on the same day and perhaps the only contemporary visual evidence of the atrocity.

Captain John Tonkin, who commanded the SAS Bulbasket mission; Lieutenant Twm Stephens, in the civilian clothes which he wore on his mission to pinpoint the petrol trains; and Lieutenant John Crisp.

although he found him very immature and desperately anxious to prove his courage. Sergeant Brown, their wireless operator, was a tall, fair Londoner with no battle experience and no French, but technically highly competent. "Mac" Austin teamed himself with a former regular French Army gunner, Raymond Leconte, a round-faced man who seemed slow-witted, but was in reality extremely sharp. Their wireless operator, Jack Berlin, was a thickset, bespectacled eighteen-year-old Jewish boy from Brooklyn who had worked his way through high school, and regarded the war as a personal crusade.

Early in April 1944, there was one of the endless wartime "flaps" at Milton. Without warning, fifteen teams were detailed to move to North Africa. Austin, Macpherson and the others found themselves trans-shipped to Oran on the liner *Capetown Castle*, and thence into the Algerian mountains for joint exercises with French commandos and Spahis to sharpen their wits before action. The Frenchmen among them exulted to be once more on their own soil. Michel de Bourbon met his father, Prince René, who was serving with the Foreign Legion. His sister, the ex-Queen of Romania, was driving an ambulance for Leclerc, and his other brother was in the Norwegian Air Force. The Bourbons considered that they had gone some distance toward redeeming themselves from the traditional suspicion of the French nation toward their family.

One night, the teams had been on an exercise high in the mountains, from which they had to march back to a grid co-ordinate. At 3 am on 5 June 1944, they pulled themselves wearily aboard the pick-up truck and found that they were being driven straight to Blida airfield. Major James Champion of SOE told Austin: "You're going tonight." They had a few hours' sleep, then the long briefing began. Austin was told that he was being dropped to a reception committee of George Starr's Wheelwright circuit, south of Sarlat. They were taking weapons for two groups of twenty men apiece. For the rest of the day, they rested and prepared their equipment, along with Macpherson's men, who were also to go that night. All the other teams had been given leave in Algiers so that they should not notice the departure of their colleagues.

That night, however, the teams stood by in vain. SHAEF had insisted that no Jedburgh should be dropped into France in uniform until the moment of invasion. When the landing was postponed for twenty-four hours, so were Austin and Macpherson. To the intense chagrin of Austin and his team, the following night also ended in anti-climax. Their Halifax failed to locate the dropping zone, and they returned crestfallen to Blida, to face much teasing from their comrades: "Did you freeze in the door, then?" On the night of 8 June they found the dropping zone, but the pilot reported that the reception comittee was flashing the wrong code letter. The Jedburgh was more than willing to risk the drop, but the airman was not. Once again they returned to Blida. It was the sort of difficulty that dogged all wartime operational flights by SOE and OSS, and caused such a high proportion of abortive missions, with all the strain and risk both for those in the aircraft and the reception committee on the ground.

By now Henry Hyde, OSS Special Intelligence chief in Algiers, had received a signal from one of his French agents, a regular army major named Jean Lescane, that the Das Reich was moving. Hyde was a lawyer like so many OSS men, twenty-nine, and educated in England at Charterhouse and Trinity College, Cambridge. To his chagrin, although he had been born in Paris and was married to a daughter of a French baron, he was turned down for agent training, and took over SI in Algiers instead. Now, the message from Lescane north of Agen was funneled into the military intelligence machine. Austin was told that there might still be time to interdict the movement of some elements of 2nd SS Panzer.

A few minutes after midnight on 10 June, Austin's Jedburgh at last saw the green light flash above the exit hole of their Halifax. After the heat and noise of the fuselage, the American was delighted by the cool fresh air and silence of the June night above the Dordogne. He landed neatly, just behind his French colleague, Ray Leconte. A shadowy figure loomed out of the darkness. Austin unburdened himself of the French phrase he had been practicing for days for this moment: "We've come to fight on your side."

"So—you're an American, are you?" said an unmistakably American voice from the darkness. The *maquisard* was a middle-aged civilian named Dick Andrews who had been brought up in France, educated at Cornell and served in the US Corps of Engineers in World War I. He was demobbed in France, and settled down to spend the rest of his life in the country. When the Germans took over the Unoccupied

Zone in 1943, Andrews sent his family to a safe refuge abroad, and joined a *maquis*.

They cleared the dropping zone and sat down to breakfast on an omelet made from fresh eggs and truffles. Jack Berlin thought some pieces of charcoal from the fire had fallen into his omelet, and carefully picked out the truffles and put them beside his plate. It was also Berlin's misfortune to dislike wine, which caused him some privation in the weeks ahead. There was nothing else to drink.

Austin began to get the measure of the *résistants*, and of the situation in the area. He was astonished to discover that the Germans were nowhere to be seen, and that the *maquisards* moved freely along the roads by *gazogène* and truck. The French talked much and bitterly about the German atrocities, but in the peace of the woods south of the Dordogne it was hard for the Americans to be infected by their anger. They found it impossible to hate the enemy. Later, when they saw a few prisoners, Austin found that he felt only curiosity. Among the *maquisards*, those with military training responded readily enough to his proposals, but the remainder were difficult to influence and impossible to order. He found his high school French confounded by their heavily accented slang. It is a measure of the isolation of the different *maquis* that this one, commanded by a Sarlatais named Albert, seemed to know nothing about the Das Reich, or about the dramatic situation unfolding not far westwards, around Bergerac. Austin proposed that they should establish some roadblocks, but the idea met with little enthusiasm, and anyway there was little enemy traffic. On the one occasion that they went to reconnoiter the Brive-Montauban road, they saw no sign of movement. Leconte started to travel the countryside setting charges on small bridges and culverts that it seemed useful to destroy. Austin began to instruct Albert's men in the use of the weapons that he had brought. There was one unseemly interruption, when the *maquisards* tortured a local man they had brought in, suspected of treachery. He died, and they sent apologetic word to his father. The man was not appeased, and passed word to the Germans, giving the location of the little chateau by the river where the group was based. The Americans were elsewhere when the German armored cars arrived. The *maquisards* beat a hasty retreat, the Germans burned the chateau, and thereafter they all lived in the woods. To his astonishment, Austin found himself desperately wishing that he had brought some books to read. Of all his apprehensions before he parachuted into France, the prospect of boredom had never been among them.

Austin learnt a great deal about guerillas in the weeks that followed—above all about their absolute unpredictability. He moved westwards and began attacking railways himself. On one notable day he was up a ladder fixing an explosive charge to the Bordeaux-Agen line beneath a bridge. He had posted a Bren gunner to cover him, a hundred yards up the track. Suddenly, he found a German bicycle patrol dismounting a stone's throw up the road, and opening a furious fire. The *maquis* party escaped in confusion, but intact. Austin learned that the Bren gunner, lulled by the hot sun, had simply gone to sleep: "Sometimes they would do marvellous things," he said, "but one had to realize that on the next operation it would suddenly turn out that they had forgotten to crank up the *gazogène.*"

Fundamentally, from the moment that he landed Austin found himself unable to carry out the job that he had been sent to do, because of the lack of Intelligence and enthusiasm among the *maquis*, and the feud between the Wheelwright circuit and the *maquis* of Soleil and the AS, armed by Poirier, which kept him ignorant and isolated for many days. Above all, the Jedburgh had come too late. The strategic decision to send the teams on D-Day may have made sense for security reasons, but was a critical handicap in tactical terms, on the ground. No man could arrive in the middle of France without previous combat experience or knowledge of the country and immediately conduct a coherent military campaign. For all their courage and enthusiasm to get into action, Austin and his colleagues were at a loss: "I didn't really know what to do. The target that I was to go after wasn't there any longer. I thought that the best thing I could do was to get on with training the *maquisards*, and go round the country meeting people until I could formulate some sort of plan. It was not what I expected it to be. . . ."

Major Tommy Macpherson jumped from his Halifax over the Corrèze on the night of 8 June with the overwhelming advantage that he spoke competent French and possessed the confidence of a man with great experience of battle and of life behind enemy lines. He had long ago

shed his 1941 "infinite capacity for belief in the infallibility of planners."
He landed into the hands of an AS leader named Bernard Cournil, who
was mayor of the tiny village of Le Rouget and owned a local garage.
Macpherson gave Cournil the codename of the *maquis* leader he had
been instructed to contact "Droite." The Frenchman said that he had
never heard of him. He himself controlled only a small group of poorly
armed *résistants*, and was delighted to have suddenly acquired his own
personal Allied mission. Bourdon did not much interest him—the
French boy seemed disappointingly young, and was obviously from an
entirely alien social background. Sergeant Brown, the wireless operator,
spoke no French at all, and found himself condemned to spend most of
his stay in France making tea beneath damp parachute canopies in the
woods, between radio schedules. Macpherson made his own assessment of the situation:

> With hindsight, it was obvious that we had been very poorly briefed.
> The impression in London was that the *maquisards* were all keen
> volunteers, but it was immediately obvious that 90 percent of them
> were there to stay away from the Germans, not to fight them. There
> was also a pretty false idea at home about what the *maquis* were
> for—there was too much Secret Army stuff, rather than concentra-
> tion on hit and run attacks by small groups. The men we found
> when we landed were neither equipped nor trained for action. It
> was only later that we began to get a flow of genuine volunteers who
> wanted to fight. I had not been given the faintest idea until I landed
> that there was a split between the AS and the FTP.

But Macpherson embodied the exact spirit that SHAEF had intended
to send with the Jedburghs. He had no interest in clandestine life—he
considered that his business was to make as much open trouble for
the Germans as possible. Thus he wore his uniform and kilt wherever
he went. When he acquired a Citroën car, he decorated the bonnet
with the Union Jack and Tricolour. Thus also, he moved at once to
take into action what men he could muster. His attitude exasperated
local SOE agents, who had spent months working in great secrecy,
and above all with concern for the welfare of the French people among
whom they lived. Macpherson troubled himself only about attacking

Germans, and wasted no time brooding about possible reprisals. He considered his instructions: "The theme of our training had been that we were to use our own judgment to create whatever mayhem could tie down enemy forces, and build up a trained nucleus of *résistants* for the 'phase of Liberation.'" In the little cluster of huts in the woods in which the *maquis* lived, he reviewed Cournil's little group. Between them, they had a few old French army rifles and one light machine gun. But Macpherson and his team had come with superb personal equipment—much of it American and extending to a money-belt laden with gold sovereigns for each man. They had also brought Brens, gammon bombs and explosives. Within a few hours of landing—and chiefly to put some life into the *maquisards*—Macpherson had mined and blown an unguarded bridge on the Aurillac-Maurs railway line, where it crossed a country road. They were short of food. Macpherson stopped a civilian lorry and hijacked four sacks of sugar. A German ration truck drove down the road shortly afterwards, and they shot it to pieces. In the back, they found two tons of chestnut puree. They carted it back to the camp.

Until the moment of the Liberation, Macpherson waged an ambitious and ruthless campaign against the Germans across the region—attacking trains and convoys, rail links and roads with remorseless energy. He was determined to compel the French to decide which side they were on. One day he drove into Decazeville and invited the mayor to join him for a drink at the cafe in the main square. The trembling Frenchman talked to him for a few minutes before there was a sudden shout that a German convoy was approaching. Macpherson and his *maquisards* leaped into the car and drove furiously out of the town, pursued by an armored car. When they reached the bridge over the road, Macpherson leapt out, climbed on to the parapet, and lobbed a gammon bomb neatly on to the German vehicle as it passed underneath, instantly halting and wrecking it.

> I felt that I had a clear role of tip-and-run disruption, getting morale right locally. I viewed part of my job as being to move the psychology of the people. The vast bulk of the people were scared stiff to help us. I remember once stopping late at night to ask somebody to come down and show us the way. "No, *m'sieu*, I cannot—the curfew," the

man called from the window. The Germans correctly judged that this was the way to deal with a guerilla movement—to make people more frightened of the penalties than of the guerillas.

The team rapidly became cynical about some of their own men. After one or two bad experiences at *parachutages*, Macpherson insisted that all containers were opened in front of himself or Bourdon. There were some *maquisards*—a small but energetic minority—who stole substantial fortunes in the course of the war by deflecting SOE money from *parachutages*, or by selling off materiel. In Macpherson's view—which would be fiercely contested by many *résistants* and some of SOE's officers—"If it hadn't been for the British officers there, the *maquis* would have done nothing. They were concerned with the necessities of life, and with establishing a power base."

To the anger of some SOE officers, Macpherson worked closely with Robert Noireau and the local FTP, simply because he felt that these men were most committed to killing Germans. Local *résistants* were also exasperated by Macpherson's assertion that, in the first weeks after his arrival, most of the local railway system was "working quite normally—indeed it was the only means by which the Germans could still move some supplies"—no doubt assisted by the fact that they had now begun to place a flatcar loaded with very old or very young French hostages in front of most of their engines.

The young Scot was a trained soldier, who regarded the situation in southern France without sentiment, merely as a military problem. He made a fine contribution to the guerilla war in the region. It is not surprising that, in doing so, he aroused fierce controversy.

But this account must focus upon Macpherson's first days in France and his contribution to the battle against the Das Reich. Shortly after they returned to the *maquis* camp with their load of captured chestnut puree—still little more than hours after their landing—word reached the Jedburgh that armored elements of the Das Reich Division were still moving up the Figeac-Tulle road. Macpherson learned later to mistrust much of the intelligence he received: "If an armoured car and a truck moved into a town, we were always told it was a battalion. If it was two half-tracks, we heard it was a Panther regiment." But for once, the news was accurate. That evening the Scot drove to within sight of the road, and glimpsed a lagered tank. He retreated to the camp: "I thought we'd better make a little bit of a show," he said. But with what? They had used most of their explosives to blow the rail bridge. They had no bazookas. Macpherson thought that they might be able to weaken a small bridge, and cover it for long enough to compel the Germans to dismount from their vehicles, with all the delay that this entailed. It was time rather than casualties that they could cause the Germans to lose.

Very early the next morning, Macpherson descended to the road with twenty-seven *maquisards*. At his bidding, two men had wrapped wet cloths around the barrels of their Stens. He had learned on the ranges in England that this caused them to sound like heavy machine guns. The men were in buoyant spirits because, unlike Macpherson, they did not appreciate the extreme peril they were about to face. They were all peasants, some wearing fragments of battledress and old French Army uniforms, surmounted by the inevitable berets. A few had put on FFI armbands. Bourdon and Brown remained in camp—there was no merit in risking the entire Jedburgh. Macpherson personally positioned each man, explaining as undramatically as possible what he wished him to do. On one side trees came close to the road; the Scot tied small charges to a succession of trunks, wired them together and gave the exploder to a *maquisard* with orders to twist it when the Germans reached the bridge. He placed ten men with himself around the bridge, and the others among the trees. On the other side, the ground was flat and open. Here, when the Germans tried to deploy upon it, he planned to have his killing ground. There was a solitary cottage by the bridge. They told the old peasant who occupied it to lose himself as rapidly as possible. Then they settled down to wait. There had been rain in the night, and in the first hours after dawn the ground was cold and wet. It was three hours before they heard the shrieking clatter of the approaching column.

It was headed by two motorcyclists, followed by a half-track and a procession of tanks, with trucks in the rear. Macpherson blew the bridge under the leading half-track, which burst into flames. Germans leaped from the wreckage and dashed back down the column. Amidst the barrage of small arms fire the first tank, battened down, paused for a moment to reflect and then crept forward. Macpherson had left a man with a gammon grenade just behind the bridge for this moment.

The gammon exploded at the rear of the tank, rupturing a track. The road was blocked.

The tanks further back along the column began to shell their position around the bridge, lumbering off the road into cover. German infantry began to work forward through the trees from the rear. There was a volley of explosions as the mined trees fell. The action lasted perhaps half an hour before Macpherson saw the infantry closing in around their flanks. He signaled the surviving *maquisards* to withdraw, supporting their walking wounded. At a rendezvous a few hundred yards away, their old lorry was waiting. They retreated to the camp.

The official report of their Jedburgh, Quinine, compiled after the Liberation, states that in their action against the Das Reich, twenty out of twenty-seven *maquisards* were killed. Macpherson's recollection thirty-six years later was that casualties were less severe. But the same lack of fieldcraft and tactical training that cost Guedin's men so dear further north and west made the Jedburgh action expensive. The *maquisards* simply did not understand the simplest principles of crossing ground under fire.

Macpherson was at pains later to remark that he did not make a practice of embarking on actions against such odds, and indeed he never did again. It was the urgent need to make an impact on the *maquisards* and on the region, above all upon the Germans, that drove him to stage the ambush. "The Germans didn't suffer much," he admitted, beyond the damage to their leading vehicles and an hour or two's frustration and delay clearing up the mess and replacing tracks. But it was from a thousand such actions the length of France in June 1944 that the confusion and strategic misjudgments of the German High Command concerning Resistance were created, and the passage of the Das Reich to Normandy delayed.

CHAPTER 8

"Panzer divisions are too good for this. . . ."

O N 10 JUNE 1944, as General Heinz Lammerding reviewed the position of his division and the orders he had received for its urgent movement, he found little cause for satisfaction. Elements of the Das Reich were sprawled across the Lot, Corrèze, and Haute-Vienne. Broken-down tanks and assault guns were lying by the roadside from Tulle to Montauban. All the staff's warnings about the technical cost of moving heavy armor by the road had been justified. The Panzergrenadier brigade was deployed in a ring covering Limoges against the terrorist attack that the panicky *Kommandantur* in the city considered imminent. The steep hills and woods made communication between all these units erratic and uncertain. The report which Lammerding now transmitted to the general commanding 58th Panzer Corps is a great tribute to the climate created by Resistance after D-Day, and a measure of the Germans' calamitous error in committing an SS Panzer division to antiterrorist operations. It is worth quoting in full:

STATE OF THE DIVISION:

The lack of adequate transport, the substantial distances to be covered in unfavourable terrain, the dispersal of units over 300 kilometres and the lack of advance preparation for operational and supply measures has weakened the strength of the division out of all proportion during the past eight days.

Unserviceability among tanks is 60 per cent, towing vehicles and half-tracks 30 per cent. The majority of the unserviceable vehicles can only be moved again when we receive the spare parts which are still missing, despite repeated requests. The division has been compelled to establish six support points in the Figeac–Tulle–Brive–Cahors area which require strong infantry protection because of the gang situation. The opportunities for commandeering additional wheeled vehicles from the gang area are negligible, because predictably the terrorists have beaten the liaison staff to it. Adequate fuel supplies depend on the arrival of the fuel convoy, which is nowhere in sight.

Only the division's wheeled elements can begin to move to Normandy on schedule. The tanks and towing vehicles require at least four days for repairs, even assuming that the requested spare parts reach the division early on 11 June. Presumably the complete crippling of rail movement by the terrorists will anyway prevent an earlier entrainment. More long marches in this sort of country can only be undertaken at further heavy cost. The Figeac–Ciermont–Ferrand–Limoges–Gourdon area is completely in the hands of the terrorists. Local German posts and garrisons are surrounded, in many cases besieged and often reduced to company strength. The French Government's forces have been completely paralysed by the terrorists. The paralysis of the German posts is quite disgraceful. Without determined and ruthless action the situation in this area will develop until a threat exists whose proportions have not yet been recognized. In this area a new communist state is coming to life, a state which rules without opposition and carries out co-ordinated attacks.

The task of eliminating this danger must be transferred to the local divisions. Panzer divisions in the fifth year of the war are too good for this. In the division's opinion, the local forces are quite capable of maintaining order if they are pulled together sharply, given transport, and led energetically. Their present isolation is a standing invitation to the terrorists. Necessary specific measures have already been reported by the division.

In view of the overall situation, the division requests emphatically:
1. that the cutting-off of German outposts should be prevented.
2. that vital spare parts for movement to Normandy be provided.
3. that the special difficulties of the division in its present state

of reconstruction, together with its supply and equipment problems, be taken into account when movement and operational orders are being issued.

Signed: Lammerding

Lammerding's report provoked a flurry of signals between the German command headquarters of France. Army Group G sent an urgent request to OKW for reinforcements to replace 2nd SS Pz on its withdrawal from Corrèze and Dordogne. They reported that, as an emergency measure, they were assembling a battle group from 11 Pz Div composed of two infantry battalions, one artillery battery and an anti-tank company: "The commander of the battle group will make personal contact with the staff of 2nd SS Pz in Tulle. His mission— restoration of peace and order and its maintenance by the strongest measures in the departments of Corrèze and Dordogne. . . ." A further signal to OKW, also dispatched on 10 June, indicated that "in view of the transport situation, entrainment of tracks 2 SS Pz Div Das Reich at earliest 12.6.44 at 00:00 Périgueux." This was a reflection of the desperate flatcar shortage and the rail cuts. Yet before the tanks could even reach Périgueux, the spare parts were essential. On 11 June, Army Group G was signaling again to OKW: "High transport losses of 2nd SS Pz Div-immediate supply of following parts to Tulle essential. . . ." There followed a list that included twelve complete tank engines, two assault gun engines, and a vast array of wheels, tracks, sprockets and oxyacetylene equipment: "Arrival of parts essential to avoid delays in transport of division's tanks. . . ." In short, the Das Reich Division was moving nowhere in a hurry.

Lammerding and his staff spent the day of 10 June at their headquarters in a villa on the Clermont-Ferrand road out of Tulle, grappling with their huge administrative problems, above all the recovery of the disabled armor on the road from Figeac.

The reconnaissance battalion, which now possessed unchallenged control of Tulle, organized several fruitless sweeps in search of terrorists north and south of the town, which achieved no more than the burning of a few farms and the execution of a handful of peasants who were slow to remove themselves from the Germans' path. The companies remaining in Tulle set about comprehensively looting the town's shops and houses while conducting further arms searches. Private Schneid and his section suffered the embarrassment of being billeted in the home of one of the previous day's widows: "Our hostess, still ignorant of her husband's death, asked us for news of him. We were cowards enough to pretend that he was not among the condemned, although he had been hanged at the corner of the next street. . . ." It was an interesting day. Ransacking one house, Schneid found an aged, moth-balled blue *poilu's* (infantryman's) uniform in a tin trunk. An elderly woman appeared at the door. He suggested that she should dispose of her husband's old souvenirs lest another less charitable searcher take it for a *maquis* uniform. The "Hascha" appeared in high spirits, driving a splendid grey car that he had liberated. Another trooper carried off a motorcycle and sidecar. One man found a gramophone with a pile of Tino Rossi records: "Ah, Tino Rossi, if you only knew how often you enabled some young Waffen SS men to forget the war. Everybody adored your voice and hummed your songs. Later there was a rumour that after the surrender of Paris the partisans had killed you, you and Maurice Chevalier. Even the Germans were horrified. . . ." Above all, the troopers seized food, and reveled in breakfast with coffee: "The last of that Tullois salami lasted us as far as St. Lo. . . . We drank the last of the coffee in front of Mons."

At 2:10 am on the tenth, the Das Reich issued the following tactical report to 58th Panzer Corps:

> Area Souillac-Figeac-Ciermont-Ferrand—Limoges in the hands of gangs, stubborn and well-armed.
> Souillac-Limoges and Figeac—Tulle roads cleared.
> Bulk of division in area Brive-Tulle-Limoges. Target for 10.6.44 Clermont-Ferrand.
> Enemy losses: 500 dead, 1500 prisoners
> Own losses: 17 killed, 30 wounded
> Heavy transport losses.

The figures for enemy losses included not only civilians shot on the road, but the ninety-nine civilians hanged in Tulle. The figure for prisoners included many Tullois men who had now been released. The decision to push east to Clermont-Ferrand was, as has been shown, almost immediately reversed. The Germans were now much more concerned about the situation westwards. The garrisons of Bergerac, Périgueux and Bordeaux were struggling to deal with the uprising inaugurated by Loupias and Philippe de Gunzbourg. They had already launched one modest attempt to relieve Bergerac from the west, which had been repulsed by the *résistants*. Now they were moving up heavier metal. Much closer to the Das Reich, on the road to Périgueux which the armored columns must travel to reach their railhead, there was a report of a strong FTP presence blocking the highway at Terrasson, a small town on the Vézère, sixteen miles west of Brive. Army Group Greported to OKW that it was essential to move to clear this gang from Terrasson at first light on 11 June. Elements of the Das Reich would do the job.

Terrasson is a pretty little town of some 3,000 people with a twelfth-century bridge, a fifteenth-century church and a prosperous peacetime trade in truffles and walnuts. Since early 1944, the FTP *maquisards* in the hills to the south-west had found it a convenient target for demonstrations and limited raids without risking an encounter with major German formations, which normally arrived only after their departure, in time to conduct reprisals against the townspeople. By June 1944, these hapless scapegoats were at their wits' end. The mayor, Georges Labarthe, proprietor of a small sweet shop, recorded the events in an unhappy letter to his mother in Paris on 4 June:

> Towards 11 pm on Wednesday evening we were woken by explosions and shooting. The town was in the hands of about a hundred men of the *maquis*, out on a punitive expedition. All the roads, all the paths were guarded, electricity cut, railways blown up. From behind our shutters, we saw men festooned with weapons moving in all directions, deploying to whistle blasts. The family in the house opposite our own were beaten and compelled to hand over their goods. It was the same at the shoe merchant's and a bicycle shop. Meanwhile they had blown open the door of the *gendarmerie* and disarmed our eighteen *gendarmes*, whose rifles and revolvers they took away. They relieved the Post Office of 150,000 francs. They went to the house of the local Fetainist Legion chief. They blew

open the door and shot him. He had been threatened and accused of informing a long time before, on many people's testimony. From there they went to a glassmaker whom they shot with his wife. She was accused of informing to the Gestapo. The whole business lasted until four in the morning. At a whistle blast everybody got back in the lorries and went away. I leave you to imagine the terror of the inhabitants. Having received the blows of one side, here one was getting them from the other. . . . I could have wished that there was no funeral [of the Legion chief], or at least that it was only a family affair, as was arranged for the *mairie* secretary. That was the accepted practise for victims of "happenings" as one now calls them (we have had fifteen). But the Prefect, consulted by telephone, wanted normal obsequies.

Ah! For the flexibility of a Talleyrand who survived the whole revolutionary process after occupying every position in sight!

But the troubles of the Mayor of Terrasson were to extend beyond agonizing about whether it was safe to attend a Vichy funeral. While the FTP's battle for Tulle was at its height, Hercules, the FTP commander below Terrasson, returned to the town at the head of his men and began setting roadblocks and putting the approaches in a state of defense. When a few local townspeople sought to remonstrate with them, Hercules shouted contemptuously: "Terrasson has 3,000 inhabitants and France 40 million! What can these here matter?" The Fourth Republic was proclaimed in the central square. Local civilians were summoned to fell trees. The FTP took away a group of "suspects," who were not seen again.

Mercifully for Terrasson, the German operation to clear the road on 11 June was not protracted. When the *maquisards* found themselves confronted by armor, and under shellfire from the SS vehicles, they retreated to their trucks, and to the hills, leaving a score of burning buildings, screaming women and children, and tumbled masonry beside the *mairie* (town hall) where it had been struck by a 75 mm shell. The Germans burnt a house adorned with a red flag by the *maquis*, and discovered only afterwards that it was the property of Denoix, the departmental *milice* chief. The entire population was then assembled in the main square, covered by smocked and helmeted troopers. They knew what had happened in Tulle, and they were certain that they were to share its fate.

The unit doctor, who to the mayor's relief spoke fluent French, pointed to the body of a *maquisard* which the SS had tossed down before them: "Does anyone recognize this man?" No one admitted to doing so. The tension increased. They watched the doctor talking to the German commander and a group of officers. Suddenly the commander laughed. The doctor turned to the mayor: "The CO is in a good mood today, because it's his wedding anniversary," he explained. Their only *maquisard* prisoner was publicly hanged, but Terrasson was spared. All that night and through the next day, as German columns rumbled through the town on the road toward Périgueux, the local firemen struggled to put out the last of the fires. To the town's utter horror, toward evening a group of *maquisards* reappeared, demanded to know what had happened, and to recover the body of their dead man. They were urged, implored and finally persuaded to leave. In an account composed on 13 June the mayor wrote:

> I profit from an armoured train which is going to Perigueux to dispatch this letter. We have seen some horrors. We are all safe, but the cost is terrible: four killed, three wounded, the *mairie* burnt, eight houses destroyed by flames or tank gunfire, the population terrorized. We have lived through two hours of terror with the whole population gathered in the square covered by machine guns, a man hanged from the next-door balcony. God willed that I main-tained a superhuman calm. . . .

In a vivid afterthought, written on 9 July, Labarthe added:

> The cycle is simple, and repeated every time: the *maquis* conduct an operation, the Germans arrive, the *maquis* disappears once more into the woods with slight losses, the civil population pay the tariff, the Germans go away and the *maquis* reappear. Where there are casualties among the Germans, the retribution is terrible. I must confess that in the circumstances it is hard to be the representative and the defender of the people!

The day that the Das Reich cleared Terrasson, 11 June, another FTP *maquis* attacked an armored train at Mussidan station, south-west of Périgueux. They were beaten off with the loss of nine killed and eight wounded. In reprisal local German forces shot fifty-two hostages, including the mayor. Army Group G was now asserting itself to restore control of the main roads and towns throughout the Dordogne. On 12 June, as the first armored elements of the Das Reich reached Périgueux, a German column smashed eastwards through the *maquis* cordon around Bergerac, killing twenty *résistants* and burning much of the village of Mouleydier. To the increasing despair of Bergeret and de Gunzbourg, it was becoming apparent that there would be no Allied parachute landings to support them. Martial, De Gaulle's departmental representative, was furious about the suicidal concentration of *résistants* facing inevitable destruction. In London, General Koenig was sufficiently alarmed by the great concentrations of *résistants* reported to be gathering that on the tenth he broadcast a somewhat clumsy request to restrain their activities: "Break contact everywhere to enable a phase of reorganization. Avoid large concentrations: form small, isolated groups." De Gunzbourg wrote:

> At the end of four or five days I admitted to myself that we would receive no Allied support, and the situation threatened to become tragic. I had to send back the men in their trucks to their various departure points, and I was constantly woken in the night by panic-stricken people.

He was doubly depressed when a *résistant* from the Gers told him that his beloved *patron*, Starr,

> . . . was displeased with me, and that I had not understood the orders given to me. Useless to say that I had suffered morally through a scarcely describable period when I believed that the country was going to liberate itself within a day or so, that the Allies had not kept their promises, that the various political factions were beginning to surface, and to dispute my action, that their leaders were seeking their own advancement through the Resistance. . . .

Thousands of men and women took to the *maquis* rather than risk remaining in their homes and face German reprisals. The great concentration of *résistants* melted away into the countryside, and the German columns smashed the roadblocks and shot down anyone foolish enough to remain visible in their path. "The British had once again become *perfide Albion* (treacherous Albion)," said de Gunzbourg sadly. "My own prestige and command of the region never recovered from their failure to arrive to support us."

Yet the people of the western Dordogne were fortunate, had they but perceived it. The Germans had neither the forces nor the time to pursue massive, systematic reprisals for the attempted uprising. The Dordogne suffered, and the *résistants* had suffered some 200 killed, but they escaped the terrible fate of Vercors a month later, where in a precisely comparable situation the victorious Germans meted out wholesale slaughter and destruction. If the attempt to liberate the region had been ill-judged, the isolation of its communications had critically hampered the Germans. The first of the Das Reich's tank trains, bearing the heavy armor north from Périgueux toward Normandy, was unable to assemble, load and depart until the evening of 15 June, although, as has been shown, OKW had demanded its movement five days earlier.

It is now time to return to the night of 8 June, to rejoin the Der Führer Panzergrenadiers crawling wearily into Limoges after their long drive north from Montauban. The city sprawls grey and unlovely on the hills above the north bank of the Vienne. Limoges is more than twice the size of Brive, an industrial metropolis dedicated to porcelain, enamel and shoe-making. Renoir made his living here for a time, painting porcelain, but it is difficult to imagine that he enjoyed himself. In AD 250, St. Martial came to convert the region to Christianity, but some ungrateful citizens of Limoges had him cast into captivity. Tradition relates that an ethereal light promptly overtook the prison, aweing his jailors and the local inhabitants, who freed Martial to stride to the temple and cast down the false idols.

No such heavenly deliverance was granted to the Limousin in June 1944. The German garrison considered itself in a state of siege. The Der Führer arrived with orders to sweep the region, clear the vital road links, and destroy *maquis* concentrations wherever they could be found. The town's railway junctions had been badly affected by determined action by *cheminot* saboteurs after D-Day. On the afternoon of the eighth the Gestapo and local garrison troops moved on the main rail depot, seeking to arrest suspected *résistants*. They opened fire, killing one apprentice and wounding another, shooting a wanted man who attempted to bolt. There had also been a string of *maquis* attacks on isolated German vehicles, whose occupants when captured had almost all been shot out of hand. At about 2 am on the ninth, the first vehicles of the Der Führer reached the nervous town, and Colonel Stadler and Major Weidinger drove to local headquarters for news. "The regiment is greeted with general relief," states Weidinger's history. "All the Germans in the town hope that it will remain as long as possible. They have been cut off for two days from the outside world. Not a single vehicle had got through the circle of *maquisards*, either entering or leaving. There is talk of a converging *maquis* attack on the town. . . ." Stadler set up his headquarters in the Hôtel Central, and gave his battalion commanders their orders. The 1st battalion, under Dickmann—which was many hours late, and had not yet arrived—would take up position on the western side, based on St. Junien. The 1st battalion of the Deutschland would cover the south. The 3rd battalion under Major Kampfe would take the east. Kampfe's initial task, at first light on 9 June, would be to push north-north-east, toward Argenton-sur-Creuse where the *maquis* were said to be in control, and north-west to Guéret, where there was word of heavy fighting and beleaguered German troops.

The AS and FTP had planned a joint attack on Argenton but, as so often, co-operation broke down. Eighty AS men from Châtillon-sur-Indre, who were intended to occupy and hold the approaches to the town, were diverted to another operation at Chauvigny. Fifty men of the FTP under Henri Lathière attacked alone. They seized two petrol trains in sidings at the station, blew the railway in several places, and moved the passengers of a blocked through train into the local school. They took prisoner twenty-three Germans from the local garrison, who surrendered promptly, and established defensive positions. They then sat down to see what happened next.

At 6:15 pm on the evening of 9 June, shooting was heard from the Limoges road. The 15th company of the Der Führer advanced into the town, firing as they came. Henri Rognon, a twenty-year-old former Vichy soldier who had joined the Resistance only on 6 June, shot it out until the house in which he lay was blown down on him. Most of the FTP retreated hastily from the area. As usual, it was the population of Argenton who bore the price for their liberation. Three elderly inhabitants of homes on the Avenue Victor Hugo died where they sat. The Germans conducted a swift and ruthless house-clearing operation. One party burst into the homes of the Vilatte family, where a mother and her two daughters were at supper. The first burst killed Gisele, thirteen, and a second disposed of her mother as she dragged her other daughter, Nicole, seventeen, wounded to the sofa. Nicole died in hospital two days later. The SS then gathered a hundred people found in the area, including the passengers from the stranded train. Six men were taken from the group and shot at once. Another group of ten, whose papers were not in order, was held aside. One of them was a sixteen-year-old *gendarme's* son. His elder brother, who had been questioned and released, asked to stay with the younger boy. His request was granted and the two were shot together, along with the others. A total of fifty -four people died during and after the recapture of Argenton.

Meanwhile, further south the rest of the 3rd battalion under Major Kampfe was advancing from Limoges to Guéret, which had been in *maquis* hands since 6 June. On the road, they had a sudden encounter with two lorries moving southwards toward them. *Maquisards* in one vehicle opened fire at once, severely wounding the officer in the leading German half-track. They then abandoned the trucks, and fled through fierce German fire. When the SS reached the French vehicles they found that these contained German soldiers and officials, together with several French collaborators captured by the *maquis* in Guéret. Two of the Germans were now dead, several wounded, and a Frenchwoman had a severe stomach wound. Putting the casualties at the rear of the convoy, the battalion moved on through the thick woods and steep hills of the Creuse. Just beyond Bourganeuf, they encountered another Resistance convoy. This time the Frenchmen surrendered, and twenty-nine were immediately shot.

There was a *Garde Mobile de Réserve* training school in Guéret, whose pupils defected *en masse* to the Resistance on 6 June. The former Prefect, who had been deposed by Vichy, was reinstalled. The town celebrated. Then, on the morning of the eighth, it was subjected to heavy German air attack. Wehrmacht units moved up from Montlu on with air support, and by the time Kampfe's men arrived at 5:30 pm on the afternoon of the ninth, the Germans had already re-established control.

The SS moved the wounded Frenchwoman to the local hospital. Kampfe then ordered Muller, the battalion doctor, to put the rest of the wounded in a half-track and return to Limoges as rapidly as possible. He left two platoons of his support company in Guéret to bolster the German perimeter. Then the rest of the battalion, tired and not a little exasperated, swung themselves back into their vehicles, and turned once more toward Limoges.

At about 8 pm, Dr. Muller's half-track was clattering along the road when it was overtaken at speed by Major Kampfe's open Talbot. The CO, in a hurry to return to his headquarters after a frustrating day, waved carelessly and swept on. He was one of the stars of the division, a thirty-four-year-old former printer and Wehrmacht officer who had transferred to the SS in 1939. Tall, very strong, and a keen athlete, he had fought with distinction and won the Knight's Cross in Russia.

At dusk on 9 June, as his car approached a road junction at the tiny hamlet of La Bussière, fifteen miles short of Limoges, he saw a lorry approaching and flashed his lights in greeting. With extraordinary lack of prudence, he halted and found himself surrounded by a ring of armed men, led by a miner from the nearby town of St. Léonard, Sergeant Jean Canou, who was returning to an FTP *maquis* after blowing up a bridge at Brignac. The group had been travelling by side roads, and were cautiously crossing the main 0941 when they chanced upon Kampfe, whom they claimed later was accompanied by a driver (German accounts hold that he was alone). Canou was not highly esteemed by his fellow *maquisards* for his brainpower, but he knew a splendid catch when he found one. Kampfe was bundled into the lorry. They could do nothing with his Talbot, for the Frenchman at the wheel of the truck was the only one among them who could drive. They said later that Kampfe showed no sign of fear, but seemed arrogantly confident that he would soon be free, no doubt because he expected to meet his own men on the main road. Within a few minutes the incident was over. Canou and his men turned up a narrow dirt road toward their camp at Cheissoux. They testified after the war that they handed Helmut Kampfe to another *maquis*, and never saw him again. To this day there is no reliable evidence of the major's fate. The only certainty is that some time after his disappearance he was killed by the *maquis*. It is a matter for speculation whether this took place immediately, or following the events of the next few days. SS records listed him: "Missing in southern France in action against terrorists."

Colonel Stadler's first knowledge of the disappearance of one of his battalion commanders—more than that, a close friend who had served as his adjutant in Russia—came with the arrival of a grim Dr. Muller. He could report only that he had found Kampfe's car, engine running and doors open, a Schmeisser without a magazine lying beneath it, but no signs of blood or violence. The battalion adjutant, Captain Weinrauch, was leading the men in a sweep of the woods around the long, straight avenue of fir trees in the middle of which Kampfe had been seized. The SS were bitterly angry. All night, frightened local peasants heard the roar of vehicles grinding down the tracks through the woods, occasionally firing flares to light the area. Two farmers from the hamlet of La Bussière, Pierre Mon Just and Pierre Malaguise, each in his forties and the fathers of five children, proved unable to provide any useful information and were shot in the ditch by the roadside. The Malaguise farmhouse was ransacked. The Germans sent for help from the Limoges *milice*, who could provide specialized local knowledge to strengthen the search.

At regimental headquarters, frustration was compounded by their inability to communicate directly either with the 3rd battalion's search parties, or with divisional HQ in Tulle. Stadler ordered Weidinger to leave at once in a Volkswagen field car with strong motor cycle escort, and report personally to Lammerding in Tulle. It was a nervous journey through the darkness. They travelled in a long, dispersed column, never faster than 30 mph for at any moment they expected to meet a terrorist roadblock. Shortly before 1 am, to their overwhelming relief they saw ahead the knife-rests and parked vehicles of the German outpost at the entrance to Tulle. They were waved through to the divisional headquarters, along the silent, heavily patrolled streets. In the lobby of the hotel where Stuckler had established his offices, among the orderlies and staff still sobered by the events of the day, Weidinger found Lammerding. He recollects only that Lammerding ordered the regiment to pursue the search for Kampfe with the utmost vigor. For the first time, Weidinger learned of the events in Tulle, and endorsed the staff view that reprisals had been entirely justified. Then he set off back to Limoges in the first light of dawn. At 6 am, he was with Stadler again.

The regimental commander's night had not been dull. In the early hours of the morning, the *Sturmgeschutzabteilung's* ordnance officer, Lieutenant Gerlach, had arrived exhausted at Stadler's headquarters dressed only in his underwear. On the morning of the ninth, Gerlach had driven with six men in three cars to reconnoiter billets for his unit in Nieul. Finding insufficient space, they moved on toward the next town. Gerlach had been specifically warned by Stadler about the terrorist menace, but raced ahead of the other cars, accompanied only by his driver. They soon found themselves alone. Becoming nervous, they turned the car and started back toward Limoges. A few minutes later, they were forced to halt in the middle of the road, and surrounded by *maquisards*. They were stripped, not gently. One *maquisard* strained his knowledge of German to shout repeatedly into their faces "SS! *Alles kaputt!*" (Everything is destroyed) and make unmistakable slicing gestures at their throats. They were then forced back into their car and driven away. The little convoy stopped and started several times that afternoon as they moved Gerlach and his driver across the Limousin countryside. They were bound for some time, according to the German, but were later untied. Then the Frenchmen stopped at the edge of a wood, and gestured the Germans to move into the trees. Gerlach testified that they were both certain that they were about to be shot. The driver began to struggle. Seizing the moment while the Frenchmen's attention was diverted, Gerlach ran headlong for the trees, pursued by a ragged fusillade. After some hours' walking, he reached the Bellac-Limoges railway line, and stumbled down it until he reached the city, and "at last his commanding officer. Stadler sent him to bed. Gerlach awoke to find another officer standing over his bed—Major Otto Dickmann, CO of the 1st battalion. Dickmann handed Gerlach the map. According to the ordnance officer's subsequent evidence, the major demanded to be shown the exact route down which he had been taken by the *maquis* from the moment of his capture to that of his release.

Every available man of the Panzergrenadier brigade was combing the Limousin on the morning of 10 June for any trace of Major Kampfe. Shortly after 10 am, at the village of Salon-la-Tour some twenty miles south of Limoges near the Tulle road, soldiers—probably from the 1st battalion of the Deutschland regiment—were approaching the village. They saw a large black Citroën approaching them, then pull up abruptly. A young boy got out and raced away into the fields. Then a man and a girl, both carrying submachine guns, broke away from the car and began to run. The Germans opened fire, and a running battle developed. A woman tending her cows by a nearby farmhouse was killed instantly by a German burst. The boy escaped, and the man vanished in the maze of dense hedges and ditches that ran back from the road. They pinpointed the girl, firing a Sten gun from the base of an apple tree at the edge of a cornfield. They worked in toward her until her gun was empty.* Then, limping from a twisted ankle and with a slight flesh wound in her arm, she was led forward and put in a staff car to be taken to Limoges. The divisional interpreter, Dr. Wache, was called to her initial interrogation by Major Kowatsch—the same Kowatsch who the previous day had acted as master of ceremonies in Tulle. She admitted that she was English, and that she had been parachuted into the area on the night of 6 June. In a subsequent statement, the interpreter claimed: "She was treated with great politeness and supplied with clean clothes. She was then passed to the SO in Limoges. I know nothing further of the treatment of this agent."

Violette Szabo had been desperately unlucky. For months, the *maquis* had traveled with impunity by car and truck across the Limousin and the Corrèze. The FTP *maquis* in the area had no knowledge of the

---

* Some former *résistants* and members of SOE were irritated by the romantic popular accounts of Violette Szabo's career which were published and filmed in the 1950s. They have suggested that she was in fact captured without having the opportunity to use a weapon. Neither German records nor surviving residents of Salon-la-Tour offer any decisive evidence one way or the other on the matter. I have therefore accepted the story of Mrs. Szabo's use of her Sten given in R. J. Minney's biography *Carve Her Name with Pride*. I have been unable to find any record of German casualties from the incident in the Das Reich files, although I did locate the previously unpublished statement of the divisional interpreter concerning Mrs. Szabo's interrogation.

presence of the Das Reich and, as so often, their lack of Intelligence was fatal. The new arrivals from French Section were driven gaily through the night of 6 June from the dropping zone to the little village of Sussac, some twenty-five miles south-east of Limoges. There they were lodged above a grocer's shop. Staunton, the commander of her party, wrote later in his report:

> When I left London I was given to understand that I would find on arrival a very well-organized *maquis*, strictly devoid of any political intrigues, which would constitute a very good basis for extending the circuit throughout the area. On arrival I did find a *maquis*, which was roughly 600 strong, plus 200 French *gendarmes* who joined up on D-Day. But these men were strictly not trained, and were commanded by the most incapable people I have ever met, as was overwhelmingly proved by the fact that none of the D-Day targets had been attended to, and that each time it took me several hours of discussion to get one small turn-out, either to the railway or the telephone line.

Sussac was in the area dominated by "Colonel" Georges Guingouin, among the most ruthless of communist leaders, in his French Army tank helmet and sheepskin jacket a familiar and feared figure throughout the Limousin. Of all the Resistance leaders in the region, he was among the least susceptible to the influence of London.

The *maquisards* of the Châteauneuf forest around Sussac did not take to Staunton any more than he took to them. They considered that he behaved too much as an English "officer and gentleman," though in reality he was a Frenchman. They preferred Bob Mortier, the more easy-going "Canadian" with him, although Mortier also was French. Staunton decided that it was essential for the mission to make contact with some of the more amenable *maquis* of the Corrèze and Dordogne. It has been suggested that he also wanted to make direct contact with Jacques Poirier. He explained that he wanted to send Violette Szabo, his courier, to liaise with them. One of the section leaders, a wild, brave young man named Jacques Dufour—"Anastasie"—volunteered to take her to a contact at Pompadour, some thirty miles south, from whence she could be passed on to local leaders.

Anastasie had a reputation for recklessness, but no one suggested to Staunton that his courier might be safer with a more prudent guide. Around 9:30 on the morning of the tenth, the two set off in the petrol-driven Citroën. One of the *maquisards* wives suggested to Violette that she would be better off with flat shoes than her high heels, but there was nothing to be done about that there. "She looked like a little doll," the woman said, "but she had a lot of guts." They waved the Citroën off. A few miles on, Anastasie stopped to pick up a twelve-year-old boy, the son of a friend who wanted a lift into the Corrèze. They strapped his bicycle on the back of the car and drove cheerfully onwards, singing and chatting. Violette was the daughter of a Frenchwoman who married a British soldier named Bushell during World War I. She was brought up a cockney and worked as a shopgirl until she met and married a French officer in 1940. He was later killed in the desert. When French Section approached her, she left a three-year-old daughter to go to France. She was adored by the men and women of SOE, both for her courage and for her endless infectious cockney laughter.

Anastasie chattered enthusiastically about the countryside through which they passed and his own boyhood. He was still talking when they came to their fatal rendezvous with the Das Reich, combing the countryside for Major Kampfe. After Violette damaged her ankle and Anastasie perfectly properly abandoned her, he hid beneath a log pile for many hours until the Germans were gone. Eventually he made his way back to the *maquis*. His boy passenger also escaped.

The *maquis* of south-east Haute-Vienne learned the identity of their latest enemies only twenty-four hours later, when one of their section commanders was examining the contents of a truck stolen from the Germans. In a crate in the back, he found a uniform bearing SS runes and the wristband of the Das Reich.

On the day after Kampfe's capture—the same 10 June on which Violette Szabo was captured—Major Stuckler issued a divisional Order of the Day to the men of the Das Reich:

> In the course of its advance, the division has already dealt with several Resistance groups. The armored regiment has succeeded, thanks to a neatly executed surprise attack, in carrying out a knife

stroke—a *"coup de filet"*—against a band organized in company strength [at Bretenoux].

The division is now proceeding to a rapid and lasting clean-up of these bands from the region, with a view to becoming speedily available to reinforce the fighting men and join the line on the invasion front.

CHAPTER 9

"... a rapid and lasting clean-up": Oradour

MAJOR OTTO DICKMANN, commanding the 1st battalion of the Der Führer regiment, had already fought through the *résistants* defending the bridge at Groslejac on the morning of 8 June, and he and his column had subsequently killed several *maquisards* and rather more innocent bystanders as they advanced through the eastern Dordogne. More recently it was Dickmann who had personally awakened Lieutenant Gerlach early on the morning of the tenth, to hear the tale of his experiences. Major Kampfe, Dickmann's counterpart of the 3rd battalion, was a close personal friend, and Dickmann was desperate for any clue to the missing officer's whereabouts.

The 1st battalion only reached Limoges, late and exhausted, at around 6:30 am on the 9 June, four hours after the rest of the regiment. "It was very rough," Dickmann told Weidinger. "After many delays and a terrible journey," states the regimental history, whose account of this, as of many other episodes, is enigmatically terse, "the 1st battalion arrives at Limoges in the morning and then moves to its deployment area. . . . During its covering movement on the left flank, it had encountered several heavy shooting attacks . . . and suffered its first losses. Many tree barriers had to be removed. The commander, Sturmbannführer Dickmann, seemed tense and strained." As soon as he had confirmed his orders, the major climbed wearily back into his car, and led the battalion south-westwards out of Limoges to the town of St. Junien, some twenty miles distant.

The German dominance of the Limousin had been as rudely challenged since D-Day as that of the Dordogne and Corrèze. On the night of 7 June, *maquisards* sabotaged and severely damaged the railway viaduct carrying the Limoges—Angouleme main line through St. Junien, a town of some 20,000 people notable for its tanneries and glovemakers. The attackers conducted a symbolic occupation of the *mairie* early on the morning of 8 June, and then took up positions covering the viaduct. That evening, a train from Angouleme halted at the southern end, and passengers began to walk across the weakened span to join another train sent from Limoges to meet them. Among them were ten German soldiers, two of whom were killed when the *résistants* opened fire. Five ran back to the Angouleme train, and three forward to go on to Limoges, where they urgently phoned their headquarters. By the time an armored train arrived in St. Junien at 9 am the next day, bearing a Wehrmacht detachment and Lieutenant Wickers of the Gestapo, the *maquis* had prudently vanished. The troops deployed through the town, and Wickers gave orders to the mayor that a hundred able-bodied civilians were to to be assembled at once with picks and spades to dig trenches round the approaches. This was a combination of precaution and punishment. Some fifty mostly elderly men eventually gathered, and dug reluctantly under the eyes of their guards until about 1 pm.

At 10 am, Wickers had received a message from his headquarters in Limoges, informing him that the SS would be relieving the Wehrmacht as soon as they could get down to the town. At 10:30, the long file of Dickmann's trucks and half-tracks crawled into St. Junien. Dickmann dismounted, exchanged brief words with Wickers and several nervous local French officials, then set up his command post in the Hôtel de la Gare. He had brought with him a notorious Limoges Gestapo officer named Joachim Kleist, a Gestapo interpreter and four *miliciens*. By the standards of the Das Reich, St. Junien escaped lightly. Germans commandeered all the petrol they could find in local garages, and conducted a grenade-throwing competition to amuse themselves. As a security precaution, all the officers slept together under heavy guard. Early the next morning— the tenth—Dickmann was back at Der Fuhrer HQ in Limoges. According to Weidinger's narrative:

. . . He arrives in an excited state and reports the following: in St. Junien, two French civilians had approached him and told him that a high German official was being held by the *maquisards* in Oradour. That day he was to be executed and publicly burnt amidst celebrations. The whole population was working with the *maquis*, and high-ranking leaders were there at that very moment. At about the same time, the Limoges SO informed the regiment that according to Intelligence from their own local informers, there was a *maquis* headquarters in Oradour. Sturmbannfiihrer Dickmann requests permission from the regimental commander to take a company there to free the prisoner. In his opinion it must be Sturmbannfuhrer Kampfe, who was a close personal friend of his. The regimental commander then informs Dickmann of the other events in the Oradour area on the previous day [the capture of Gerlach], and immediately grants permission for this plan with the additional order that Dickmann must try above all to take *maquis* leaders prisoner in case Kampfe was not found. He intended to use any prisoners for negotiations with the Resistance to release Kampfe in an exchange. . . .

Dickmann also spoke directly to Gerlach, from whom, according to post-war testimony, he received an indication that he believed his own captors had taken him through Oradour. In the regimental history, Weidinger also recounts a bizarre attempt to make contact with the *maquis* and bargain for the release of Kampfe by freeing a prisoner held by the Limoges SD. Weidinger claims that the freed *maquisard* telephoned once to say that he was doing his best to find Kampfe, but was then never heard from again.

Dickmann was back in St. Junien by mid-morning. He held some discussion with Kleist of the Gestapo and the *milice*, then ordered his 3rd company, commanded by Hauptsturmfiihrer Kahn, to prepare to move out for an operation. At about 1:30 pm Dickmann, Kahn and 120 men in a convoy of two half-tracks, eight trucks and a motor cycle drove eastwards out of St. Junien on an indirect route to Oradour-sur-Glane, via St. Victorien. Dickmann himself rode in his commandeered Citroën *deux chevaux* (2CV) with his young Alsatian driver and his adjutant, Lange. According to some—not surprisingly hesitant and confused—post-war testimony, they halted *en route* for Dickmann to give a cursory briefing for a "search and destroy" operation of the kind that they had several times undertaken from Montauban. But an NCO named Barth was said to have implied that this would be something special when he declared buoyantly: "You're going to see some blood flow today!" to a group of young recruits, adding: "And we'll also find out what the Alsatians are made of."

There is today no longer any prospect of discovering the definitive truth about Dickmann's motive in moving against Oradour-sur-Glane. Some of those who knew are dead. Others, in the shadow of war crimes trials, have always had the strongest possible motives for lying. There are survivors of Dickmann's company alive and living in Germany today who undoubtedly know some of the answers, but will never reveal them. Some of those with whom the author corresponded in researching this book know the whereabouts of men who were in the convoy that left St. Junien that afternoon, but they have no intention of disclosing them.

Certain key points can, however, be brought into focus. First, it has sometimes been alleged that a tragic error was made—that Dickmann's men moved against Oradour-sur-Giane, whereas the *maquisards* whom they sought were to be found around Oradour-sur-Vayres, twenty miles south-westwards near the forest of Rochechouart where the FTP had killed a number of German soldiers in recent weeks. There is no evidence to support this view. Oradour-sur-Vayres is geographically even more distant than Oradour-sur-Giane from the seizure of Kampfe and all the activity concerning the Das Reich. Second, some Germans allege to this day that the *maquis* had perpetrated an abominable atrocity against Wehrmacht soldiers—some say against an ambulance convoy—near Oradour. Had this been the case, it is unthinkable that the Das Reich and for that matter the propaganda apparatus of Berlin would have failed to proclaim the fact at the time, as they did the alleged killing of prisoners at Tulle. This possibility can be discounted. Third, the evidence is overwhelming that there was no *maquis* presence in or around Oradour-sur-Glane. The nearest *maquis* camp was some seven miles south-westwards.

Yet is is impossible to believe that French historians have been justified in asserting so often since the war that Oradour was the victim of an entirely arbitrary, blind stroke of savagery by the Germans. Even at their most ruthless moments, the SS contrived to pursue a policy that in their own terms possessed some logic. With so many scores of villages from which to choose for Dickmann's purge—many of them with well-known links with the *maquis*—why should he have chosen Oradour? It seems most probable that Dickmann acted upon misplaced intelligence received from some deluded or malignant French source. The Germans, in their mood of frustration that day, were questing urgently for a clue to a target. Someone in Limoges or St. Junien placed the finger upon Oradour. Once the hint had been given, Dickmann showed no interest in confirming its accuracy. A pretext was enough. It seems almost certain that his officers expected Dickmann to do little more to Oradour than they had done to scores of suspect French villages that summer—search, and make an example with a clutch of salutary executions and burnings. But from the unhesitating conduct of the major that afternoon of 10 June, it seems equally clear that, in his own mind, Dickmann drove into Oradour knowing precisely what he proposed to do.

Englishmen or Americans would describe Oradour-sur-Glane as a small town rather than a village. Its 254 buildings included two small hotels and more than a score of shops. The tramway to Limoges, built in 1911, had marred the appearance of the main street, the Rue Emile Desourteaux, with overhanging cables and pylons, but it had also provided electricity and brought the village within easy commuting distance of Limoges. It was a community of twentieth-century suburban architecture and privet hedges—never beautiful, but set in the perfectly rural woods and fields of the flat countryside west of Limoges.

There was a strong leavening of bourgeois and professional families among its inhabitants—some of them were lingering over an expansive Saturday lunch at the Hôtel Milord on the afternoon of 10 June, for the black market ensured that there was no shortage of food for those able to pay for it. In the past four years of war, the population had become swollen with the sort of ragtag of refugees who had descended upon even the most remote French rural communities to escape persecution, or to put as much distance as possible between themselves and Allied bombing targets. The BBC French Service had been warning since

16 April that "all vital points on the railways in Belgium and France will be subjected to attack in the coming weeks. Get away from them." Some of those in Oradour on 10 June had paid heed. There were Jews and Alsatians; Parisians and Lorrainers; a group of thirty Spaniards, flotsam of the Civil War who had taken local manual jobs. The town was crowded, and not discontented. Like every other community in France, it had received the news of the Allied landings as the promise of an end to the long struggle, and the fighting was far enough distant to present no threat or cause for fear. Many people had drifted into the village to collect their tobacco ration, issued every ten days, or to do the weekly shopping. The three schools were full, because it was the day of a medical inspection and vaccination. The boys' schools opposite the tram station held sixty-four children, while the girls'—divided into three classrooms—held 106. There was also a special school for the little Lorrainer refugees. Every circumstance conspired to ensure that Otto Dickmann found the village crowded with people. By early afternoon the farm workers had come in from the fields. A few weekend fishermen had ridden the tram from Limoges to try their luck on the Glane. There was the usual Saturday foraging party from the city, seeking food that was more readily available in the countryside. The streets were still damp from a morning shower, but the sky had cleared and the sun was shining, warming the gray, creeper-clad houses. Oradour was a drab, unprepossessing place, but in the midst of war, occupation and so many troubles and uncertainties it seemed a haven of sanity. "This place," a young refugee named Michel Forest wrote in his diary, "is pervaded by a classical tranquillity, in which one can live as a human being should. Everything here is done in moderation in the best sense of the word."

He was a twenty-year-old law student, the son of a philosophy teacher, Professor Forest, who had been born in Oradour, and had now returned to find some peace and quiet with five of his six children—the eldest was an STO evader with a *maquis* in George Starr's area. In March 1944 the Germans had closed all the universities in France, and Professor Forest moved into the pleasant little Château de Laplaud, a mile west of Oradour, rented to him by a family friend, the Vicomtesse de Saint-Venant. Michel, a deeply religious young man, was to take his first communion on 11 June. On the afternoon of the tenth he walked into Oradour with his six-year-old brother Dominique—the family favorite—to get a haircut and see his grandfather. Professor Forest took the other three children with him on the tram to Limoges.

An insurance agent from Avignon was also on the Limoges tram that afternoon. M. Levignac had just moved his sons to Oradour because of the intense Allied communications bombing. An overshoot from the railway yards killed their neighbours in their own home, and M. Levignac decided that enough was enough. His eldest son Serge, sixteen, was now billeted with a farmer on the edge of Oradour, and the younger, Charles, twelve, was staying with two elderly women. M. Levignac himself had travelled up from Avignon on the afternoon of the ninth to visit the boys, and had spent the night in the Hôtel Avril. He scribbled his wife a postcard to say how well he found them: "I feel I am giving our sons life itself." Then he left them for a couple of hours, promising to be back by early evenmg.

Another refugee was the wife of Robert Cordeau, a French POW working as a forced labourer near Danzig. The family came from Paris, but found life there very difficult during the Occupation. Mme. Cordeau originally came from Oradour and after discussing the matter in letters with her husband, she decided to return to the Limousin. She found a job as secretary to a Limoges doctor, and her sixteen-year-old daughter Bernadette began to learn dressmaking in Oradour. On the afternoon of the tenth Bernadette was in the village, while her mother was in Limoges because the doctor was on call.

Denise Bardet, a twenty-four-year-old teacher at the girls' school, was one of the few people in Oradour who knew that the SS were in the area. The previous day she had boarded the rickety *gazogène* bus to St. Junien with a little group of her girls who had to sit an examination in the town. They arrived to find a company of the Der Führer billeted in the classrooms, and SS troopers striding through the playground. The first thought of any woman in France when she saw Germans sweeping the district was fear for the men—they could be seized as hostages or carried off for forced labour. Denise Bardet was engaged to a young man in Limoges, and her brother was at the teacher training college there. She returned safely to Oradour on the evening of the ninth, but lay awake for hours in the big bed that she shared with her widowed mother in her cottage outside the village, discussing the alarming scene in St. Junien. The next day she was at school as usual. She returned home for lunch, then mounted her bicycle and pedalled unhurriedly back to the classroom to supervise the afternoon medical check.

Here then, at 2:15 on the afternoon of 10 June, the tableau is frozen for the rest of history: an undistinguished Limousin town, its normal population of 330 swollen to some 650 by the pressures of war, lingering over the remains of its lunch on a sunny early summer afternoon; a community that had hitherto glimpsed the German Occupiers only as a convoy roaring past upon the main road, or a handful of officers slipping out from Limoges for dinner at the Hôtel Emile. There had been no battles around Oradour, no descents by the Gestapo, no brutalities. Insofar as life in France in June 1944 could anywhere be declared to be normal, in Oradour it was so. The men tilled the fields beyond the little back gardens of the town with their two-seat privies and neatly tended bushes. The women eked out the erratic food supplies and complained about the chronic queues and shortages, but there was no real hardship in Oradour.

Two young trainee teachers from the college in Limoges finished lunch at the Hôtel Milord and strolled to the edge of the village together before one, who was on an assignment with one of its schools, turned back to her classroom. The other, making for a hamlet a little way off, waved, turned, and disappeared down the road. She was the last French civilian to leave Oradour at peace that afternoon.

The spectacle of Otto Dickmann's trucks and half-tracks grinding up the main street of Oradour, laden with helmeted and camouflage-smocked infantry covering the houses with their weapons, caused immediate astonishment and bewilderment. "Let's hide," said a motor mechanic named Aimé Renaud to his eldery wine merchant friend M. Denis. "I am not afraid of the Germans," replied Denis phlegmatically. "They're only ordinary men like us, and anyway I am too old to be frightened anymore."

But some people in Oradour had reason to be terrified by the very sight of Germans. Martial Brissaud was a teenager from Les Bordes, just arrived to visit a friend, and appalled by the thought of being seized for forced labor. Dr. Desourteaux, mayor of Oradour like his father before him, sought to reassure the boy when he ran to him in the street, but Brissaud was not persuaded. He fled homewards and took refuge in the loft. He tried in vain to persuade his family that they were all in urgent danger, then took to the fields and stayed there all afternoon. Other parents were more prudent. "Hide! Hide!" shouted Mme. Belivier to her eighteen-year-old son, who also fled into the fields. A Jewish couple staying at the Hôtel Avril frantically drove their two daughters of eighteen and twenty-two, together with their nine-year-old son, into a bolthole under the staircase just by the garden door. A Jewish dentist from Rennes named Lévy ran for his life to the fields. His wife was already in a concentration camp. His lunch companion, a Mme. Jeanne Leroy from St. Malo, remained composedly at her table. Her papers were perfectly in order—she had been driven out of St. Malo when her home was taken over by German workmen strengthening the fortifications. She had nothing to hide or fear.

One of Dickmann's men led Dr. Desourteaux to the major, who spoke briefly to him. M. Depierrefiche, the town crier, was hastily dispatched through the handful of streets escorted by two SS troopers, beating his drum and calling on the entire population to assemble instantly in the Champ de Foire, the little central square, bringing their identity papers. Apprehension gave way to relief and irritation. After all, it was only another identity check. But as the troopers fanning out through the town began to fire in the air, to hammer doors with their rifle butts and push and jostle families through the streets, uncertainty increased again. A strange convoy appeared at the end of the road: families from outlying farms and hamlets were being herded towards the Champ de Foire—a pretty enough place with its trees and a covered well—by impatient, dead-eyed infantry. A local tenant farmer named Jean Rouffranche was in the crowd with his wife Marguerite, their son Jean and their daughters Amélie and Andrée—Amélie pushed a pram bearing her seven-month-old daughter, and behind her came their eighty-year-old grandmother. The Le Lamand family came with their small grandson and granddaughter, maid and elderly mother. Their son and daughter were away at a wedding. Other men were being driven in from the fields. Mme. Binet, the principal of the girls' school, was ill in bed, but now appeared with a coat thrown over her nightdress. Another sick old man was carried by his two sons. The Abbé Lorich, the Lorrainers' own priest, was pushed out of his house with his sister and a friend.

SS troopers burst into the school classrooms calling *"Alle 'raus!*

(Everyone out!)" The teachers hurriedly mustered their charges and bustled them in orderly crocodiles towards the square. Some cried, but they were hurried onwards, because everyone in Oradour that afternoon was desperate to be compliant. It is a rule of civilized or even semicivilized existence that if threats and provocation are met only by submissiveness, the aggressor has no pretext for resorting to violence.

When a seven-year-old boy named Roger Godfrin shouted to his sisters in the rush from the classroom that they should all bolt, he was ignored. He himself ran away: "I was very frightened, because I was from Lorraine and I knew what they were like." He lost a shoe scrambling through a hedge at the edge of the schoolyard, then found himself pursued by a volley of shots. He rolled over and lay limp. A soldier kicked him in casual confirmation of death and moved on. The boy, uninjured, lay motionless, listening to more shooting. Then he leaped to his feet and fled onwards out of the village. He glimpsed a mechanic named Poutaraud being shot by two soldiers, sagging to the ground at the foot of a fence. One of the Germans saw the boy, and fired again. But Roger Godfrin scampered on and on until he reached the river, and fell panting under the safety of its bank. There he lay until silence fell, many hours later, and he crept on through the woods until he reached a farmhouse where he found safety.

It was now about 2:45. The entire population of Oradour except a few of the old, the crippled or the fugitive, who still lingered in their beds or hiding places, faced each other across the Champ de Foire, men on one side, women and children on the other. German machine gun teams had set up their Spandaus covering the square, the gunners lying at their weapons, ammunition belts curling into the breeches. Some of the women and children were crying noisily, but many simply stared in bewilderment, clutching each other's hands.

The men stood in their faded blue peasant overalls, grey or black suits, much-mended shoes. The local *gendarme*, Duquerry, was in uniform. Boucholle, the old baker, had come directly from his ovens and stood naked to the waist, covered in flour, impatient to be back at his business. After a few minutes, he asked a German NCO if he could go back and do something about the pastry that was still baking. "Don't worry, we'll take care of that," said the soldier shortly. Suddenly, into the centre of the assembly drove Dr. Jean Desourteaux, the mayor's son, back from visiting a patient. Covered by an SS man, he hurried from his car to the corner where his father was talking to an officer, probably either Kahn or Dickmann. A witness afterwards claimed to have heard the German demanding that the mayor select thirty hostages. In the background, all of them could hear sporadic shooting. They could not know that isolated civilians were already dying, but they were acutely conscious of danger.

The Germans suddenly began to move decisively. All the women and children were to be taken to the church, they announced. Herded by an SS detail, rifles at the port, the long procession of old and young, mothers clutching their babies and grandmothers supported by their families, shuffled across the road and a few yards down the hill to the tall church with its red Romanesque tiles and turreted spires, its crucified Christ upon the outer wall. Inside, it was cool and dim, but bright with flowers for next day's first communion. Oradour was not a notably religious community—indeed, for years attendance at Sunday services had been sparse. Abbé Chapelle was old and sick, and had few personal friends in the village. Each day he walked three miles in all weathers to his other parish, Javerdat, to hold its masses. Ironically enough, he had always spoken warmly of Marshal Pétain from his pulpit, and offered prayers for the victims of Allied bombing. Now, while he waited with the men, the nave and altar steps of his church filled with women and children, and their nervous cries and whispers echoed from the walls.

The men were ordered to seat themselves in three rows, facing the wall of the houses flanking the Champ de Foire. An SS trooper, probably an Alsatian, shouted in fluent French: "There are concealed weapons and stocks of ammunition in this town that have been hidden by terrorists. A house-to-house search will be conducted. While this is going on, you will be assembled in barns and garages to facilitate operations. If you know of any place in which weapons are stored, you must report the fact immediately!" An elderly farmer named Jean Lamaud called out that he possessed a shotgun and a police permit for it. "We're not interested in that," said the trooper. The men were ordered to their feet. Forty and fifty at a time, they were marshalled by the Germans and led briskly out of the Champ de Foire. One party was directed into Mme. Laudy's big coach house fifty yards up the street. One by one, the other groups filed into five other garages and barns whose doors had been thrown open to make way for them. They huddled together, like all threatened animals, at the furthest end from their captors. It was about 3:30. There was a single shot from the square. Shouting like men advancing to the charge against the enemy, the Germans began to pour fire into the crowds of Frenchmen in their execution chambers.

An eighteen-year-old boy named Yves Roby had been seized as he cycled up the road past Oradour. He was one of those herded into the Laudy barn. He became one of the only five male survivors of the executions who lived to testify about events in Oradour that afternoon:

> As soon as we got there the Germans made us haul away two carts that stood in the way of the doors. Then they forced us at gunpoint to go inside, and four soldiers covered us with their machine gun. We reckoned this was to keep us from running away. They talked to each other and laughed as they checked their weapons. Five minutes after we had entered the coach house . . . the soldiers began howling, and opened fire on us.

The first men to fall were protected from the shots that followed by the bodies of those who fell over them. Roby threw himself flat on his stomach and hid his head in his arms. As the roar of gunfire echoed ceaselessly through the coach house, the air filled with choking brick dust, fragments from the ricochets, and wounded men's screams for their wives, mothers and children.

Then the shooting stopped. The Germans strode forward to the mound of prostrate bodies, and began shooting with pistols each one that moved or groaned. Roby lay terrified, waiting for the shot that he expected to finish him. It caught his left elbow. He lay motionless until at last the groaning died away and the shooting stopped. Soldiers began to move around them again, dragging in straw, hay, brushwood and saddlery and heaping it upon the bodies. Then they tossed down a match and left the building, closing the doors. Flames began to race through the coach house.

Roby found himself fighting to pull his body from the weight of those above it, as a handful of other survivors did likewise. Several more lay badly wounded and covered with blood, yet visibly alive. There was nothing to be done for them. Struggling frenziedly despite his smashed arm, Roby at last fought free. He clambered to his feet, expecting a shot, and saw that the Germans had gone.

> It was now becoming impossible to breathe, but I found a gap in the wall, quite high up. I slipped through it and hid in the next door barn. There I found four friends—Broussardier, Darthout, Hebras and Borie. I crawled under a pile of straw and beans. Borie and Hebras hid behind a woodpile. Broussardier huddled in a corner. Darthout had four bullet wounds in the legs, and was bleeding from all of them. He asked me if there was room for him beside me. We huddled together like brothers, and lay listening carefully to every sound from outside.

A German suddenly stepped into the barn, put a burning brand to the straw that covered them, and walked out again. The Frenchmen lay motionless as flames leaped up, scorching Roby's feet. He cautiously put up his head, to see Broussardier dashing across the barn—he had seen a way out. The two men dashed through a rear door, and found themselves in a tiny yard containing a big rabbit hutch. They crawled into it, and burrowed deep into the earth and straw at its base. There they lay for three hours.

But the fires now enveloping Oradour at last reached the rabbit hutch. Almost choked with smoke, brushing away burning fragments that singed his hair, Roby forced his way out, followed by the coughing, spluttering Broussardier. They crept furtively towards the Champ de Foire. Broussardier slipped forward to look for Germans. He saw none. The two men burst into a run, fleeing towards the graveyard, and at last into the safety of thick undergrowth. "We were so overjoyed at coming back to life that we kissed each other. I spent the rest of the night in a rye field, and returned home to Basse-Foret the following day, Sunday, at about eleven o'clock."

Jean Darthout, the man shot in both legs, also miraculously survived with two others. But many more who had neither been killed in the initial firing, nor dispatched by *coup de grâce*, died in the flames that were now enveloping Oradour. German troopers ran from house to house, starting fires. Here and there they discovered fugitives who had escaped the initial round-up. Some were dispatched where they lay. A few belatedly discovered women and children were pushed into the burning barns and shot, their bodies falling among those of the men. Five young men and a girl, seized when they cycled up just as the executions began, were shot against the wall of the forge.

The three young Jews who had hidden under the stairway of the Hôtel Avril were driven to bolt from their refuge when flames and smoke overwhelmed the building. Late in the afternoon, surrounded by the horror of the burning town, they ran across the yard behind the hotel and into the arms of an SS trooper. The oldest girl asked him simply: "What are we to do?" The soldier stared down at her for a moment in silence, then swept his arm aside in an urgent gesture of dismissal. The three ran through the houses, across the fields, and many hours later to a chateau where they found shelter. It was an almost unique gesture of mercy among the events of the afternoon.

The Beaubreuil boys were the children of the local carpenter and, since one of them was an STO evader, their father hid them immediately under the living-room floor when he heard that the Germans were in Oradour. There they lay listening in terror to the sound of boots, shouted commands and shots. They heard a neighbour cry: "*Nous sommes perdus!*" ("We are lost!") There were screams. There was a smell of petrol or paraffin, and suddenly choking flames. The boys crawled from their refuge, and ran four miles to St. Victorien without stopping, and miraculously without encountering a German soldier.

Hubert Desourteaux, a twenty-nine-year-old car dealer and escaped prisoner of war, had also hidden under a stairwell when he heard the Germans arrive. He was the only survivor of the mayor's family. His mechanic, Aimé Renaud—the man who scented danger the moment he saw Dickmann's convoy roar up the main street—had hidden with his wife in the yard behind the Desourteaux' house. They lay there all that afternoon and into the night, listening to the screams, the gunfire, and later the explosion of grenades. They were convinced that they were to die. Jeannine Renaud's mother and her four-year-old daughter were with the other women in the church.

Something over 400 women and children were crowded into the church by the time the doors were slammed upon them. Two SS remained inside, covering them, until the doors opened again to admit a group of soldiers carrying a heavy box. One woman, Marguerite Rouffranche, was struck by how very young they looked. They dumped their load at the intersection of nave and chancel, lit the fuse protruding from it, and retired down the church. Thick black smoke began to pour from the box, which appeared to contain some incendiary device. Women and children screamed and started to struggle for refuge. The Germans at the west end of the church cocked their weapons and stripped the tape from their grenades. As the first bursts of fire echoed through the town from the barns where the men were dying, the SS began hurling grenades and emptying gunfire into the great throng of women, children and babies. To their anger, they suddenly saw that the door to the vestry lay open. Fugitives were fighting their way through it. Troopers ran forward, firing as they came. They pushed through the door and began machine gunning those lying and crouching inside. Mme. Rouffranche saw her daughter fall dead. She herself slipped to the ground and lay still. Two boys of ten and twelve who ran into the confessional were shot in the neck at point-blank range. One Levignac boy had already died with the men in the barns. The other, along with little Dominique Forest, the four-year-old Renaud girl, Lucien and Marcel Boulestin whose mother had scrubbed them in the tub under the apple trees to be clean for medical inspection, Bernadette Cordeau, Roger Joyeux, four, Henri Joyeux, five, eighteen members of the Bardet family aged from sixty-four to four months, Marie Claude Milaud, four months, Mme. Leroy whose papers were in order, Mme. Belivier who had sent her sons to hide, the Jewish mother who had left her children beneath the stairway—died with some 400 others that afternoon in the church.

Prams, chairs and the confessional were riddled with bullet holes, the walls pock-marked with gunfire in the dreadful cacophony of screams and shooting. Women and children with their clothes on fire ran shrieking hopelessly in search of refuge. The SS heaped straw and chairs upon the bodies of the dead and wounded, fired it, and finally departed. The flames spread rapidly, and soon the entire building was blazing, the roof timbers cracking and collapsing into the nightmare spectacle beneath.

One woman, Mme. Rouffranche, escaped. Behind the high altar she noticed three windows. Hauling herself up on a stand upon which the Abbé stood to light his candles, she climbed on to a buttress above it and flung herself from the window. She fell ten feet, and looked up to see another woman attempting to jump behind her. Henriette Joyeux was clutching her seven-month-old baby. Suddenly it slipped from her grasp, fell, and screamed. The Germans turned, caught the scene and fired at once. Mme. Joyeux fell back dead into the church, and the child was killed where it had fallen. Marguerite Rouffranche fled for her life along the chancel wall, stumbling as bullets struck her—she was hit five times—but scrambled frenziedly on. Between the rows of peas in a tiny vegetable garden she found a refuge and literally buried herself in the earth until, many hours later, the silence of death descended upon Oradour.

In the countryside around the town the distant sound of gunfire and the columns of smoke from the village of fire aroused puzzlement rather than alarm. There was no *maquis* anywhere near the village, so there could scarcely be a battle. The fires appeared to be burning in the woods beyond Oradour. Towards late afternoon, the mystery deepened. Where were the children, due back from school? Little knots of mothers began to gather and chatter at the roadside, gazing towards the distant smoke. Mme. Forest, at the Château de Laplaud, waited at the tea table with her husband for Michel, Dominique and their grandfather. A certain M. Deschamps had the most extraordinary, almost spectral experience of the afternoon. When he came in from the fields to his home at La Fauvette and found his wife beginning to worry about the children, he walked into Oradour to look for them. At the moment that he reached the school on the eastern edge, the Germans were fully occupied in the centre. He found the school deserted, the childrens' possessions still in their places, their caps and satchels in a neat row on their pegs, yet no sign of life. It seemed that Oradour had been evacuated. He glimpsed German soldiers at the other end of the street, and beat a prudent retreat.

A little later another parent, Mme. Demery, mother of three children at the schools, had almost the same experience. She too visited the schoolhouses and escaped unmolested. But by this time she saw flames and heard screams and shooting. The news that she carried back across the fields heightened the growing alarm. Other intruders were less fortunate. A young miller named Antoine cycled towards Oradour despite warnings from the roadside—"Don't go into the town! They're shooting in there!" Antoine shrugged cheerfully: "The Germans had me as a prisoner of war. I know them—they don't frighten me." Waving his white handkerchief high in one hand, he rode towards a German picket covering the approach to the village. There was a single shot and he fell. A trooper finished him with a pistol.

Around 6 pm, when the shooting had subsided, Marie-Leon Foussat walked towards Oradour, despite advice to stay away. He also waved a handkerchief. He also was shot. So was the driver of a small maintenance tram who arrived from Limoges late in the afternoon. Jacques Boissou, a farmer from Mas de l'Arbre, was fired upon as he approached the village, and pursued as he fled. He lay in a little stream until nightfall, seeing one man killed as he did. When he returned to his own home, he found that his mother and grandmother had gone to Oradour. Blanche Taillander had an extraordinary escape. Dickmann's men burst into the house where she was having lunch with a woman friend, shot the friend, but spared Mme. Taillander because her identity card showed that she was from Paris.

When the tram bearing M. Levignac and all the other weekend shoppers back from Limoges reached the edge of Oradour, they gazed up at the hill in utter horror at the palls of flame and smoke, and the infantry still moving briskly among the houses, tossing in grenades. A German picket boarded the tram and began to check papers. When he found a man whose card showed that he lived in Oradour, the German said briefly: "That's bad." Another SS trooper doubled away up the hill, obviously for orders. He returned a few moments later: "All residents of Oradour must dismount. All others will remain in the car and return to Limoges."

Twenty-two terrified men and women dismounted slowly and walked into a ring of SS men around the car. They were separated by sexes, and their papers were inspected again. Then they were put together once more. There was a heated debate between several of the Germans. The agonized minutes dragged on. It was hideously apparent that the lives of the tram passengers were at stake. Suddenly a German turned to them and shouted: "Disappear! Into the country—not into Oradour!" Another French-speaking trooper cried after them: "You're being let off! Believe me, you're lucky!" There was a last, grotesque afterthought. A German noticed from one girl's papers that she lived many miles away. Picking up a bicycle that he had seized from one of the doomed houses of Oradour, he offered it to ease her journey.

M. Levignac, the insurance agent from Avignon, dismounted from the tram as soon as it was once more out of sight of Oradour, and lingered on the road in an agony of terror for his children. Professor Forest, the philosopher, walked from Lapland to Oradour at about 7 pm. The church and much of the town were still burning fiercely. He approached a sentry and asked in German where his children might be. The trooper—probably an Alsatian—replied in French, to Forest's surprise, that all the women and children were off in the woods: "They're safe." They were standing twenty-five yards from the church, perhaps fifteen from Mme Rouffranche's hiding place. Professor Forest turned and walked uncertainly back to Laplaud.

All that night, frightened mothers scoured the woods around Oradour for their missing children. The conviction that they were somewhere in the countryside was strengthened when the exhausted Aimé and Jeannine Renaud, escaped from their hiding place in the Desourteaux yard, stumbled into a farmhouse at La Place and announced simply: "All the men were shot, and all the women and children were led away."

Very early on the morning of the eleventh, a handful of brave and intolerably apprehensive people made their way towards Oradour, determined to get news. M. Lévèque, at Orbagnac, was missing not only his children but his brother and the family maid. He was one of the first to return from the terrible scene with a blurred but definite picture: everyone in Oradour had been killed. Professor Forest made his second journey at about 5 am. "Where are the children?" he asked a sentry. "*Alles kaputt* (Everything is destroyed)," said the German succinctly. M. Levignac reached the house where his eldest son had been staying and found it intact, but abandoned and looted. The couple who had gone to a wedding returned to their home to find the table still set for lunch, but their parents and children nowhere to be found.

At about 11 am on Sunday morning, Dickmann's men drove out of Oradour, their vehicles loaded with loot and livestock. One truck was towing a car taken from the street which suddenly snapped its cable, careered into a pylon and crashed, injuring the SS driver. Then they were gone, and the last vestiges of doubt about what had taken place were removed from the minds of the region's inhabitants. A farmer from Le Breuil named Hyvernaud, with two sons of thirteen and six at the school in Oradour, made his way into the smoking, deserted church:

> I went to hunt for my children, and I actually found one of the boys. He was my youngest. He lay on his side and was half-charred. . . . He still had one of his wooden shoes on. His other leg was completely out of joint and twisted behind his back. His throat was half cut through.

Hyvernaud walked home to Le Breuil, gathered his wife and some sheets, and returned to the church to fetch back the little body:

> . . . I went on searching for my other son. I knelt down and peered at the stiffened faces of the children, one after another, wherever there were features that could be recognized. But I did not find my older boy. Behind the altar, crammed closely together, lay at least twenty small children who had tried to find shelter there. . . . They had all been suffocated by smoke or burned to death. I also saw prams with dead infants in them. Some were burned, others were riddled with bullets. Then I went home. That evening we dug a grave for André in our little yard.

On the morning of Monday, 12 June, as the news of Oradour spread by word of mouth across the horrified Limousin, a Wehrmacht convoy drove into Oradour and worked for some hours digging two mass graves, and carrying into them some of the bodies. Towards lunchtime the Germans departed, taking with them many of the loose beasts and fowls not already appropriated by the Der Führer. That afternoon, the first of many volunteers from among local doctors and sanitary workers, civil defence teams and priests moved into Oradour and began the dreadful task of removing and identifying the bodies, already corrupted by two days of warm sunshine, or crumbling to ashes at the touch. Even for experienced medical teams it was a terrible task to work among the debris on an entire community—its burnt-out cars and sewing machines, crockery and cutlery, scorched living-rooms and charred bedding, straying cats and dogs, discarded children's toys. At one moment, the medical team saw that another lorryload of Germans had halted in the middle of the main street, and were busy loading the Frenchmen's bicycles, lying against the houses. The Germans obviously imagined that previous looters had overlooked these. The medical team remonstrated with them. The Germans unloaded the cycles and drove away.

CHAPTER 10

Excess of Zeal

FOR WHAT IT IS WORTH, this is the manner in which the regimental history of the Der Fuhrer, compiled by Major Weidinger, records the first news of Oradour:

> Late in the afternoon the same day [10 June], Sturmbannführer Dickmann returns to the regiment and reports the following: the company had met resistance in Oradour and had come across several bodies of murdered German soldiers. The company then occupied the town and had promptly started a search of the houses. Unfortunately they had not found Kampfe, though they had discovered hidden ammunition and weapons. So Dickmann had all the men of the town who could be identified as *maquisards* shot.
>
> The women and children had been locked into the church during this time. Then the town had been set on fire; in nearly all the houses hidden ammunition had exploded. The fire then suddenly spread to the church, which also had ammunition hidden in its steeple. The church burnt down very quickly, and the women and children died.
>
> Staf. Stadler is deeply shocked at this report and tells Dickmann: "Dickmann, you could pay heavily for this. I shall request that you be court-martialled immediately by the division! I cannot let something like this rest on the shoulders of the regiment!"
>
> Staf. Stadler was also furious that Dickmann had not carried out his orders to bring back *maquis* prisoners should Kampfe not

be found. Deeply disturbed, he sends Dickmann away to draw up a detailed report. Dickmann does not defend himself, but obviously expects to do so at the military hearing. Immediately after the arrival of the divisional commander, Brigadeführer Lammerding, Stadler reports the events in Oradour-sur-Glane and requests the court-martial of Dickmann. This is promised as soon as the situation allows for a trial to be arranged. . . .

The 1c [Kowatsch] overhears a radio message sent by a senior *maquis* staff officer after the events of Oradour and Tulle, ordering that all fighting against the Germans is to cease until the division Das Reich has left central France. Resistance has become pointless in the face of the great sacrifices which it has provoked in Tulle and Oradour. These sacrifices bore no relation to successes achieved. Another message on an enemy wavelength claims that Kampfe has been shot to avenge the destruction of Oradour. . . .

The fact that Dickmann went far beyond his commander's orders and took a personal initiative can no longer be regarded as an excess. First, it must be realized that Dickmann wanted to free his friend Kampfe. If he did not find Kampfe and did not take hostages, as he had been told to, he must have concluded that Kampfe could no longer be alive and therefore could not be released. . . . In his judgment Dickmann also had to consider the general instruction of OB West [the Sperrle order] and the special order of the corps concerning terrorists. Eyewitnesses reported that Dickmann did not take the decision lightly. . . . The destruction of Oradour cannot, therefore, be blamed upon the leadership of the Der Führer regiment, or of the Das Reich Division, or on any other German authority.

The logic of these remarks may be judged by the reader. Only two points of substance need to be made. First, since no Resistance group possessed radio-telephone, it is impossible that Kowatsch could have intercepted such messages. It is possible, though unlikely, that he could have intercepted Free French signals to or from London, but there is no evidence that any traffic of this nature was ever passed. Second, although Dickmann was indeed brought before a court-martial (which never reached a verdict) in Normandy, he remained in command of his battalion until his death. The first action of a commander in any army who is seriously displeased by the action of a subordinate is to relieve him of his command. Stuckler asserts that he never heard of events in Oradour until he arrived in Normandy. The Der Führer's war diary, and the situation reports signalled to division, assert blankly that "the town of Oradour-sur-Giane was surrounded, and ammunition found stored in almost every house. Results: 548 enemy dead. Our casualties: one dead, one wounded." In reality, as far as the investigators were ever able to ascertain, 393 residents, 167 people from the surrounding country-side, thirty-three from Limoges and fifty-five from other places were killed—only fifty-two bodies were identifiable. Remarkably enough, Dickmann's detachment had indeed suffered casualties: falling masonry from the church injured one man and killed another, Lieutenant Knug. He was reported to his family as: "Died for the fatherland."

The balance of circumstantial evidence suggests that the Das Reich Division made nothing of Dickmann's doings at Oradour until forceful inquiries from Vichy officials and army headquarters caught up with them in Normandy. The local garrison commander in Limoges, General Gleininger, realized as soon as he heard the news that the SS had over-reached themselves at Oradour, and offered effusive apologies to the Bishop of Limoges and other local dignitaries. The Germans also made clumsy attempts to conceal the nightmare. The local censor imposed a blanket ban on publication of any news of Oradour's fate in the region's newspapers. The Gestapo instituted a mercifully unsuccessful search for survivors. They realized, as the officers of the Das Reich did not, that this had been something special.

Dickmann and his battalion spent the night of 11 June in new billets at Nieul, six miles east of Oradour, attracting nervous local attention by their conspicuous array of loot. While the 1st battalion was at Oradour, Kampfe's 3rd battalion had been engaged in a number of minor skirmishes with *maquisards* as they patrolled the area east of Limoges. The *maquis* situation all over southern and central France was causing acute concern. On 12 June, General Von Biaskowitz, commanding Army Group G, took over personal tactical direction of the anti-partisan war, and requested OKW that the south-west be formally designated a battle zone. On the eleventh—before divisional headquarters became aware of Oradour—the 2nd SS Pz signal led Army Group G: "Mopping up operations in the region Limoges, St. Leonard, Ambazac, Bellac, Rochechouart. Provisional balance sheet: 337 killed, 36 prisoners. The road Tulle–Seilhac–Uzerche free of the enemy."

That day, the units of the Das Reich in Tulle abandoned the town—they were relieved by the battle group from 11th Panzer division and moved north to Limoges, laden with loot from the town. Early on the morning of the twelfth, once again preceded by the reconnaissance battalion, the roadborne elements of the division moved north out of Limoges, under orders to proceed with all speed to Normandy via Poitiers and Tours.

The scale of the tragedy at Oradour dwarfed other, isolated killings by the division on 10 and 11 June: Jean-Baptiste Legressy, a thirty-four-year-old workman; Charles Prima, a farmworker, twenty-four; Roger Bayard; Henri Dijoux, nineteen; Adrian Girette, twenty-one, tortured and hanged at Buissière-Poitevine; Marchal Roger, thirty-five; Achille Maren, forty-six; Henri Villesange, a coachbuilder's apprentice, sixteen. The last, alone among all these, identified himself as a *résistant*, a member of an FTP *maquis*. Exact responsibility for their deaths cannot be pinpointed within the division. It is known only that the Frenchmen were shot by members of the Das Reich in the performance of their duties. Major Weidinger's account declares simply:

> There are further concentrations, attacks and losses. Only in the area of the 1st battalion of the Deutschland is there complete peace. . . . The 3rd battalion carried out one more operation, in search of an armed French *gendarmerie* unit which had defected to the *maquis*. The approach of German troops had obviously been noticed and reported by civilians. When they reached the camp in the forest, they were able only to arrest two or three Frenchman and release several German soldiers. The bulk of the *gendarmerie* unit had escaped. The rest of the day was spent preparing for the march. . . .

It would be absurd not to acknowledge that the efforts of the Das Reich made a profound impression upon the population of Haute-Vienne. On the morning of 12 June, Gaston Hyllaire— "Leonie"—the departmental commander of the *Armée Secrète*, paid a secret personal visit to Oradour. Major Weidinger was perfectly correct in asserting that a strong body of opinion among the local Resistance commanders now held that no gesture in arms was worth such a terrible price. Jean Sennemaut, commanding the AS unit around Bellac to the north-west, recalled that until the moment of Liberation, senior local AS officers opposed any attempt unilaterally to seize and free towns, lest the horror of Oradour be repeated. The FTP—and above all Guingouin's *maquisards* southeast of Limoges—were rather less troubled by these risks. But it is surely significant that while the communists of Haute-Vienne had been discussing a full-scale attack on Limoges for months, in the event they did not move to take over the town until the Germans were in full retreat from the region. "Action taken during the passage of the Das Reich Armoured Division through Limoges and its surrounding countryside has made a visible impression on the population," noted the war diary of the 19th SS police regiment, based on Limoges. Painful though it may be for humanitarians to accept, a policy of unlimited repression can be formidably effective. Oradour made a lasting mark on the Haute-Vienne. If the exercise had a weakness from the SS point of view, it is that it was not publicly announced as a reprisal for the seizure of Major Kampfe. It seems certain that if the Das Reich had been available to continue carrying out such appalling acts in reprisal for every operation carried out by the AS or the FTP, *maquis* commanders would have come under enormous pressure from the local population to desist absolutely from attacks. Mercifully, however, the Das Reich was compelled to move on.

The division suffered only one further clash with *maquisards* after moving north from Limoges. Jean Sennemaut's AS company, deployed in the north-west of Haute-Vienne through which the divisions passed, was not even aware of its existence until, early on the morning of 12 June, their commander risked slipping home to Bellac from his *maquis* in the woods to collect some clothes. He heard the clatter and roar of a large German convoy moving up the *route nationale*, and at one point a burst of firing. He vanished hastily back into the fields, toward his *maquis*.

An hour or two later a small group of FTP *maquisards*, approaching a junction just north of Bellac in a lorry, glimpsed a German truck halted on the main northbound road. Only a short stretch of the highway was visible to them, and thus they could not see the great mass of German vehicles halted on each side. The *maquisards* dropped from their lorry and closed upon the single parked truck, firing as they came. Their Moroccan Bren gunner fired only one burst before his gun jammed. He then turned to his haversack of grenades, and hurled one at the truck. But now, to their consternation and dismay, the little group of Frenchmen—commanded, ironically enough, by yet another Alsatian—found themselves engulfed by the ferocious return fire of several hundred extremely wakeful Germans of Wulf's *Aufklärungsabteilung*. Five *maquisards* were killed in a matter of moments, before the others fled back into the woods, abandoning their vehicle.

When the shooting began, Private Schneid and his young comrades of the anti-tank platoon hurled themselves for cover behind the body of their half-track. The furious "Hascha" hurled them bodily from this refuge and made them deploy to return the fire. "We won't win the war with soldiers who hide behind their vehicle at the first shot!" he shouted. Then he motioned Schneid to follow him, and as the *maquisards* retreated, slipped forward into the fields to reconnoiter. They found a dead man on his front in the grass, a bandolier over his shoulder. "Turn him over," said the "Hascha." He picked up the Sten that lay under the man's body, and gazed at the dead face. "They're all the same, these bloody characters . . . ," Kurz muttered to Schneid, who was surprised to notice in his voice ". . . a kind of respect. . . ." They picked up the bandolier. Then the two men strode briskly back to their half-track and, at a signal from the front, the column rolled slowly away again toward Poitiers.

One eddy from the wake of the Das Reich's operations reached the city a few hours before them. The 311 men who had been loaded into the lorries in the courtyard of the Tulle arms factory on 9 June, informed that they were being taken to the Hôtel Moderne, were in reality driven to the old cavalry barracks in Limoges, where they arrived at 3 am on the tenth. For the remaining hours of the night they were obliged to stand under the guns of the SS guards while their fate was discussed. Then the Wehrmacht relieved the sentries, and conditions improved. The prisoners were allowed to sit down, to eat and to receive visits from French Red Cross nurses. In whispered snatches of conversation, they heard for the first time that the Allied beach-head in Normandy was now firmly established. Towards 5 pm, the SS and a group of *miliciens* reappeared. The senior *milicien* announced: "The German authorities have allowed us to collaborate with them to separate the corrupt elements from the town of Tulle. We have done this work as good Frenchmen. *Vive le maréchal! Vive Darnand! Vive le milice! Vive la France!*" ("Long live the marshal! Long live Darnand! Long live the *milice*! Long live France!") It never proved possible to discover by what process of logic 162 of the detainees were now released, while the other 149 were selected for deportation. These were loaded aboard trucks once more, and driven north to Poitiers on the evening of the twelfth to await entrainment for Germany.

They joined some 250 other Frenchmen, already herded for the night in the courtyard of Gestapo headquarters at 13 Rue des Ecossais. At about 1 am, the RAF's Bomber Command attacked Poitiers railway yards, causing panic and substantial damage to the town. Not surprisingly, as bombs rained down within a few hundred yards of their prison, the desperate French captives tried to fight their way over the railings, or at least into the shelter of the building. The SS guards opened fire at once from the cover of the headquarters, killing six and wounding thirty-five. Four others were wounded by bomb fragments. Order was thus restored, and the prisoners were left to their own devices without food, water or medical assistance until 2 pm the following afternoon. On the evening of 13 June they were transferred to Compiègne, and taken from there by rail to concentration camps in Germany, arriving at Dachau on 5 July; 980 of the 2,521 prisoners on the train died during the three-day journey. In all, of 149 Tullois deported, forty-nine lived to come home in 1945.

The German-controlled press reminded the citizens of Poitiers in forceful terms of the source of their troubles. *Centre et Ouest* headlined its account of the RAF raid: "POITIERS PAYS ITS OWN TRAGIC TRIBUTE TO THE WAR." Its front-page story went on:

At 1:30 am today Poitevins were brutally hauled from their slumbers by huge pillars of fire which embraced the city. You will remember the pamphlet dropped upon Billancourt two years ago that proclaimed, "Don't be afraid, we know our business"? They knew it so well that, two hours later, there were six hundred dead. At Poitiers also, the Anglo-American pilots knew their business so well that today we are celebrating the "final liberation" of about a hundred of our people. . . .

On the night of 12 June, on a hill a few miles outside the city, Major Heinrich Wulf and his men lay beneath the camouflage nets covering their lagered vehicles, watching the flashes and shock waves enveloping Poitiers. Somebody murmured: "Well, let's thank God we're not down there. . . ." In the woods just a mile or two away, another little uniformed group also saw the distant raid. Much the same thoughts passed through their minds. These were officers and men of the British 1st Special Air Service Regiment, who were to cause the Das Reich Division its last significant inconvenience before it became enveloped in the battle for Normandy.

CHAPTER 11

The SAS: Bulbasket

IF THE ALLIED STAFF at SHAEF headquarters had been given a free choice in the matter, it is unlikely that the forty men of 0 Squadron, 1st SAS would have been anywhere near Montmorillon on the night of 10 June. The roadborne elements of the Das Reich would have reached Normandy one, perhaps two or three days earlier than they did. SAS operations against the rail links south of Poitiers must also have contributed to the interminable delays suffered by the 2nd SS Pz tanks on the move from Périgueux via the city. An SAS-directed attack on the petrol dump at Châtellerault destroyed huge reserves upon which the Wehrmacht had relied to refuel the Das Reich's wheeled elements for the last phase of their march to the coast.

An impeccably-bred Englishman who fought with distinction in Europe said afterwards: "The great thing about the 1939–45 war was that everybody did what they liked." By this he really meant that a few thousand Englishmen with access to the bars of the great St. James' clubs proved able to organize their own military destinies sometimes even their own campaigns—in a manner impossible in any war before or since. The Special Air Service was among the most celebrated of the array of "private armies" that emerged during the war. Almost all were conceived and partly officered by those with privileged access to high places. A posting to Phantom or the commandos was passionately coveted by a dashing young man. If the risks were greater than those of

186

regimental soldiering, so were the fun and the company and the opportunity for extraordinary adventures.

In 1940–1, the "private armies" were tolerated by the service hierarchies as playthings for the Prime Minister and some irregularly minded generals. But as the great confrontations of massed armies upon the battlefield developed, so did the impatience of the staff with the pirate forces on the fringes. Critics claimed that they threatened service discipline; were a grossly uneconomic drain on resources, even unto warships and air transport; and employed thousands of outstanding officers and men who might otherwise have stiffened rifle and armored regiments on the main battlefield.

All these criticisms had some weight. The contribution of special forces of all kinds was always marginal. It is not surprising that in 1944, as SHAEF prepared for one of the great battles of history, its planners had little time or enthusiasm for any force that threatened to divert attention or resources.

Like the Special Boat Service, Popski's Private Army, the Long Range Desert Group and the Special Interrogation Group, SAS was spawned in the desert, that happy hunting-ground of buccaneers and individualists. David Stirling conceived his force in 1941, to bring havoc to the enemy rear areas. In fourteen months of spectacular activity, he and a handful of other daring spirits destroyed hundreds of enemy aircraft on their landing grounds and created a legend throughout North Africa. Stirling himself was captured in February 1943, but the SAS had by then expanded into a force of two regiments, one of them commanded by his brother Bill. They were among the first Allied troops ashore in Sicily and Italy.

Early in 1944, the survivors were brought home to prepare to take part in the invasion of France. Reinforced by volunteers from Home Forces, they were now designated the SAS Brigade, with strong French and Belgian elements. They were based in central Ayrshire in Scotland, and put under the command of Brigadier Roderick McLeod, a regular gunner. In the Scottish mountains they began intensive fitness, parachute and battle training in readiness to go into Europe.

But where and for what to send them? General Montgomery inspected SAS without enthusiasm one morning. He was shown the Phantom GHQ reconnaissance squadron, attached to provide radio links for SAS in the field. "Don't use 'em!" snapped the general, and passed on. Beyond the conventional skeptics, there were other thoughtful officers who believed that if "private armies" were to make an economic contribution to the war, they must be kept small and intimate. David Lloyd Owen, the brilliant commander of the Long Range Desert Group, wrote of SAS in North Africa: "I believe that after David Stirling began to expand the SAS, the balance sheet showed too great an excess of expenditure over achievement." John Hislop, who parachuted into France with an SAS Phantom team in 1944, wrote later:

> When small successful private armies such as the SAS in its early stages, come into being, two tendencies in particular emerge: they expand beyond their capacity to keep up the necessary standard of personnel; and the army, which has never viewed unorthodox forces with favour, takes a closer hold upon them. In the first case the private armies become less effective, and in the second their flair is liable to be hamstrung by red tape.

Hislop suggested that Brigadier McLeod in the spring of 1944 was "quite out of his depth with SAS officers and men, and simply did not know what had hit him when he took over."

Any regular officer might have been forgiven for finding difficulty coming to terms with such men as the commanding officer of the 1st SAS, Lieutenant-Colonel Paddy Mayne. A pre-war rugger international of enormous size, physical strength and courage, Mayne had personally destroyed more German aircraft than any British wartime fighter ace in his raids on the African airfields with Stirling. He treated the regiment as his personal fiefdom. Those of his men who did not adore Mayne were utterly awed by him. He landed on the fire-swept beach in Italy at the head of his unit, with his hands in his pockets. Sober, with his slow upper-class Irish drawl, his Irish songs and sentimentality, his charm was famous. Drunk, he could be ruthless and very dangerous. "Where's so-and-so?" he asked mildly, looking around one evening in the mess to find an officer missing. "Has he gone to bed without saying goodnight?" He led the others purposefully upstairs, slipped into the room of the sleeping officer, lit a bonfire under the bed and opened the betting on how long it would take the man to wake up. Under Mayne's captaincy, regimental football games were fought out with terrible violence. He was one of the great fighting machines of the war, a man who found himself perfectly in his element at the head of men in battle.

"He was everything that we all wanted to be," said one of his men, Corporal Sam Smith. Smith was another soldier who had achieved complete happiness in the SAS. A tough young Liverpudlian who left school at fourteen, he escaped a court-martial after a brawl by volunteering for the commandos, and later transferred to SAS in Egypt. He became almost a professional "only survivor" of operations. On one occasion, he and another man were left alone in a sandstorm with a broken-down vehicle, to discover later that the other twenty-five men in their party had all been captured or killed.

It was a ruthless war. One day, they stopped a truckload of Italian soldiers, searched their vehicle, and then allowed it to proceed. But they had quietly drooped two Mills bombs in the back as it drove off. Smith remembered a morning in Italy, with the troop pinned down by fire on a hillside. A brick-tough former booth boxer lying beside him suddenly noticed all the women of the nearby village sheltering under a bridge fifty yards away. Scorning shouted protests, the man "belted for the bridge, had one of the women, and was back inside three minutes." Their small arms instructor punctuated his lectures with shots into the ceiling, and once indented for the use of some nearby Italian prisoners for target practice (he was refused). Their pride in their unit, and in their style of warfare, was intense. Sam Smith, a veteran at twenty-one, was perfectly content: "I was in love with the SAS. It was my life. Our greatest fear was that we might be sent back to our units."

But many of the men posted to the SAS Brigade early in 1944 had no battle experience. At thirty-two, Lieutenant Peter Weaver was older than most. His father, a regular Indian Army officer, had been killed in World War I. After public school, he enjoyed a checkered career through the 1930s, trying various small businesses, a spell as a private soldier in the army (from which he bought himself out) and a great deal of rugger and cricket, to which he was devoted. "The war came as a great relief to me," he said. He was briefly commissioned in the Dorset Regiment in 1940 before being transferred to one of the secret auxiliary units that were formed as "stay-behinds," to continue resistance to a German invasion if the regular army had to give ground. They were intensively trained in fieldcraft and demolition, but as the threat of invasion receded, monotony set in. In vain they sought a transfer to the commandos. At the beginning of 1944, when they were at last given the chance to go to SAS, Weaver and most of his men seized it eagerly.

But as the Brigade entered its last weeks of training at Darval, the argument at SHAEF and at Special Forces HQ about its employment continued more fiercely than ever. SHAEF was consumed by one over-whelming preoccupation: the need to get the Allies ashore on 5 June, and to keep them there. For security reasons, 21st Army Group would not entertain any plan that involved putting uniformed Allied troops into France before D-Day. But when the moment came, the French Resistance could not be expected to concentrate to much effect in the immediate battle area. Small groups of highly trained SAS dropped into Normandy on the night of D-Day might wreak havoc behind the immediate fighting front.

It was a clearly suicidal assignment, and senior Special Forces officers argued that it was not even the most useful way of employing SAS troops. All forms of irregular warfare must be regarded as strategic, not tactical weapons. SAS should be dropped far behind the lines, where they would have the freedom and flexibility to operate for months, attacking the enemy's communications with the front. SHAEF now asked what SAS could do to interdict the first, critically important German units expected to move toward the battlefield, the Das Reich prominent among them. "2nd SS Panzer Division will be concentrating in a forward area by D+3," argued a pessimistic SAS appreciation of 19 May, "and SAS troops cannot affect that move unless dropped on D-1, which is impossible." The SHAEF proposal that SAS should impede the German armor by defending road blocks with small arms exasperated the Brigade.

In the middle of the row Bill Stirling, the volatile CO of 2nd SAS, was compelled to resign. One of his officers, Roy Farran, wrote:

This was a serious situation for a volunteer unit, since our main allegiance was to our Colonel. . . . It was ridiculous to think that scattered parties of parachutists could do anything much to delay the arrival of panzer divisions. Perhaps we might have caused some confusion for a day or two, but there was no way in which we could have been resupplied so close to the front, and we would therefore have soon become ineffective. . . . These arguments proved such lack of understanding of our role that our confidence in the new command was severely shaken.

In the last days before D-Day, plans for the use of SAS changed repeatedly. Bill Stirling's resignation stood. But only a handful of men—five three-man Titanic teams—were to be dropped immediately behind the beaches to spread confusion among the defenses. A larger (finally costly but useful) operation was to be mounted by 115 men of the French SAS Regiment in the Breton peninsula, to cause maximum uncertainty to the enemy about Allied intentions. The bulk of SAS was to be dropped deep behind the lines as aircraft became available after D-Day.

Something of the flavor of the argument about the use of the Airborne Army in the last months of 1944 had crept in. SAS were demanding to be employed because they were ready and keen. The case for the French operation in Brittany was self-evident. But the rest of the Brigade were to be used as large-scale Jedburghs—stiffening Resistance forces and carrying out sabotage and target-finding missions. The value of small parties of officers and NCOs in this role was obvious. But the decision to drop SAS squadrons in parties large enough to attract urgent German attention, but too small to be capable of self-defense, flew in the face of every principle of irregular warfare. It was the end-product of a succession of bad-tempered arguments and compromises. After many months in which other units had prepared for their invasion role in minute detail the Brigade moved to Fairford in Gloucestershire at the end of May in the confusion of a first-rate "flap." They were imprisoned under tight security in a heavily wired camp close to their airfield, still ignorant of their part in the assault on Europe.

For Captain John Tonkin, the young officer who spent the evening of D-Day making jigsaws with Violette Szabo, the monotony of idle waiting was broken on the morning of 30 May. Paddy Mayne informed him that he was to be dropped with his troop of four officers and thirty-nine men, a five-man Phantom wireless team and an RAMC corporal, near Poitiers, in the Vienne. The SAS's "Amended Instruction No.6" ordered: "You will now concentrate on building up secure bases in the area north-east of Château Chire, codename Houndsworth, and west of Châteauroux, codename Bulbasket, from D-Day onwards with a view to strategic operations against the enemy lines of communication from the south of France to the Neptune area as occasion may occur, or as developments in the main battle may dictate. . . ." Tonkin was about to start briefing his men when another "flap" broke out. He was summoned to the CO and told that he himself would be dropped into France that evening with Lieutenant Richard Crisp, as a reconnaissance party. They worked far into the night, drawing and preparing equipment, maps and money. Then they received the message: "All scrubbed." The Titanic teams were also told that their operations were cancelled. Tonkin and his colleagues, who had been telling the young Titanic officers for days how much they envied their exciting assignment, at last dropped the mask and shared their relief that these suicidal missions had been dropped. Then two Titanic commanders were told that they were "on" again. "I can remember the two of them coming out of Paddy's tent as white as sheets," wrote Tonkin. Of six SAS men who dropped with an army of parachute dummies at the south-east corner of the Cherbourg Peninsula to double-bluff the German defenses, three miraculously survived. They diverted an entire German brigade for the morning of 6 June.

Tonkin and Crisp were sent to London with other key SAS officers destined for France, to be briefed by some of SOE's experts. John Hislop remembered being invited to choose equipment from an exotic assortment of edible papers and pens that used invisible ink—"as if, when a boy, I had been taken into the novelties department of a large store and been given *carte blanche*." Tonkin and Crisp, each escorted everywhere by a security officer, were told to memorize the faces and codenames of SOE agents whom they would meet in central France. A Jedburgh team was being parachuted with them, but would operate independently on the ground. A middle-aged Frenchman who was in London "resting" talked to Tonkin for some hours about the laws of survival in Occupied France: "He gave me much useful advice that I recognized as being from the horse's mouth, and paid good heed to." Hold a gun in your right hand and a bar of chocolate in your left, advised the Frenchman figuratively. If you must seek help or advice from a farm, wait for the old mother of the family; do not accost the young. Expect nothing from those *maquisards* who are merely avoiding the STO; look to the

FTP and AS to do the fighting, but remember the mutual jealousy and ambition that dog them.

On 3 June Tonkin, Crisp and a handful of other SAS officers who were being dropped in advance of their main parties moved to Hasell's Hall, the house near Sandy in Bedfordshire from which SOE dispatched so many of its agents into Europe. There they waited through the three long days of expectation and postponement, to final departure. "The fifth came, and we learned that Titanic and ourselves were definitely 'on'. It was a horrible day for a jump—low dark clouds and far too strong a wind—but the complete absence of any sign of activity, our peaceful house with its jigsaw puzzles, and the general holiday atmosphere made the greatest operation in history seem completely unreal," Tonkin wrote afterwards. At 8 pm the cars came to take them to Tempsford. The RAF dispatchers fitted their parachutes and equipment. Then they waddled out to the waiting Halifax. In the darkness of the fuselage, they lay drinking coffee and chewing sandwiches as the aircraft slowly gathered height over the Channel, and below them the vast invasion armada closed upon the coast of Normandy.

For Tonkin, there was no novelty about going into action. At twenty-three he was a veteran of extraordinary adventures with the SAS in Italy. He had been born in Singapore of Huguenot stock, studied civil engineering at Bristol University, and volunteered for the Royal Engineers in 1939. He spent a frustrating three years searching in vain for action—with the RE, the Northumberland Fusiliers, and the Middle East Commando. Then in June 1942 he joined 1st SAS in North Africa. He spent four months on raids behind enemy lines in the desert, and later took part in four assault landings in Sicily and Italy. On the last of these, at Termoli in October 1943, his squadron was cut off after pushing too deep behind the German lines. They were surrounded by the German 1st Parachute Division, and compelled to surrender when they ran out of ammunition. To Tonkin's astonishment, as a fellow-parachutist he was invited to dine with General Heidrich, the German divisional commander, who talked for hours about the Russian campaign, and how the British withdrawal from Crete began just after he had ordered his own men to start pulling out of the bloody battle. Then Tonkin was removed to another headquarters. A German major told him: "It is my unfortunate duty to inform you that we have orders that we must obey, to hand you over to our special police. I must warn you that from now on the German Army cannot guarantee your life." It was the first that Tonkin knew of Hitler's "commando" order. He realized that he must escape, or die. The following night, when the lorry carrying him northwards up the frozen mountain roads stopped for a moment in the darkness, he slipped through the canvas at the front, on to the cab, and away into the hills. He walked for two weeks toward the sound of gunfire before he heard feet stumble on rocks, and a single brief English obscenity. He had walked into a British night attack. A few weeks later, he was back with 1st SAS.

The men who remember Tonkin from those days speak of him as "the classic English public schoolboy"; a keen shot and rugger player, compulsively energetic and cheerful, an enthusiastic practical joker off-duty. Like all the SAS, he was immensely fit, and bursting to carry the war to the Germans.

A few minutes after 1 am on 6 June, the mid-upper gunner of the Halifax slipped from his turret and moved up the fuselage, softly shaking the five men awake. They finished their coffee, climbed to their feet, and fitted the huge rucksacks to the quick-release clips below their knees. Tonkin, the first man out, groped his way to the jump hole in the floor of the aircraft. Gazing below him in the light of the brilliant moon, he began to identify the ground details he had spent so many hours memorizing. The engines cut, and the aircraft started to glide. The gunner shouted the "Go" signal and swept down his arm. Tonkin slid forward:

It was the nicest exit I've ever had. Before I knew I was out of the plane, I felt the chute tugging at my shoulders and then I was swinging in the air in the bright moonlight, with only a faint breeze to mar the dead silence. I lowered the rucksack and then had a look round for the other four and the containers. They were dropping into a wood. . . . I was drifting into a tree-edged lane. For a moment I thought I was going to land in a tree, but I just missed it. My parachute caught, and I came to rest with my feet just touching the ground. I doubt if I'd have broken an egg if I'd landed on it.

The reception committee was just three men—the farmer who owned the land, his son and a farmhand. They were nervous about interference from a nearby German night-fighter field, and indeed they had scarcely finished bundling and hiding the great white parachute canopies when an aircraft droned overhead, and circled for several minutes. The team dozed in a barn through the dawn of D-Day. At around 7 am, a quiet dark-haired young man carrying a Sten gun arrived. There followed one of those conversations that always made those taking part feel slightly absurd. "Is there a house in the wood?" asked Tonkin in French. "Yes, but it is not very good," answered the visitor.

Tonkin had recognized him from a photograph he had seen in London, even before he heard the password. This was "Samuel," one of SOE French Section's outstanding agents. Major Amédée Maingard de la Ville-es-Offrans was a twenty-five-year-old Mauritian of aristocratic background, who had been studying accountancy in London when war broke out. He volunteered at once for the 60th Rifles, and it was there that Selwyn Jepson's talent scouts sought him out and asked if he would go to France. He was parachuted into the Indre in April 1943 to assist "Hector"—Maurice Southgate. After Southgate's arrest, Samuel and the redoubtable Pearl Witherington divided his area between them, and built up two of the most effective networks in SOE, blowing scores of rail links on the eve of D-Day and in the weeks that followed.

That D-Day morning, news of the invasion had still not reached Samuel or his assistants. For some hours, after so many months of impatience and disappointment, they were frankly disbelieving of the parachutists' report that the invasion had begun. But Samuel was due to receive a *parachutage* many miles away that night, and Tonkin and Crisp and the Jedburgh team were to receive a further SAS party on the night of 7 June. At 7:30 am that morning they left the farm by car—two hours before German troops arrived to comb the area unsuccessfully for evidence of a drop. On 7 June, some forty miles south-eastwards, Tonkin was joined by Lieutenant Twm Stephens and eight more SAS. The Jedburgh team moved east, to begin demolition and *maquis* training around Leblanc. The SAS, eleven strong, then moved a few miles by truck to yet another dropping zone, this time close to the main Limoges-Poitiers road, south of Montmorillon.

Tonkin now spent the first of many hours with Samuel and local Resistance leaders, emphasizing the urgency of concentrating attacks on railways and petrol supplies, and discussing how best to assist the training of the *maquis*. There were some 2,800 FTP and 6,400 Gaullist *maquis* in the Vienne, most of them under-armed and all of them under-trained. Before D-Day, the local Resistance had concentrated upon assisting the escape of shot-down Allied aircrew, and there had been little sabotage. The flat, open country did not lend itself to guerilla war as in the Dordogne and the Lot, until the Germans had been thrown decisively on to the defensive. Colonel Bernard, the local AS chief, seemed to many *résistants* too regimental and orthodox to make the best use of his forces. He had attempted some measure of co-operation with the communists but relations between the FTP and the AS were as usual jealous and fractious.

To the British soldiers, among whom only Tonkin possessed any command of French, the *maquis* seemed exotic and somewhat bewildering. John Hislop, further east with another SAS unit, described them bluntly as "obscure of purpose, jealous of their position and unco-operative." The Bulbasket team were chiefly perturbed by the excessive French zeal to get into action. Tonkin, in a strange country and utterly unfamiliar conditions, quickly decided that the only reasonable course was to trust the *maquis* in almost everything. He and Samuel took a conscious decision that, since it was impossible to keep secret the arrival of a large body of uniformed men, they should seek to capitalize upon it for intelligence, propaganda and prestige. Samuel believed that his men could keep the railways cut east of Poitiers. The SAS would concentrate on the vital Poitiers-Bordeaux and Poitiers-Tours lines south of the city. The SAS would camp with groups of *maquisards*, to whom they could give weapon training, and rely on the *résistants* and local people for warning of a German attack.

On the morning of 10 June, in Tonkin's words "a small, very frightened and therefore highly courageous French civilian (I think he was a railway employee) arrived at our newly established base. He told us that there were eleven petrol trains on a well camouflaged and heavily guarded series of sidings about a kilometre south-west of Châtellerault." London had told them repeatedly that petrol was a priority target. But before calling for an air strike, it was essential to pinpoint and confirm the existence of the trains.

Lieutenant Twm Stephens was a fierce, wiry little Welsh regular soldier who had transferred to the SAS after meeting John Tonkin in a transit camp in North Africa after his escape in Italy. Stephens, too, had been a prisoner of war. He came to France with a passionate hatred of all things German, and a determination to erase the indignity of surrender. Although he spoke no French it was agreed that he should accompany the railway man and another *résistant* to reconnoiter the petrol trains. A civilian suit was found for him. Despite Stephens's withering comments on French transport, he accepted the loan of a bicycle. The three men set off on the thirty-five-mile ride to Châtellerault.

They returned, exhausted, late the following morning. At 5:17 that afternoon, Special Forces HQ logged a cipher message from Bulbasket, giving the map reference of the petrol trains. The message was at once passed to 2nd Tactical Air Force. Shortly after 8 pm that night, twenty-four Mosquitos of 487 RNZAF, 464 RAAF and 107 RAF squadrons took off from their bases in southeast England to attack the sidings at Châtellerault.

Late that evening, Tonkin and his men stood by the unlit bonfires on the dropping zone, ready to receive the main party of SAS. To their consternation, they saw approaching northwards on the main road from Limoges a great column of lights. It was clearly a major German troop movement. There was a quick debate. They decided that if they moved quickly to clear the DZ, there was just time to handle the drop. The drone of the Stirlings closed on the field. The fires were lit, and parachutes began to bloom above them. Then, to their horror, they saw colored lights suddenly burst forth on the containers in the sky. It was the fruit of an ill-conceived technical innovation in England, to make containers immediately visible on the ground. The lights were supposed to switch on only at impact, but something had gone disastrously wrong. As the containers touched, soldiers ran desperately forward to smash the light bulbs. *Résistants* urged forward the bullock carts to move the great 500 lb. containers, 16 tons of supplies in all. On the road, the German convoy had extinguished its lights. They were vehicles of the Das Reich. Mercifully for the British, they made no move to intervene.

Tonkin met Sergeant Jessiman, commanding the new arrivals. There had been yet another change of plan, reported the NCO. There had been a request from SHAEF for attacks on the railways west of Poitiers, too distant for Bulbasket to reach. Two officers and fourteen men had therefore been dropped "blind" on the vital lines, with orders to march to join Tonkin after they had laid their charges. As Tonkin's men settled for the remainder of the night in a farmyard, they could see the great glow in the sky to the north-west, from the flames of Poitiers. Still further north, beyond their vision, more fires were burning. 2nd TAF's Mosquitos had attacked Châtellerault in three waves at very low level with cannon, forty-eight 500 lb. bombs, and perfect accuracy. The petrol trains, more precious than gold to Germany's battle for Normandy and to the movement of the Das Reich, were blazing beyond salvage.

The RAF's 38 Group made disappointing practice of dropping the four SAS "blind" parties. Lieutenant Morris landed to find one of his troopers missing—he was never seen again, and they assumed a parachute failure. Sergeant Holmes landed successfully near Airvault, blew a stretch of rail and joined Tonkin later. Corporal Kinnevane and his team were dropped, disastrously, in the middle of the town of Airvault. One man vanished and was never heard of again. The others were compelled to abandon all their explosives and equipment in order to escape. They reached Tonkin only much later.

Lieutenant Peter Weaver, with three men from his old auxiliary unit, landed almost 100 miles from Tonkin's camp. They were equipped with pistols, wireless and explosives, but no food. They were told that they could live off the country. Weaver asked for portable bicycles to be dropped with them, but the request was refused. None of his party spoke a word of French, but they were ordered to communicate with the French only in emergency. As soon as they landed, they discovered that they were many miles off target. They hid up through the hours of daylight, then walked all night toward the railway. At dawn, they heard the sound of a train. Once more they took cover through the day, in a cornfield where they had the disturbing experience of watching the farmer harvesting around them, until they were left at dusk like rabbits in the tiny patch remaining. In the darkness, they slid down to the line, laid their charges, and retreated a few hundred yards. They waited hours before they were rewarded with an explosion, the hiss of steam and much shouting from the line. Then they set off eastwards toward Tonkin.

They had been told to walk through the fields and avoid roads, but in darkness they found this much too slow. They marched for ten nights, growing very hungry. Occasionally they would separate for an hour, each foraging in a different direction. Once, one of them found a goose, but more often it was only an egg or a few vegetables. One day, in a wood, they were astounded to hear American voices. They stepped cautiously into a clearing and found a major and sergeant in American uniforms sitting alone, surrounded by a great mass of equipment, food, wireless gear and, above all, money—they had a fat chest of French francs, Swiss francs and American dollars. They said that they had been sent to supply money to the Resistance, but had yet to find any suitable beneficiaries. They asked the British if they would like some. Weaver politely declined, on the grounds that they were overloaded already. They marched on.

When at last they reached the rendezvous, to their dismay they found no sign of Tonkin and his men. Desperately, they approached a farmhouse and asked for news. They were lucky in their choice. The farmer pedaled off on his bicycle, and some time later a car loaded with heavily armed *maquisards* raced up in a cloud of dust. They were taken to a local village, where a crowd fell upon them. Girls kissed them, wine was thrust upon them, and their desperate hunger was appeased. "Don't worry about the Germans, they're all in Poitiers," said a *résistant* lightly when Weaver showed his unease. They were carried in triumph to the *maquis* camp, and at once put to work instructing the Frenchmen in small arms: "They hardly knew how to throw a grenade," said Weaver. They had weapons, but little idea what to do with them. For four days, the *maquisards* insisted that they knew nothing of any other British soldiers. Then it dawned on Weaver that the French were simply so delighted to have acquired a private weapon-training team that they were concealing the truth. The SAS insisted upon being taken to the rendezvous. Very well, said the *résistants* flamboyantly, but on the way they would attack a cafe that the Germans used. They crowded into their cars and set off. To the intense relief of the British, the cafe proved empty. They drove without incident to the SAS camp.

For almost three weeks, Tonkin and his men had been among the *maquis*. Four jeeps armed with Vickers K machine guns had been parachuted to them. By night, they patrolled the area or carried the sabotage teams to within easy reach of rail targets perhaps twenty miles away. They had attacked the lines a dozen times. Richard Crisp, young and perhaps too gentle for this kind of war, had nonetheless taken out successful expeditions to mine the roads for German convoys, spreading dirt across the road at intervals in front of the mines, to compel the enemy to stop and sweep constantly after the first explosion. Tonkin himself went out repeatedly to lay charges. The one serious mishap was that the Phantom team, dropped at a DZ some miles away on 12 June, had failed to link up with Tonkin's men, and were reportedly stockpiling weapons for the *maquis* from their own base. Tonkin unsuccessfully tried to get them to join him, but was able to maintain contact with London through his own wireless operator, Corporal Chicle.

Tonkin's officers and NCOs were working desperately hard at all hours of day and night. But for the men, many of whom did not go out on the sabotage operations, the greatest problem was the boredom of life in the camps. They ate eternal tinned steak and kidney puddings, varied with some local produce. Once they bought a calf, although nobody enjoyed the necessity of clubbing it to death and butchering it, to avoid the noise of a gunshot. They learned to light fires with the ferocious local spirit, *gnôle*, and to barter with soap, which was almost non-existent in the area. They found that hard cash was also an essential lubricant to Resistance co-operation. They cooked, occasionally patrolled, but mostly lay on their backs smoking, talking to the *maquisards* in broken French or English among the trees. They thought little about the distant battle in Normandy, but took it for granted that they would be overrun by the advancing Allies within a matter of weeks. They lived in their own private world. The chief excitements of each day came at radio schedule time. As their code tune, "Sur le Pont d'Avignon," echoed across the clearing, it became a standing joke for the men to jive to the beat.

John Tonkin himself was very tired and some of his men thought that he tried to do too much. The size of the party made it essential for him to spend much of his time grappling with administration and supply problems. 38 Group missed half Bulbasket's resupply drops during their time in France. Petrol for the jeeps was always chronically short, and so sometimes were explosives. They found that the German habit of running either an empty wagon or an explosives scoop in front of their railway engines made impact detonators useless. The lines could be very quickly repaired. Instead, Tonkin or one of his men would lie, sometimes for hours, with an ear to the line listening for a train, before connecting a pull switch to be fired from cover, or setting a timer. Then one of the jeeps overturned after a brief clash with a German patrol. The driver, O'Neill, badly injured his hand. Tonkin's medical orderly amputated some mangled fingers with a pair of scissors, but the wound became gangrenous. In desperation one night, Tonkin, a local Resistance leader named Jean Dieudonné and one other trooper drove O'Neill by jeep into Poitiers to leave him with a doctor. As they drove home, they stopped to wire up a railway bridge on the edge of the city with explosives and time pencils.

They moved camp four times, when the *maquis* said that the Germans were coming too close. The British had been warned at briefings that informers were a deadly threat, and they saw five alleged double agents shot by the *maquis* during their time in France. For some days, a girl who had fraternized with the Germans was held prisoner in the camp. She was in her thirties, a graduate of Poitiers University who spoke perfect English. She had no great fear for her own fate, for she did not think her crime serious. She sewed shirts from parachute silk for some of the SAS men, and they chatted amicably enough to her. Then early one morning a *maquisard* woke Sam Smith and asked if he wanted to see an execution. They walked to a clearing where the *maquisards* dug two graves. The girl was brought first. She simply asked that her ring be given to the local farmer's wife. Then a Belgian prisoner was brought, dragged screaming on his knees for mercy. When he realized that there would be none, he stood up quite calmly and said: "Don't shoot me in the throat." Then five *maquisards* shot them with rifles. Smith felt guilty later that he had watched without attempting to stop the executions, but at that moment he was merely a spectator of other men's war. The *maquisards* often remarked that it was easy for the SAS to be merciful, for if they were captured they faced only a POW camp. For themselves, capture meant death. Smith tried to show solidarity by sewing FFI flashes in his tunic.

Perhaps the root error that the British made was to think of themselves simply as soldiers doing an exciting and romantic job. They had scarcely glimpsed a German since arriving in France. They found the French that they met overwhelmingly friendly, despite all the cautious advice they had received before leaving England. Their Phantom officer wrote a charming and enthusiastic description in his report of a characteristic evening with the *résistants*:

> There was nothing clandestine about my first what the French call "*un parachutage.*" Once the containers were released from the aircraft there was considerable drama. Albert (the local *maquis* chief) began the proceedings by shouting "*Attention*! Everyone! The *bidons* (cans) descend." Everyone present repeated this advice to Bobo or Alphonse or Pierre, or whoever was nearest, to "have a care that the sacred *bidons* do not crush thee!"
>
> Once the containers had landed the parachute stakes were on. The winner was whoever could roll and hide away the most parachutes before being spotted by someone else. The bullock carts then came up with much encouragement from the drivers such as: "But come, my old one, to the *bidons* advance." Then began the preliminary discussions as to how the first container would be hoisted on to the cart and who should have the honour of commencing. I found that I had to go through the motions of beginning to hoist one end myself before, with loud cries of "But no, my captain! Permit!" or for example "My captain, what an affair!" my helpers would then get on with the job.
>
> Once, however, the drill for clearing the DZ was understood, the helpers were of the greatest value, and we succeeded one night in clearing the DZ in seventy minutes. This was very good as it included four containers that had fallen in trees.

The *maquis* "should be treated unreservedly as friends and Allies," the same officer continued in his report, "and the greatest trust can be put in them. Any mistakes they make are from over-enthusiasm and willingness to help." Once Weaver and two others went to attend the funeral of three Canadian airmen of Bomber Command whose bodies had been found near a village thirty miles away. They were deeply moved to find the entire community in the little street, following three oxcarts heaped with flowers to the graves. The Germans now appeared confined to the major roads and cities, overwhelmingly preoccupied with the battle for Normandy. Tonkin wrote in his report:

> One point to be watched carefully is the general state of alertness. It often happened that we went for several days without a flap. When driving around in daylight all the villages were very friendly, and the girls looked very nice. No Jerry was seen in the area, consequently the men tended to forget they were behind the lines and liable to be attacked at any moment. They wanted to stop in the villages and there was a general tendency to relax. . . . The highest discipline must be maintained to prevent them wandering away from camp. The British soldier's aptitude for scrounging will make him see no harm in going to the nearest farm for eggs, whereas such a thing is highly dangerous. . . . The chief danger is that the locals" talk will reach the enemy through the village collaborator. . . .

There were breaches of security that might have been acceptable in the inaccessible reaches of the Lot, but were highly dangerous in the Vienne. A local Resistance leader reported to Tonkin that two SAS men had wandered into a local cafe for a glass of wine. The SAS, in holiday mood, photographed each other around the camp. Much more seriously, one night when Sergeant Eccles and two troopers attempted to place charges at a railway junction just south of Poitiers, the NCO returned to report that the other two had disappeared, and almost certainly been taken prisoner.

One evening, Sam Smith and two troopers were driven by jeep with a Resistance guide to a drop-off for another railway attack. Smith and his mate, Trooper Fielding, had approached Tonkin, and asked to be allowed to take on a demolition job to relieve the monotony of the camp. Tonkin warned them: "You may be flogging a dead horse, because the Resistance say there are no trains running on the line." But they set off with rucksacks and explosives and their pistols. To their fury they found that the jeep driver had lost his way, and put them down even further from their target than the camp. They began walking fast, soon leaving their guide far behind—they never saw him again. They passed a black-pudding factory. Once they saw a man lowering his trousers in a field, who glared up in astonishment as he saw them. They caught sight of a patrolling German, riding a white horse. Then, as they approached the railway line in the darkness, there was a sudden hammer of machine gun fire close at hand. They beat a hasty retreat, and lay up for the rest of the night and through the following day. The next evening, Smith worked his way to the edge of a cutting some way south of their original attempt. The next sensation he remembered was waking from a doze to find that he had slipped over the edge, and was rolling down the bank. He heard feet moving toward him, set his charges, broke the time pencils, and ran for it. Like most of the SAS railway attacks, this one only damaged a straight stretch of line which could be repaired in a few hours. But Tonkin had concluded that stations and junctions were now too dangerous to attack. It was the repetition of attacks—for Samuel's *maquisards* were maintaining a steady flow of rail-wrecking operations parallel with those of the SAS—that interrupted traffic. The wilder claims of the *maquis*, that rail traffic had stopped altogether, usually proved unfounded. Some trains carrying priority loads almost always kept moving. But German schedules and troop movements were hopelessly dislocated.

The three Englishmen began the long walk back to the camp. They found it hard to keep to their road, for the *maquis* had turned around many signposts to confuse the Germans. When Smith knocked on farmhouse doors to ask for directions, to his fury the inhabitants again and again closed them in his face. But at dawn, in the garden of a house they saw a group of civilians deep in conversation, and asked for help. The French told them simply that they should not go near the camp in the forest of Verriers, because there had been trouble there. After some discussion, they set off for a farmhouse near the drop zone for their jeeps, where they assumed that they would find friends and news. Smith knocked. An almost hysterical woman appeared. She identified them, and shouted something about her son having been caught and shot with the British. Then she slammed the door. They were walking away, confused and alarmed, when by extraordinary good fortune a car loaded with *maquisards* overtook them. They hailed it, and were taken at once to a farmhouse where they found Samuel, a group of Resistance leaders and a wretched captured *milicien* pedaling the generator for the SOE wireless. They fell asleep in the barn. When they woke, one by one a handful of other SAS men arrived to join them, and reported the news of the catastrophe that had overtaken Bulbasket.

Tonkin had always been aware of the dangers of remaining too long in one place, where rumor and German radio direction-finding might pinpoint the camp. But he was restricted by the need to remain within reach of supply dropping grounds, and the difficulty of finding camps close to water for a hundred men, in that exceptionally dry summer, for there were anything up to a hundred *maquisards* with them at any one time. Tonkin had also summoned all the shot-down Allied airmen from camps in the area, and offered them the chance to join the SAS. One, an American fighter pilot named Bradley, at once volunteered for operations: "Captain, I see no reason why the lack of an aircraft should stop me fighting," he told Tonkin, and became a popular and respected member of the unit. Most of the others preferred either to return to the *maquis* camps from which they had come, or to press on down the escape line toward Spain. But when disaster struck there was one American, Lieutenant Lincoln Bundy, in the SAS camp, along with thirty-nine British soldiers and some fifty *maquisards*.

They had been camped for some days in the forest of Verriers, in a thinly wooded valley beside a stream. They moved for security reasons to another base, only to find the lack of water a chronic problem, so they moved back to Verriers. Tonkin went out to reconnoiter a site for a new base, and did not return until the small hours of morning.

Soon after first light, mortar bombs began to burst upon the men in their sleeping bags, and machine gun fire started slashing through the trees. Peter Weaver sprang up to see a cook running half naked through the trees, shouting: "They're coming! They're coming!" Tonkin, followed by Weaver and Jean Dieudonné, ran to the edge of the trees and saw scores of German troops working rapidly along the hedges toward them, under heavy covering fire. Tonkin dashed back into the camp and shouted to his men to scatter and make their own way to safety. By one of most extraordinary, indeed almost fantastic misjudgments of the operation, the entire SAS party had been sent from England with only .45 pistols as personal weapons. Beyond the Vickers guns on their jeeps, they had no means whatever of resisting the German attack. Weaver glimpsed Richard Crisp bandaging a wounded man's leg, and heard somebody shout to him that there was no time for that—it was every man for himself now. Of the fifty-odd *résistants* in the camp, seven were killed in that panic-stricken action in the wood. Many more, with most of the SAS troopers, disappeared in a milling herd into the valley and into the arms of the German cordon. Almost all surrendered.

Tonkin broke the time pencils into their explosives bin, and vanished westwards into the forest. He lay motionless behind a rock as a line of advancing Germans passed before him, listening to the bursts of fire in the woods as little parties of *maquisards* and British troopers were rounded up. Two other officers and six men who made a dash for safety uphill, away from the stream in the same manner as Tonkin, also escaped. Peter Weaver watched his section run downhill with the main body, but himself moved in the opposite direction. At the edge of the trees he met Twm Stephens "almost berserk with rage." Weaver said to him: "There's nothing we can do. I'm going through this cornfield." They parted, and Weaver crawled into the wheat as a line of Germans began sweeping toward him. They fired. He ran zigzagging into some trees, the Germans in his wake. He felt a passionate thirst. Jumping a stile, he saw a small waterfall before him and paused for a second to splash his face in the blessed cool water. He was revived. Choosing a thick thorn bush, he scrambled into its center. There he lay for many hours, pistol in hand, "feeling that I was prepared to stay there for the rest of the war." Night came. It began to rain. He crawled across a field, and suddenly found himself eyeball to eyeball with a large dog. He moved hastily away into cover, and fell mercifully asleep.

When he awoke, it was a beautiful morning. He climbed to his feet and walked into the yard of a nearby farmhouse to find, to his astonishment, John Tonkin. "Thank God you got through," said Tonkin. Only eight of his men had survived. Thirty-one—four of them wounded, including Richard Crisp—had been taken prisoner, together with Lieutenant Bundy of the USAAF, and the two SAS troopers captured four days earlier on the railway. The next afternoon Tonkin walked into the village of Verriers, almost dazed with shock, to find that the Germans had gone, taking their prisoners. Twm Stephens had been wounded and captured. The Germans tied him to a tree, paraded the village past and then beat him to death with their rifle butts. The other SAS prisoners, together with Lieutenant Bundy, were executed on

7 July, presumably in accordance with Hitler's "Commando Order." Their secret mass graves were uncovered after the Liberation. In all, of 100 SAS captured by the Germans in France during the operations after D-Day, only six survived.

John Tonkin wrote thirty-six years later: "I have always felt that the Geneva Convention is a dangerous piece of stupidity, because it leads people to believe that war can be civilized. It can't." There were many paradoxes about Bulbasket. Trooper John Fielding remembered that when they were briefed before they dropped, the SAS were clearly informed that they could not take prisoners, because there were no means of holding them. It is extraordinary, first, that no one reflected that such a policy might be reciprocated; and second, that the SAS were allowed to drop into France under the illusion that the war they were being sent to join had something to do with ordinary soldiering. Special Forces HQ failed to emphasize to the SAS their likely fate if they were captured. Had they been aware of it, it is unlikely that so many men would have surrendered.

SOE agents who met SAS parties in the field, notably Philippe de Vomécourt, considered that they behaved with some carelessness in the thick of enemy territory. They were sent knowing little of France or of the Resistance war, and, according to Colonel Barry of SOE, regimental pride made them reluctant to accept over-much guidance from Baker Street. The SAS of that period were better trained and certainly men of higher abilities than British line infantry, but they were not remotely comparable in quality and expertise with the post-war SAS. Bulbasket's lack of armament is a measure of the misconceptions surrounding the operation. John Tonkin said: "We were simply not intended to fight pitched battles with the Germans." But it was absurd to imagine that a party of fifty men in enemy territory ran no risk whatever of encountering the enemy. The *maquis* lacked the training and ability to protect them. After the disaster at Verriers, the British searched bitterly for evidence from which they could pin blame for their betrayal. John Tonkin believes to this day that a foreign-born officer of the SAS (not mentioned in this story) betrayed Bulbasket to the Germans to take pressure off his own team. John Fielding thinks that two men on a motorcycle who passed the camp one day when he was on guard were in reality German agents.

The truth will never be known. But it seems much more likely that, when thousands of villagers over a wide area knew of the existence of the SAS party, the Germans received a local tip-off. Resistance historians in the Vienne who have studied the episode remark that the SAS were incautious, for instance in taking a jeep into Poitiers. The Germans at that period were not seeking confrontation with the Resistance unless it was thrust upon them, but the presence of a uniformed British force, flaunting its presence around the country, was evidently an intolerable challenge to their authority. It cannot have required very ingenious intelligence work to locate the camp at Verriers, when the SAS had been there on and off for eight days. Although contemporary SAS reports speak of the final attack being carried out by SS units, Resistance historians say that, in reality, Verriers was taken by the 158th Security Regiment from Poitiers. Seizing thirty-three men armed only with pistols was scarcely a demanding task, and it was a tribute to the Germans' fumbling that Tonkin and eight others escaped.

The survivors of Bulbasket, at last joined by the Phantom team, remained in France for almost five weeks after the disaster at Verriers. For much of that time they were awaiting fresh supplies of explosives and equipment from England. The shock of the attack lifted surprisingly quickly from the minds of the eighteen young Englishmen who survived, but their mission's back was broken. "We'd written ourselves off," Weaver said. "I never expected to get back to England." Tonkin, unfailingly energetic, made four more railway attacks, but with only one jeep—which had escaped Verriers because it was away for repairs—they lacked mobility for more ambitious operations. On 7 and 10 August the SAS group, together with Samuel and eight USAAF aircrew, were evacuated to England in two airlifts by Hudson, from an improvised landing ground.

Contemporary opinion on Bulbasket was divided. In a War Office report dated 10 August 1944, the Director of Tactical Investigation who compiled after-action assessments wrote brusquely:

> In comparison with the achievements of the other SAS groups, Bulbasket has not, on the evidence available, been so successful as a source of information. This group has from time to time reported

a few bombing targets, and also the results when the targets were taken on by the RAF. There is nothing to show that SAS troops have taken any part in arming or organizing the *maquis* in this area.

But he added:

Bulbasket has, however, played an important part in making the movements of German troops in the area difficult, in conjunction with RAF bombing. . . . They have also employed many German troops in action.

Hindsight suggests that the report should have been inverted: Bulbasket probably did little more to occupy the attention of German troops in the Vienne than the Resistance could have done without them. But Stephens's pinpointing of the German petrol trains at Châtellerault was a classic example of liaison between an air force and behind-the-lines observers.

Yet could not Tonkin with a tiny handful of officers and NCOs have accomplished as much, or more, without risking the disaster that took place at Verriers chiefly because a large body of men required a conspicuous fixed base? Hislop wrote, after his own experience with SAS in France: "In retrospect, it seemed to me that the same result could have been achieved with fewer and more carefully selected men." There was a fundamental confusion among the planners who deployed uniformed regular soldiers—albeit with special forces training—in a profoundly irregular situation.

But war is about the balance of advantage, the final net gain or loss when the casualty returns are in. The Director of Tactical Investigation did not possess the advantage of seeing the desperate signal intercepted by the British Ultra decrypters at Bletchley Parle "Urgent request for allocation of fuel for 2 SS Pz Div from army fuel depot Châtellerault addressed to AOK I at 1100, 13 June." In the cold accountancy of battle, this alone was an achievement purchased cheaply by the loss of a platoon.

CHAPTER 12

Normandy

THE DAS REICH Division's battle against Resistance effectively ended at Bellac, on the road to Poitiers. *Maquis* groups further north did not attempt to attack such an overwhelmingly powerful force in unfavorable country. London had never expected that *résistants* would be able to achieve much against major formations in areas approaching the battlefront. The division was not even aware of the existence of the SAS detachment which caused the destruction of their petrol depot. To most of the men of the Das Reich, there was simply another of the interminable checks and delays which had wasted so much time since Montauban.

Now, as the division approached the Loire, they entered the region of France in which most havoc was being achieved by the Allied communications bombing. "Our operations in Normandy," wrote Rommel, "are rendered exceptionally difficult, and in part impossible to carry out, by the . . . overwhelming superiority of the enemy air force." Between 6 March and D-Day, the Allied air forces had poured 62,000 tons of bombs on to the ninety-three key rail centers chosen for attack by Eisenhower's air and transport specialists. By ruthlessly sweeping aside civilian traffic throughout the French rail network, the Germans continued to be able to run some priority trains, but the chaos and delays were appalling. All the lower Seine bridges were destroyed. 2nd Panzer Division arrived in Normandy only on 13 June after a journey of 150 miles, and required a further seven days to regroup before going into action; 17th SS Panzergrenadiers did not arrive until 17 June, having struggled the 200 miles from Bayonne; 9 and 10 SS Panzers arrived from the Eastern Front only on 25 June. German wireless networks were overwhelmed with pleas for fuel, transport, new routings, bridge repairs and locomotives. The Wehrmacht was bleeding terribly in Normandy, losing an average of 2,500 and 3,000 men a day, yet the reinforcements were crawling across France with fatal sluggishness, lapsing into confusion after they crossed the Loire and entered the most deadly fighter bomber target zone. The Allies were dispatching an average of almost 600 fighter bomber sorties a day on roving commission to attack moving trains and convoys wherever they were found in northern France. These inflicted terrible damage on the Germans. North of the Loire, the Germans were compelled to resort almost exclusively to the roads for the last phase of their forward movement, becoming even more vulnerable to air attack. Almost every German who fought in Normandy conceded that the Allied air attack was the decisive factor in the Wehrmacht's defeat. It was the air forces which inflicted the most important delays upon most German reinforcements approaching Normandy. No other major battlefield formation was permitted to waste as much time upon Resistance as the 2nd SS Panzer.

The Das Reich Division trickled into the rear areas of the battlefront piecemeal, between 15 and 30 June 1944. The elements which had remained at Toulouse under Major Wisliceny followed on 7 July. To the intense chagrin of its officers, units were committed independently to shore up the sagging German front. The division did not begin to fight as an integral force under Lammerding's command until 10 July, by which date it had already suffered heavy losses.

Sufficient petrol was found to move the reconnaissance battalion and the Der Führer regiment across the Loire on 13 June, by the bridges at Saumur and Tours, which were still intact despite the intensive Allied air bombardment. Other units followed as they could over the next week. The tank units did not even begin to move from Périgueux until 15 June, a great tribute to Resistance and the Allied air forces. On the sixteenth, a SHAEF G-3 report stated: "In spite of our efforts to delay it, Panzer division Das Reich, units of which reported Perigueux, left in fifteen trains, thirteen last night, two this morning, for Poitiers." Their progress up the railway was painfully slow. Fritz Langangke, coming from Germany with his newly equipped Panther company, travelled a great circle around France for a fortnight before catching up with them. The tanks were compelled to detrain at Angers, more than a hundred miles from the battlefront, and to move forward by night, with all the delays and breakdowns made inevitable by another prolonged road march.

From the moment that they crossed the Loire the Germans were appalled by the utter dominance of Allied air power, the "*Jabo** (German slang for fighter bomber) fairground in the sky," as Ernst Krag called it. In Russia, the enemy air force had presented no serious threat to movement. But in France, questing fighter bombers fell on them ceaselessly. The convoys of the Das Reich were compelled to abandon daylight movement after Saumur and Tours, and crawl northwards through the blackout. At dawn on 14 June they were halted by the roadside near LaFleche. A signal was handed to Colonel Stadler. The commander of the 9th SS Hohenstaufen Panzer Division had been killed in action. Stadler was to replace him immediately, handing over command to Major Weidinger. The headquarters group were making hasty arrangements for the transfer when an Allied fighter bomber section smashed into the column, firing rockets and cannon. Within minutes, as men struggled to train the light flak guns and swing the vehicles under cover, sixteen trucks and half-tracks were in flames. Thereafter, they camouflaged the vehicles with deadly care. The tanks moved only as a "walking forest," as they called it, blanketed in foliage. When Otto Pohl's company lagered in an orchard, he had his men scythe the grass behind the tanks to conceal the tracks. The crews cursed that "they couldn't even step into a field for a crap" without drawing a *Jabo*. Again and again, as they inched forward through the closely set Norman countryside, the tankmen were compelled to leap from their vehicles and seek cover beneath the hulls as fighter bombers attacked. Their only respite came at night. To their astonishment, after Russia where much of the most bitter fighting took place at night, they found that "after 10 pm the American left us strictly alone." In the merciful peace of darkness they could redeploy, rest and re-arm until daybreak brought the return of shelling and the fighter bombers. There were other lessons about a new kind of war. Moving into action in his Panther for the first time in

---

* *Jagdbomber*—fighter bomber.

Normandy, the young Das Reich tank officer Fritz Langangke swung around the corner of a building to find an extraordinary panorama stretched out before him: a Norman village street littered with the debris of fierce fighting—burning vehicles, American and German infantry and anti-tank guns confronting each other 200 yards apart. But not a man was firing. Between the lines, American and German stretcher-bearers were scuttling to and fro, removing the wounded. "It was the first hint that this war would be different," said Langangke. "In Russia, we would have driven straight over them. . . ."

Weidinger and other veterans arrived in Normandy expecting to take part in a great counter-attack to force the Allies back into the sea. To their astonishment and dismay, they were ordered simply to plug a gaping crack in the line, alongside the remains of the superb Panzer Lehr Division commanded by Bayerlein. Bayerlein laughed when they talked to him about their hopes of taking the offensive. "It will be a miracle if we can stand where we are," he said laconically. The Das Reich's divisional staff had wanted time for a few hours' tactical training behind the line, or at least a spell in a quiet sector. But there were no quiet sectors. "Where is the German Air Force?" men asked those who had arrived before them in Normandy: "There is no more German Air Force." The newcomers were dismayed to see the exhaustion and sagging morale of units coming out of the line—the open defeatism and crippling casualties, the strain of incessant bombardment and the roaring—like so many trains—as the huge shells from the warships offshore tore past them into the rear areas. Experienced officers were shocked to discover that they had a significant desertion problem, chiefly among the Alsatians.

But it would be false to suppose that the Das Reich was an enfeebled fighting unit in Normandy. The only redeeming merit of the SS was that they were among the most dogged, fanatical soldiers in the world. Fritz Langangke, sitting battened down in the turret of his Panther under artillery fire one afternoon, cursed the code of his corps when he saw the Volkswagen field car of their commander, Tyschen, dashing up the lane toward him, with the major standing erect and exposed behind the windscreen. Langangke was compelled to leap down from his turret and stand at attention before Tyschen to receive his orders while shells shattered around them.

The Der Führer regiment lost 960 men—almost half its strength in the first four days of battle. Shelling accounted for most of them; regimental headquarters received a direct hit which killed nine men and a visiting war correspondent. They became unwilling to gather company commanders for briefings in case they should all die under a single hit. Runners had to carry all messages between positions. The use of radio appeared to be instantly detected by Allied locators and met with artillery fire. It was futile to lay telephone wires under constant bombardment. Major Stuckler came to visit them in their positions, and was appalled by what he found. With Pak guns and Teller anti-tank mines, they halted one British tank attack within yards of regimental headquarters. Just as in Russia, they found that the postal service collapsed, and they spent weeks without letters from home, with all the corrosive consequences for morale.

It was in the line in Normandy that the division at large learned some of the details of the reconnaissance battalion and the Der Führer's accomplishments at Tulle and Oradour. Unheard-of requests for inquiries and courts-martial were being forwarded through Army Group B. But in the first weeks in Normandy there were two very convenient casualties in the Der Führer regiment. Captain Kahn was in a group of men hit by shellfire, and was badly wounded, losing an arm. He disappeared from the division and was never traced again. On 30 June Major Otto Dickmann foolishly moved outside his bunker one morning without his helmet, and was caught by a shell splinter in the head which killed him instantly. There was some speculation among his comrades that Dickmann had lost the will to live, to commit such a suicidal act. It is difficult to imagine that he was stricken by remorse. But it is possible that he was exasperated by the inquiries being pursued into his actions. With his death, these could reasonably be allowed to lapse, to the relief of the Das Reich and, no doubt, of Army Group B.

The thirtieth was the day of Von Rundstedt's celebrated telephone conversation with Führer headquarters. Keitel asked: "What shall we do? What shall we do?" Von Rundstedt replied: "Make peace, you idiots—what else can you do?" and was replaced three days later. Did not even the SS now begin to feel that their lives were being sacrificed in a hopeless struggle? "Could we allow anyone to say that we were only willing to fight abroad, that we would not fight on in defence of our own country?" asked Weidinger. "The English would have done the same."

Wisliceny's regiment met sixty-four American attacks in eleven days, fifty-six of these without armored support. There was a chronic shortage of Pak anti-tank ammunition. The stench of dead cows made the forward positions almost intolerable in the summer heat. The men read, talked, and played chess and scat between attacks. Lammerding was wounded by a splinter in an air attack, and relinquished command of the division.

Major Heinrich Wulf's reconnaissance battalion went into action for the first time to reinforce the western flank against an American attack. A reserve infantry regiment was cracking under pressure. Three times Wulf and his men with their armored vehicles persuaded the infantry to move back into positions from which they had retreated, and three times they did so under intense shelling. On 8 July, Wulf reported to Stuckler that he had only 200 men left: "If we do this again, you'll be looking for a new CO." Stuckler brushed aside his fears. If they could simply restore the line once more, he promised Wulf, the battalion could be relieved. A few hours later, Wulf and his staff were at their headquarters in a dairy when a 105 mm shell blew off the roof, wounding almost every man in the building. A splinter severed the nerves in Wulf's left leg, while another tore off a finger. Wulf never fought again on the Western Front.

Only one man in three from the Das Reich Division came out of Normandy with his unit. They suffered terribly at Falaise, where among many others one of the hangmen of Tulle was blown up while asleep in a barn, beside a half-track load d with Teller mines which was hit. Fritz Langangke ended up swimming the Seine to escape, leaving his gunner and loader dead behind him. Otto Pohl was in his Panther when it was blown bodily from the road by a Wehrmacht anti-tank mine, killing his driver. "At Falaise," wrote Eisenhower, "the SS element fought to annihilation."

Not long after, Colonel Karl Kreutz was handed a signal by his adjutant announcing that he had been awarded the Knight's Cross. Kreutz remained expressionless. "Aren't you pleased?" asked his adjutant, puzzled. Kreutz pointed to the skyline, torn open by one of the great American bombardments. "Pleased? How can I be pleased? Look at that."

"For the first time," he said thirty-six years later, "I knew that we had lost."

The march of the Das Reich Division to Normandy began to achieve the status of a legend as early as 16 June 1944, when the daily Intelligence summary to SHAEF G-3 reported: "An organization in the field claims that Resistance succeeded in delaying the departure of 2 SS Pz Div for over a week. . . . The results achieved by the FFI have far surpassed those generally expected. Wherever armament is sufficient, they have displayed unity in action and a high fighting spirit."

"The movements of German formations to the battle area have tended to be slow on the whole," wrote the British War Office Director of Tactical Investigation in a report in August 1944. "In the south and south-west, the reason had been, for the most part, effective action on the part of French Resistance groups, while in the case of those divisions obliged to cross the line of the rivers SEINE and LOIRE, the hindrance has been bomb damage to bridges etc. . . ." The same report, turning to information derived from prisoner interrogation, gave the first hints of the troubles of the Das Reich on its journey northwards: "It is estimated that on this move, most elements took twice, and some thrice as long as the distance warranted. Considerable delay was caused to the rail party by the bridge at TOURS being damaged by bombing. On 7 June a company of the Panzer Grenadier Regt was attacked by partisans at SOUILLAC, and a similar incident occurred to this unit on 11 June. Casualties were suffered, and troops deployed to deal with the partisans. . . ."

After the Liberation, the story achieved a special place in the canon of Resistance. Characteristically, it was André Malraux's vision which scaled the highest peaks of rhetoric, when he delivered the oration at the tomb of Jean Moulin:

> Poor tortured king of the shades, see your shadowy people rising in the June night. . . . Listen to the roar of the German tanks moving up toward Normandy amidst the long-drawn out complaints of the awakened cattle; thanks to you, those tanks will not arrive in

time. . . . Look, fighters, at your own rabble crawling out of their oak *maquis* and with their peasant hands trained in the use of bazookas, holding up one of the foremost armored divisions of the Hitlerian empire—the Das Reich. . . .

For many years there has been a misunderstanding, that on 8 June 1944 the 2nd SS Panzer division left Montauban under orders to proceed immediately to Normandy. This was not so. There has also been an attempt to give solely to Resistance (or for that matter, by passionate advocates of air power, to the RAF and USAAF) the credit for the crippling of movement to Normandy. But as Churchill wrote in one of his most brilliant commentaries on the nature of war: "All things are always on the move simultaneously." It is impossible precisely to divide credit for Allied victory in Normandy between the Allied deception plans, the invading troops and their commanders, the blunders of the German High Command, the air forces and the achievements of Resistance.

French historians and former *résistants* have wildly exaggerated the material damage inflicted upon the Das Reich in action against *maquisards*. There is no reason to doubt the division's casualty return for 8–9 June—the days on which it was most heavily engaged—of seventeen killed and thirty wounded. Even adding Kampfe, Knug, Gerlach's driver and a generous allowance for Terrasson and other minor incidents on the road in the days that followed, it is easy to believe that the SS lost no more than thirty-five killed in all, out of some 15,000 men.

But casualties and material damage were never the matters at issue. The highest ambition of the Allied commanders before D-Day was that Resistance might unbalance the German forces in France, delay the passage of reinforcements and divert strength from the Normandy battle. In all these things the *résistants* of the Lot, Corrèze, Dordogne and Limousin succeeded. If the German decision to commit the Das Reich to a *ratissage* operation two days after the invasion was profoundly foolish, it was a decision to which they were goaded by Resistance. The *maquis* and the AS created a climate before and after D-Day which provoked the Germans to divert eight divisions— admittedly, as Professor Foot has said, their worst eight—to suppress the "terrorists."

The officers of the Das Reich today make light of their difficulties on the march, and the OKW War Diary professed that internal guerilla war in France after D-Day developed less dramatically than the staff had expected: "The terrorist movement which had already crippled parts of France before the invasion did not increase to the extent expected." But the scale of the German response and the almost hysterical note of some of the German signal traffic emanating from Army Group G belie these statements. SHAEF Intelligence wrote of the Das Reich's march from Montauban: "It has been estimated that on this movement, most elements took twice and some thrice as long as the distance warranted under favourable conditions." It is difficult to follow Professor Foot so far as to suggest that the arrival of the Das Reich in Normandy ten days earlier might have tipped the balance of the battle against the Allies, but it would certainly have made their task significantly harder. This book does not attempt to assess the overall achievement of Resistance. But it is useful to stress that its contribution to Allied victory in France must be judged chiefly by what it did in the first weeks after D-Day, and not by its later and more glamorous successes. Much nonsense has been written about the Resistance "Liberation" of cities and departments in August and September 1944. These achievements were generally made possible simply by German withdrawals. Most of the garrisons that surrendered to *assistants* were low-grade reserve troops, unlikely to be missed.

But the story of the Das Reich Division may have helped to demonstrate the courage—the often reckless sacrifice—with which the Resistance compensated for its lack of military skill. It is worth noting the total wartime casualties of *résistants* in Region R5, where most of the actions with the Das Reich were fought: Corrèze: 248 killed, 481 deported; Creuse: 123 killed, 190 deported; Dordogne, 771 killed, 308 deported; Haute-Vienne: 957 killed, 373 deported. Lest anyone should imagine that Oradour and Tulle were entirely isolated occurrences, the following numbers of hostages and prisoners were executed by the Germans: in and around Paris: 11,000; Lille: 1,113; Angers: 863; Orléans: 501; Reims: 353; Lyon: 3,673; Nice: 324; Limoges: 2,863—and so on across France. In all, 100,000 French men and women died in Resistance activities and German reprisals.

Because the FTP's ruthlessness and political objectives seemed so distasteful, I believe that they have been given insufficient credit for their contribution to Resistance's achievements. It was their relentless, widespread campaign of violence in the Corrèze and the Limousin before D-Day which provoked the Germans to dispatch the Das Reich. The restrained military policy of the *Armée Secrète* was more rational, and sought to spare the civil population from many terrible reprisals. But I believe that it contributed less to the climate of chaos which so exasperated the Germans around D-Day. When *résistants* embarked on major military operations—as admittedly the FTP attempted in Tulle—they usually failed, or provoked a catastrophe.They could never face crack trained troops. But when, in Jacques Poirier's perfectly apposite phrase, they simply set out to "make a mess," the Germans were often goaded beyond endurance. "Resistance is small business," said Macdonald Austin reflectively, recalling his Jedburgh experience. "Any attempt to make it anything more than that is bound to go wrong." General Dick Barry, Gubbins's former chief of staff, looked back on the entire effort of SOE/SO and said: "It was only just worth it."

But Barry was considering merely the military balance sheet. Much more than this, much more than the number of days that the *maquis* delayed the Das Reich, every man and woman who played his part and survived was exalted by the experience even through the terrible layer of pain. The great contribution of Resistance—that which justified all that SOE did and made worthwhile the sacrifice of all those who died—was toward the restoration of the soul of France.

There is one further matter upon which there should be some reflection here: the conduct of the Das Reich Division in southern France. It is ironic that, to find a ready historical parallel for the way in which Hitler's army sought to suppress Resistance in Occupied France, it is necessary to look back to the manner in which Massena's army dealt with the guerillas of Spain in 1808–9: "In Spain . . . the French military leadership responded as leadership always will. It resorted, when it seemed profitable, to terror," in the words of a modern historian. The French today display an undiminished reverence for the memory of Napoleon and his armies. Yet until the coming of Hitler no leader in modern European history had ruled conquered people with such savagery, or inflicted such misery.

Regular armies have always detested guerillas. In the Franco-Prussian War, some 58,000 French *franc-tireurs* killed around 1,000 Germans, and compelled the Prussians to deploy 120,000 men—a quarter of their army—to cover the lines of communication. "We are beating them down pitilessly," declared Bismarck. "They are not soldiers. We are treating them as murderers."

A British liberal historian, Thomas Arnold, wrote in 1842:

> The truth is, that if war, carried out by regular armies under the strictest discipline, is yet a great evil, an irregular partisan warfare is an evil ten times more intolerable; it is in fact to give licence to a whole population to commit all sorts of treachery, rapine and cruelty, without any restraint; letting loose a multitude of armed men, with none of the obedience and none of the honourable feelings of the soldier. . . .

Field-Marshal Bernard Montgomery, commanding the British 21st Army Group in 1944, was a Brigade-Major fighting the Irish guerillas in 1921. "My whole attention was given to defeating the rebels," he wrote, "and it never bothered me a bit how many houses were burned. Any civilian or Republican, soldier or policeman, who interferes with any officer or soldier is *shot at once.*"* Until domestic public opinion compelled them to rescind the order, the British employed a policy of Official Reprisals against the rebels, including the burning of houses of those who assisted them. General Maxwell executed the leaders of the 1916 uprising, and sent their followers to camps in England. "My own view," Montgomery reflected later on his Irish experience, "is that to win a war of that sort you must be ruthless; Oliver Cromwell, or the Germans, would have settled it in a very short time."

It is interesting that while General Eisenhower paid fulsome tribute to the contribution of the French *résistants* after the Liberation, Montgomery never displayed either interest in or respect for them. He always seemed to retain the regular soldier's distaste for irregulars, whatever cause they fought for." He might have felt a sneaking sympathy for those Wehrmacht officers who asked during the

---

* Montgomery's emphasis.

Occupation in France why, if it was just for the British to shoot Sinn Feiners in 1921, it was unacceptable for the Germans to shoot French *résistants* bearing arms when their own government had signed an armistice with Germany?

This, of course, was the professed opinion of the SS in France in 1944. It is worth recalling that not all their dreadful killings were illegal by the accepted usage of war. General Eisenhower could not reasonably expect the Germans to accept his broadcast demand that all captured *maquisards* be treated as prisoners of war. Historically, civilians in arms have always been liable to summary execution, whatever the Hague Convention may say in defense of those equipped with brassards or other distinguishing marks. The Das Reich was within its rights, for instance, to shoot the captured twenty-nine *résistants* on the road to Guéret; to hang the captured *maquisard* at Terrasson. The Germans were entitled to execute Violette Szabo and any other SOE agent who fell into their hands. It would be foolish to make too much of German looting—horrible though it was for the communities that had to endure it—when Allied forces were equally liable to appropriate anything not nailed down or within immediate sight of its owner. The Liberating armies were no more popular with civilians in many parts of France—above all, Normandy—than were the Occupiers, "levelling everything in front of them on the ground, towns, villages, monuments; and distributing to the civil population in the same breath chocolate and phosphorus shells," as Tillon wrote acidly.

Yet beyond all this, when every conceivable allowance has been made for the circumstances of war, the march of the Das Reich will always be remembered among the most dreadful episodes of World War II.

There is not a great deal that anyone other than a philosopher or a psychiatrist can say about the men who carried out the massacre at Oradour. To those with knowledge of Buchenwald and Auschwitz, it is not surprising that the leaders of the SS detachment, Dickmann and Kahn, were capable of ordering such an act. They were young men who since their earliest years had been imbued with the spirit of Nazism and of the SS. Dickmann was a product of a National Socialist cadet school, said by his comrades to have a pleasantly infectious laugh. Long before his operations on the road through the Dordogne on 8 June, he had commanded a *ratissage* (sweep operation) at Fraysinnat-le-Gelat, when the Das Reich was still quartered at Montauban; 400 civilians had been assembled in the central square in much the same fashion as at Oradour. A frightened old woman who fired a shotgun at the German intruders was hanged, along with the two nieces who shared her house. Their bodies were thrown into the flames when it had been fired. Ten hostages were chosen and shot, and when a father among them asked permission to embrace his fifteen-year-old son for the last time, the imaginative Kahn shot them together as they stood in each other's arms.

It seems almost certain that neither General Lammerding nor Colonel Stadler gave Dickmann an order that could be said to have authorized the destruction of Oradour. But throughout their years in the SS, Dickmann and his fellow-officers and NCOs had been shooting civilians as an almost routine exercise. On 3 February 1944, Field-Marshal Sperrle signed a notorious order to the Occupation forces in France, decreeing the most ruthless attitude to civilians at the slightest sign of attack or recalcitrance: "There will be an immediate return of fire . . . immediate burning down of the houses. . . . If thereby innocent people are hit that is regrettable, but entirely the fault of the terrorists." General Lammerding had issued repeated orders demanding savage reprisals in terrorist areas.

No authority had ever suggested to Dickmann or his colleagues that there was a precise moral and military limit, beyond which a certain number of executions or burnings became unacceptable. In Fraysinnat, Dickmann had killed thirteen people and this had been considered a proper performance of his duty. In Tulle, the division had hanged ninety-nine people without a single officer suggesting that this was unreasonable. Why should Dickmann have supposed that if he killed 642 people in Oradour, he would be considered to have exceeded his discretion?

It has been found surprising that Dickmann's soldiers, many of them young recruits, so readily carried out his terrible orders on 10 June. But many of these, too, had previous experience of shooting civilians, albeit in smaller numbers. Again and again it has been shown that the chief motive forces in war are the example of one's fellows, and the fear of revealing weakness before them. These were seen in the most grotesque form at Oradour. Even young Alsatians -half-countrymen of those they killed—found it easier to press their triggers alongside their comrades than to show revulsion or to flinch from the slaughter. Had they done so, they knew that it was possible -even probable—that they themselves would have been before a firing squad within hours. The SS made a fetish of toughness from the moment that a young recruit joined their ranks. It made them the most formidable fighting soldiers of World War II, and its perversion on such occasions as 10 June 1944 also made them the most detested. Again and again the SS showed that there were no limits to their concept of their own duty, or to their ruthlessness. I have made little in the account above about some of the more extraordinary stories told of Oradour: the baby said to have been burnt in the baker's oven, the breaking open of the champagne in the grocer's shop and the round of accordion music as the troopers waited for the fires to finish their work, the grazing horse left tethered to the outstretched arm of M. Poutaraud's corpse, because, as with all horrifying historical events, the story of Oradour was allowed to grow extravagant sideshoots and to develop its own emotional myths as the tale was told afterwards. I have omitted a number of stories and remarks which seem to bear the scent of retrospective garnishing. And yet all the evidence of SS history shows that the story of the baby in the oven could conceivably be true. Even thirty-seven years later, I find myself hoping desperately that it is not.

In the years after Oradour, countless acres of paper were filled and gallons of ink spilt in exploring the motives of the men who did these things. Even after so many other terrible tragedies that were inflicted upon France in World War II, this one developed a fascination of its own. I will quote only one passage from the trial at Bordeaux in 1953 of twenty-one men of Dickmann's company. Joseph Busch from Strasburg was a former Hitler Youth, forced by his father—an ardent Nazi—to join the Waffen SS in February 1944. He subsequently deserted from the Das Reich Division in Normandy in July.

"When we were one kilometre from Oradour, all the officers and NCOs were called forward to Major Dickmann and Captain Kahn, from whom they got instructions."

"What instructions?" asked the Court President.

"We couldn't hear what was said. But some papers were passed to them."

"Then what?"

"My squad drove directly to the market place. We picked up the people we met along the way, and then we helped separate them into groups and stood guard over them. I was there when a group was led off to Desourteaux' barn. We had orders to shoot when Captain Kahn fired his pistol."

"And then you fired?"

"Yes, Herr President—three or four times."

"You obeyed orders like a machine, like a mechanism that someone else operates?"

"Yes, Herr President."

"Then what happened?"

"Well, people fell over."

"Yes, but what did you do next?"

"Well, then we threw the timber and brushwood in on top of the people."

"Were these people still alive?"

"Well, they may have been, Herr President. I didn't pay too close attention. . . . I was not especially interested."

"Then you started the fire?"

"Yes, sir, Herr President."

"All in accordance with orders?"

"Yes, sir, Herr President."

"Then what?"

"We were ordered to go to the church, where I was placed on guard duty."

"Did you see anything there?"

"Yes. Two women came looking for their children. We told them to get out of there, or they'd be shot. But then Sergeant Boos and a German came along. They dragged the women into a barn and shot them."

It is important to remember that if Oradour was an exceptionally dreadful occurrence during the war in the West, it was a trifling sample of what the German Army had been doing on a national scale during the war in the East, since 1941. Of Russia's 20 million war dead, a countless number were killed during massacres as terrible as Oradour.

Russia was where Otto Dickmann had learnt his soldiering, and become accustomed to the manner in which Hitler's Germany fought its wars.

To emphasize this, it is worth reporting a conversation that I had with an SS officer—of the Death's Head, not of the Das Reich Division—while writing this book. He told me that, long after the war, he met a fellow SS veteran who had taken part in the destruction of Oradour. The other man spoke of his astonishment about the international uproar which followed the revelation of the massacre. Speaking as one old SS man to another, said Dickmann's officer confidentially, ". . . in our circle, Herr Muller, it was *nothing.*"

General Lammerding's defense of his own and of his division's conduct, made after the war to his former subordinate Colonel Weidinger, is worth quoting only for the record:

> It was necessary to provoke terror among the *maquisards* to deprive them of the support of the civil population. The remedial method was cruel, but it was war, and I do not know any army in the world which would have done otherwise in a similar situation. . . . I assume that it is useless to recall that the Geneva Convention formally forbids the actions of *franc-tireurs*, and warns that all will be shot. I assume that it is equally useless to recall that General Sperrle . . . had given precise instructions for reprisals to be carried out in areas where the civil population attacked the German military. . . . It was a matter of life or death for the German Army, and I approve of Dickmann's action in shooting the men and burning the houses in which *maquisards* had hidden, or in which arms and ammunition had been stored, conforming to the orders of General Sperrle. But Dickmann also left several hundred women and children to burn in the church, and that I cannot accept. It was a crime. I recognize it.

Curiously enough, at the time of a post-war trial, a Frenchman was among those who considered the guilt of the Das Reich with most sympathy. In a long, carefully reasoned essay in *Monde Nouveau* in March 1953, Pierre Boisseau wrote:

> It is impossible to say that Oradour was "useless." Let us recall a few facts: on 6 June 1944 the Allies landed on the coast of Normandy. The

2nd SS Das Reich . . . received the order to move toward the enemy.
They were delayed for four days on their march by incessant guerilla
attack by a clandestine army, ubiquitous, impossible to engage,
which caused explosions, hit outposts, cut communications. . . .
This division defended itself by the only available means which
would act quickly and effectively against the partisans: they took
reprisals on such a scale as to convince everyone that any further
operation would be to the disadvantage of those who attempted it.
We know today that the terrifying example of Oradour added to
that of Tulle prevented a surely successful attack that the *maquis*
had planned on Limoges. We may assume that it also prevented
many other *coups de main*.

. . . From two points of view one must choose one: either all
violence is always part of the one vast unity—thus, there is no longer
any question of war crimes. There is the crime of war which begins
with the mere bearing of arms. All recourse to force is forbidden
and punishable.

. . . Alternatively, two or several sovereign states employ violence
against each other, and thus the ruins of Oradour are paid for by
those of Berlin, Dresden, Hamburg, by the labour of prisoners
of war, by the political division of Germany, by the dismantled
factories, by Occupation, by the children of France well-fed in the
Black Forest, by a certain number of summary executions, by the
last mopping-up operations of the war.

It might have been worthwhile to offer, in 1945, to all those
gentlemen dressed in black who are presiding at the Oradour trial,
a trip to Germany. They would have seen enough ruins, widows,
orphans to assess sufficient reparations and return with dry eyes.

In short, could the bombers of Dresden justly try the destroyers of
Oradour? But that is a dilemma of morality, not of history, which I am
grateful to be able to leave the reader to resolve.

CHAPTER 13

Afterwards

MOST OF THE SURVIVORS of the Das Reich Division were in Hungary or Austria when the war ended, still fighting alongside such flotsam of the Third Reich as a unit of Dresden firefighters, who said that there was nothing useful left for them to do at home. Some of the SS reacted to news of the surrender like Ernst Krag's wireless operator, who put one pistol bullet into his set and a second into his own head. Many others began an epic struggle to fight their way alone across Europe to their families—and out of the path of the Russians. Most were rounded up by the Allies and imprisoned. The French, naturally, claimed most survivors of the Das Reich, and several hundred were held in the prison ships at Bordeaux until the late forties or early fifties, awaiting trial or release. Otto Pohl, the young tank officer, found himself acting as assistant to the prison dentist, Captain Reichmann, late of the 95th Security Regiment in Tulle. Pohl's father, the SS Inspector-General of Concentration Camps, was hanged at Nuremberg.

The war crimes trials of the 2nd SS Panzer Division, when they were finally held in 1951 and 1953, proved unsatisfactory to everyone concerned. Twenty-one NCOs and men of the 1st battalion of the Der Führer were indicted for their part in the massacre at Oradour. But Dickmann was dead, and Kahn could not be found. More senior officers such as Stadler were never tried.

Even more embarrassing from the French point of view, fourteen of the accused were Alsatian. A formidable protest movement was launched in Alsace, so lately and uneasily reunited with France. The Alsatians castigated the French Government for permitting the trial of young men whom they considered almost as much the victims of Nazism as the dead of Oradour. Six of the fourteen had surrendered to the British in Normandy and told everything they knew about the massacre. Two had subsequently served with the French Army in Indochina.

On 12 February 1953, after weeks of horrifying evidence, the Military Tribunal at Bordeaux delivered its verdict. An Alsatian volunteer named Sergeant Boos was sentenced to death; nine other Alsatians received hard labor and four prison terms, none exceeding eight years. A German warrant officer, Lenz, was sentenced to death. One German was acquitted and the remaining five received prison terms of ten to twelve years. Forty-two other Germans were sentenced to death *in absentia*. France was racked by the storm that now followed—first from the relatives and survivors of Oradour, outraged by the leniency of the sentences, and second from the people of Alsace-Lorraine, convinced that their young men were being made scapegoats.

It was all too much for a French government struggling weakly to re-create national unity. All the Alsatians except Boos were amnestied. Both death sentences were commuted. Five of the seven Germans sentenced were repatriated at once, having already served more than their time while awaiting trial.

Only three people were available for trial for their part in the hangings at Tulle: Major Heinrich Wulf, the hangman Otto Hoff, and the interpreter Paulette Geissler. The defense—the only conceivable defense—was that the executions were an unfortunate but justifiable act of war. Private Schneid gave evidence of his own role, and felt that the court missed the point. He demanded of the official interpreter: "'Ask the court if they knew what an order was in the German Army... ! He told me that he could do nothing about it, that justice must take its course." Wulf was sentenced to ten years, Hoff to life, Geissler to three years. All were set free within a matter of months, in 1952.

If the leniency of the courts in 1951 and 1953 seems remarkable, it is necessary to remember the mood of the time. The world had been sated with international justice and ritual retribution at Nuremberg. There was growing doubt and uncertainty about matters of absolute right and wrong, when the Russians had been allowed to sit in judgment on the Germans for barbarities which scarcely rivaled their own. There was a sense that somewhere, the search for the guilty must stop, that the time had come to look forward, rather than forever back. Above all, perhaps, there was the embarrassing knowledge that the most notorious figures had not come before the Tribunal. General Lammerding and Major Kowatsch were sentenced to death *in absentia*. Some SS men claimed that Kowatsch had died in Normandy. But it was well known that Lammerding was alive and well and building a prosperous engineering business in Dusseldorf. He sent a sworn statement to the Military Tribunal during the Oradour trial, before taking temporary refuge in Schleswig-Holstein. He then moved to the American zone until the hunt for his life had abated, and finally returned to Dusseldorf where he remained in prosperous security until his death in 1971. The British would take no action to extradite Lammerding or other wanted Nazis to France "unless there is incontestable evidence that the accused has committed murder." In Lammerding's case, there was thought to be doubt.

Most of the Das Reich officers who survived the war are today prosperous and vigorous men for their age: Weidinger, Stadler, Wulf, Stuckler, Krag and Kreutz—to name only the most senior. They keep in regular contact with each other, and argue with fierce passion that there is nothing in their wartime service for which they have cause to reproach themselves.

Most of the survivors of Resistance have also prospered. In the years after the war, a record as a prominent local *résistant* proved a passport to commercial and professional success for many Frenchmen (although it is interesting to notice how many Vichy officials were able to continue their careers uninterrupted by the Liberation). Over the years it has been forgotten who joined Resistance in the dark days of 1942 and 1943, and who came hastily to the cause in June and July 1944.

But it should also be remembered that some Frenchmen still harbor a bitter private hatred for the *maquis*. One afternoon in June 1980, I sat in a pleasant house in the Dordogne hearing an elderly *vicomtesse* (viscountess) explode with passion about her memories of the depredations and murders allegedly committed by local *maquisards*. I heard of a priest in Brive, not many days later, who rendered great assistance to Resistance *by* bearing messages and concealing explosives. After the war, it is said that he was denied a bishopric because the church hierarchy so vividly remembered his activities during the Occupation.

After the Liberation, Prince Michel de Bourbon was summoned hastily to the *chateau* of one of his relations on the Loire, which the local Resistance were ransacking on the grounds that its owner had been a collaborator. De Bourbon, in uniform, produced his credentials, signed personally by De Gaulle. He demanded that they desist. Their leader tore up the letter, imprisoned him in a barn and promised to shoot him the next day. De Bourbon was fortunate to escape during the night.

Jacques Poirier was summoned equally urgently from Paris one day after the Liberation, by a prominent Limoges businessman who had provided Poirier with a safe house for many months, while posing as a collaborator. Now, George Guingouin's men had promised to kill him. Poirier arrived in Limoges too late to prevent the blowing-up of the man's garage business, but in time to save his life by some very tough talking to Guingouin and his cohorts.

There was a terrible national settling of scores in the months following the Liberation. M. Robert Aron suggests a total of more than 20,000 summary executions, most of them the work of former *résistants*. Simply to have served in the Resistance was not enough to provide safety in many regions—it was necessary to have been with the right faction.

Among the most prominent characters in this book, Jean-Jacques Chapou, who led the FTP attack on Tulle, was killed in action a few weeks later. Lieutenant Walter Schmald was captured by *résistants* in July and shot—some say more painfully killed. Soleil, Georges Guingouin and Robert Noireau are all alive, after quarrelling for years after 1945 with the French communist party. Violette Szabo was shot at Ravensbruck concentration camp early in 1945. Anastasie was killed in Indochina. Harry Peulevé survived Buchenwald.

Maurice Buckmaster became a successful businessman. George Hiller took up the diplomatic career that he had promised himself before the war, and served as a British ambassador before his death in 1973. Jacques Poirier and Peter Lake accepted the surrender of Brive in August 1944, while George Starr drove into Toulouse with his *maquisards* as the Germans abandoned it. Poirier became an oil company executive, retiring in 1980. He now lives with his beautiful wife in a delightful flat in Paris. André Malraux, of course, became De Gaulle's Minister of Culture before his death. Baron Philippe de Gunzbourg still lives in enviable splendor, and has not lost his affection for Britain, while lamenting her decline. Peter Lake and the late George Starr became consular officials. In 1945, Starr had the satisfaction of entertaining to lunch his former commanding officer from the days when he was sergeant in charge of Phantom's pigeons in 1940. His CO had finished the war as a major. Starr was a colonel. Several other members of the French Section transferred to the Secret Intelligence Service after the war. It would be tactless to say which.

René Jugie lives in a large house on the edge of Brive crammed with documents on Resistance and such sentimental keepsakes as a gammon grenade, detonator and Schmeisser sub-machine gun. Marius Guedin retired from the French Army as a general. The Verlhacs are dead, but the Brus are still in the enchanting village of St. Céré, and Odette Bach and her family prosper in Souillac.

Prince Michel de Bourbon was parachuted into Indochina in 1945, handed over to the Vietminh by the Japanese, and held prisoner until he escaped and walked for weeks through the jungle to Thailand. He now lives in a house at Versailles lavishly decorated with photographs of his relations among the royal families of Europe. Tommy Macpherson transferred immediately from France after the Liberation to further adventures in the Italian campaign. "Mac" Austin lives on Hilton Head island, South Carolina. His wireless operator, Jack Berlin, is an ordained Baptist minister.

John Tonkin of the SAS travelled compulsively after the war, and took part in an expedition to Antarctica with Paddy Mayne, who later died of a heart attack. Tonkin is now a businessman in Australia. Sam Smith runs a cafe in Liverpool. John Fielding is an estate agent in Norwich. Peter Weaver lives in retirement on the south coast. Amédée Maingard built a large business in his native Mauritius before his death in 1980. Almost all those named above were decorated for their deeds in 1944.

The ruins of Oradour–sur–Glane have been preserved as they lay on 10 June 1944, a French national monument. A sadly drab new village has been built near by, in which, astonishingly enough, Mme. Rouffranche chose to spend the rest of her life.

In the town of Tulle, on 9 June each year a visitor will notice garlands hanging from many balconies and lamp posts. This is not a gesture to decorate the streets. Each one marks the spot upon which a citizen of Tulle was hanged by the Das Reich Division in 1944. Tulle has not forgotten, even though each year now a great army of German tourists passes through the Dordogne and Corrèze; as far as anyone can observe, without a hint of self-consciousness.

Appendix A

2 SS-PZ Division
Das Reich

Order of the Day

Divisional HQ
9 June 1944

The Position with Regard to Guerilla Bands and Tactics for
Combatting Them

1. The guerillas have occupied the area Figeac–Clermont–Ferrand–
Limoges–Gourdon which, until now, has only been weakly held by
German troops. The *maquis* who have appeared there have exclusively
communistic tendencies. The small number of *Armée Secrète* are also
communists and are also to be treated as gangs *[Banden]*. All instructions, orders, etc. should aim to incite the civilian population against
these guerilla bands and make our action appear protective. The threat
from these gangs can have the most far-reaching consequences if we
are unable to instill it into the minds of the population that these men
have no national feeling, and also impress upon them that they are
nothing more than highway robbers. On the other hand, it is necessary
that our own troops behave in such a way that the civilian population
is convinced of our good intentions and also of the character of our
Division as an elite formation. Looting will, if necessary, be prevented
by force. In every case regimental or battalion commanders will decide

what is to be done with captured material. Standing orders regarding dress, behavior on vehicles, maximum speed, maintenance of vehicles, remain in force. To minimize casualties, personnel will remain seated in recce cars.

2. The following special instructions are laid down:
   a. Curfew from 2100 to 0600 hours. Handing in of all arms under threat of death penalty. Orders concerning the provision of supplies are to be enforced in all places.
   b. The mayor and police are to be reinstated in all areas and will be made personally responsible for carrying out orders.
   c. Houses from which shots have been fired, together with the neighboring houses, will, in every instance, be burned to the ground.
   d. Captured documents will not be destroyed but will be handed in to the Division.
   e. Persons whose participation in Resistance is undoubted will be treated as criminals. It may be a good idea to throw them in irons in the sight of civilian population.
   f. The inhabitants of every community will be assembled together for a count, and will be treated during this process as prisoners.
   g. In every instance units will hold the following as prisoners:
   All men who have reached the area only a short time ago.
   All men whose identity cards or worker's cards are obviously faked.
   All those who can be proved to be members of gangs.
   After examination, the men should generally be released. Prisoners should be handed over to the local army establishments concerned with the movement of workers to the Reich, for employment there (via Limoges and Montauban).
   h. In all cases attempts at escape must be made more difficult by removing the men's braces etc. Permanent and adequate pickets must be established. Whenever possible, rooms on the first floors of houses should be used. Windows will be nailed up. The local mayor must be made responsible for supplying food to prisoners.
   i. Executions are to be carried out on the order of regimental or other commanders by hanging, only in such places where guerilla units fight to hold up our troops or commit atrocities (shameful treatment of wounded or dead, use of dum-dum bullets, etc.). As

a rule, the proportion to be applied is as follows:

For every wounded soldier . . . 3 guerillas

For every dead soldier . . . 10 guerillas

j. Executions are in no way a public spectacle, but a punitive measure. Troops must therefore be kept at a distance until the order for the execution is carried out. Orders should be given at short notice to detail men for execution squads, and a public announcement should be made, Priests may attend executions and carry out their religious functions, provided these are not of a demonstrative character (this is very important in France).

3. Operations:

Guerilla units are highly mobile and can withdraw quickly. The only effective tactic against this is to surround and surprise them, working round their flanks and rear while pinning them in front by fire. Their objective is invariably to pick off isolated soldiers and to seize weapons and supplies. Operations which fail because inadequate forces are employed should be avoided. It is vital to ensure that German soldiers do not fall into the hands of guerillas because of careless security measures on the march, or when men are acting as couriers or sentries.

Appendix B

PRINCIPAL WEAPONS OF THE *MAQUIS* AND THE 2ND SS PANZER DIVISION

The Maquis

The Bren: (Fig. 1) by general consent the finest light machine gun in the world of its period, and the most useful weapon provided to the *maquis*. A .303 gas-operated gun fed by a 30-round magazine, it was accurate up to 1,000 meters, and could withstand immense maltreatment and unskilled use. *Résistants* were constantly pleading for maximum drops of Brens.

The Sten: (Fig. 2) the standard British sub-machine gun of the war, a 9 mm blowback-operated gun fed by a 32-round magazine. The Sten was

Fig. 1

Fig. 2

highly unreliable, prone to jamming, and inaccurate beyond 30 meters. It was unsuitable for guerilla operations in open country because it encouraged waste of ammunition, and was useless at average battle range. But it was easy and cheap to produce—a gun was said to cost fifteen shillings—and was supplied to the Resistance in huge quantities.

The Gammon grenade: an improvised hand-thrown bomb used by the Home Guard, the Special Air Service and the Resistance, especially suitable for the destruction of aircraft or vehicles. An explosive charge was wrapped in fabric and sewn to an impact fuse that detonated on sharp contact.

Resisters were also supplied with large quantities of British and captured Italian rifles of varying efficiency; revolvers and automatic pistols; the British 36 grenade—the Mills bomb—the standard anti-personnel shrapnel weapon; and modest quantities of plastic explosive. They also made extensive use of French Army rifles and light machine guns, mainly stolen or retained from Armistice Army stocks, and captured German 9 mm Schmeisser SMGs. One of the most serious problems for all Resistance groups was the disparate range of arms for which ammunition had to be found.

Fig. 3

Fig. 4

Fig. 5

2nd SS Panzer Division

The Panther V, (Fig. 3) of which the Das Reich had an establishment of 62 in 1944, was one of the outstanding battle tanks of the war. Weighing almost 45 tons, with a crew of 5 and a 75 mm gun, it was first introduced in 1942 as a counter to the Russian T-34. It remained at the forefront of German armored units until the end of the war.

The *Panzer IV*, (Fig. 4) of which the DR had an establishment of 64, was the most widely produced German tank of the war. It weighed 23 tons, with a maximum road speed of 25 mph against the 34 mph of the Panther. By the opening of the Normandy campaign, the *Panzer IV* was obsolescent, but from necessity the Germans continued to use it extensively. The upgunned version, with a 75 mm gun, remained a very powerful weapon.

The *Sturmgeschutz III* (Fig. 5). This self-propelled assault gun, with which one battalion of the DR was equipped, was essentially a turretless tank, constructed upon the chassis of the *Panzer III* tank. Armed with a 75 mm gun, it provided close fire support for the infantry. Although produced principally as a "poor man's tank," a cheap substitute when attrition on the Eastern Front began to destroy armor faster than Germany's factories could make *Panthers* and *Panzer IVs*, the *Sturmgeschiitz*, with its low silhouette that provided a difficult target for enemy tanks, and its heavy armor and hitting power, was a formidable weapon.

The armored half-track personnel carrier, (Fig. 6) universally known within the German Army as the SPW, was produced in scores of variants. An armored division such as the Das Reich possessed more than 300 of them, some mounted with mortars, 75 mm anti-tank guns or flamethrowers, others armed only with machine guns, for use as infantry personnel earners.

The *Schwerer Panzerspahwagen* (Fig. 7) was armed with a 20 mm cannon, carried a crew of 4 and possessed a maximum speed of more than 50 mph. The DR's *Aufklärungsabteilung* possessed one company of these armored cars.

In addition to the above armored vehicles, the DR possessed a further armored battalion of *Panzerjaeger* self-propelled anti-tank guns, 4 battalions of self-propelled guns and howitzers, 1 self-propelled antiaircraft gun battalion, and some 50 towed flak and field guns. The division had a total establishment of more than 3,000 vehicles, 359 of them armored, in addition to the tanks.

Fig. 6   *Fig. 7*

2nd SS Panzer Division Das Reich, Spring 1944

Div. HQ
    8 x M/C
    32 vehicles
    141 men

SS-Pz Regt 2
    62 X PzKw V
    64 X PzKw IV
    8 x 3.7 em Flak
    6 X 20 mm Flak
    53 X M /C
    313 vehicles
    2,401 men

SS-Pz—Gren Regt 3 "Deutschland"
    88 x M/C
    6 x 15 em G/H
    12 x 10.5 em G/H
    24 X F/T
    12 x 12 cm Mor
    527 vehicles
    3,242 men

SS-Pz Art Regt 2
    12 x 17 em G/H
    6 X 15 em SPG
    12 x 15 em G/H
    12 x 10.5 em SPG
    12 x 10.5 em G /H
    40 X M/C
    534 vehicles
    2,167 men

SS-PZ Jäg Abt 2
    31 x 7.5 em SPG
    12 x Pak 40
    17 X M/C
    135 vehicles
    513 men

SS-Recce Abt 2
    13 x 7.5 cm SPG
    35 X 20 mm Pak
    6 X F/T
    22 X M/C
    193 vehicles
    942 men

SS Pi Abt 2
    3 x 20/28 mm Pak
    3 x 20 mm Pak
    20 x F/T
    52 X M/C
    212 vehicles
    984 men

SS-Sig Abt 2
    14 X M/C
    114 vehicles
    515 men

SS-Pz-Gren Regt 4 "Der Führer"
    As above

SS-Flak Abt 2
    12 X 8.8 cm
    18 x 20 mm
    16 X M/C
    181 vehicles
    824 men

SS-StuG Abt 2
    30 x StuG III/IV
    11 x M /C
    100 vehicles
    344 men

SS—NblW Abt 2
    18 X NblW
    8 X M/C
    107 vehicles
    473 men

Abbreviations

Pz = Panzer

M/C = motorcycles

men = officers, NCOs and men

Regt = Regiment

Abt = Abteilung (Battalion)

Pz = Panzer Grenadier

G/H = Gun/Howitzer

F/T = Flamethrower

Mor = Mortar

Art = Artillery

SPG = Self-propelled gun

NblW = Nebelwerfer

StuG = Sturmgeschütz

Reece = Reconnaissance

Pi = Pioneer

Sig = Signals

Note: These figures are for the division at full establishment. In June 1944 the DR's vehicle strength was substantially lower. Excluded are medical and MP units, etc.

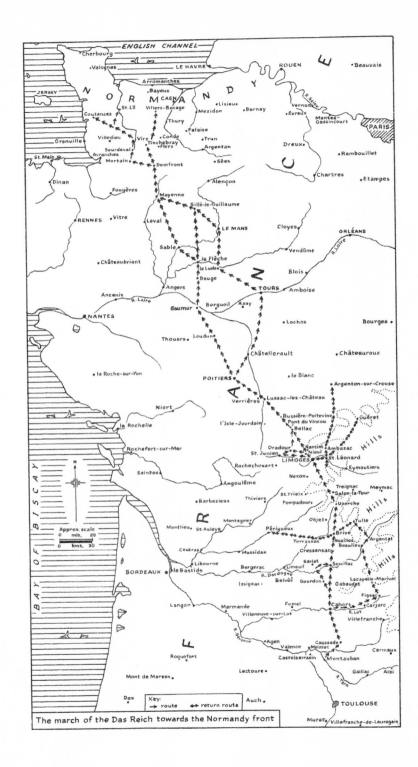

The march of the Das Reich towards the Normandy front

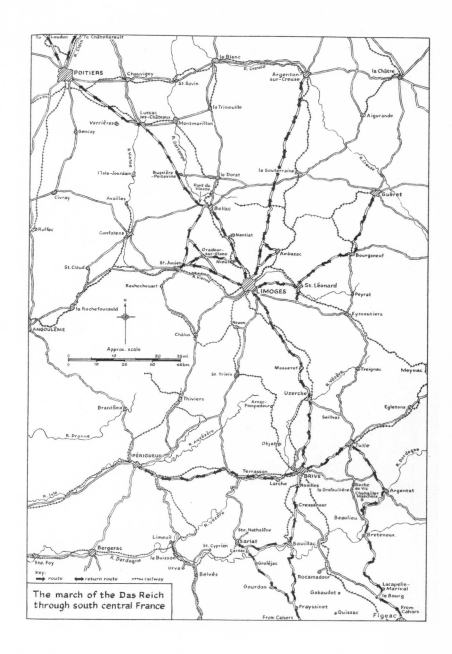

To Loudun · To Châtellerault
R. Clain
To Châtellerault
POITIERS
Chauvigny
le Blanc
R. Creuse
Argenton-sur-Creuse
la Châtre
St. Savin
la Trimouille
Aigurande
Lussac-les-Châteaux
Verrières
Montmorillon
Gençay
R. Vienne
R. Gartempe
R. Creuse
l'Isle-Jourdain
Bussière-Poitevine
le Dorat
la Souterraine
GUÉRET
Civray
Availles
Pont du Vincou
Bellac
Ruffec
Confolens
Nantiat
Oradour-sur-Glane
Ambazac
Bourganeuf
St. Claud
St. Junien
Nieule
Rochechouart
R. Vienne
LIMOGES
St. Léonard
Peyrat
la Rochefoucauld
Eymoutiers
ANGOULÊME
Châlus
Nexon
Approx. scale
0   10   20   25ml.
0   10   20   30   40km.
St. Trieix
Masseret
R. Vézère
Treignac
Meymac
Thiviers
Uzerche
Egletons
Brantôme
Arnac-Pompadour
Seilhac
R. Dronne
R. Auvézère
Objat
Tulle
R. Dordogne
PÉRIGUEUX
Terrasson
Larche
BRIVE
Noailles
Roche de Vic
Chehailler Mascheix
Argentat
R. Isle
la Grafouillère
Cressensac
Beaulieu
R. Vézère
Ste. Nathalène
Bretenoux
Limeuil
SARLAT
Souillac
St. Cyprien
Carsac
Bergerac
le Buisson
Urva
Groléjac
Rocamadour
Lacapelle-Marival
Ste. Foy
R. Dordogne
Belvès
le Bourg
Gourdon
Gabaudet
Figeac
Frayssinet
Quissac
From Cahors
From Cahors

key:
→ route   ⇒ return route   ⊢⊢⊢ railway

The march of the Das Reich through south central France

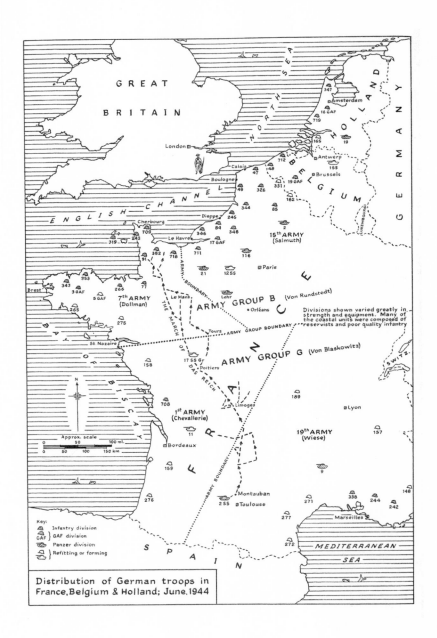

Key:
Infantry division
GAF division
Panzer division
Refitting or forming

Distribution of German troops in
France, Belgium & Holland; June, 1944

Bibliography

and a Note on Sources

THE PRINCIPAL SOURCES for this book have been interviews with the survivors of those whose story it is. Some inner files of SOE remain closed in perpetuity, but I am grateful to the Foreign Office archivist, Colonel E. G. Boxshall, for providing the answers to certain specific questions from these records, and above all for copies of the relevant Jedburgh team after-action reports. The German Army's archives at Freiburg supplied the surviving relevant signal traffic and situation reports from the War Diaries of Army Group G, 66th Reserve Corps and 58th Corps. The Public Record Office contains many of the files of Special Forces HQ, G-3 SHAEF and the SAS Regiment, including the reports and signal logs of Bulbasket. I have made extensive use of scores of regional Resistance publications, especially the journal *R4*. Baron Philippe de Gunzbourg loaned me a copy of his unpublished memoir *Souvenirs du Sud-Ouest*. Mrs. Judith Hiller allowed me to read and hear the marvelous notes and tapes that her husband George made for his unwritten memoir.

The books listed below are not a comprehensive guide to Resistance literature, which would be enormous, but a selection of those which I have found most helpful. Their inclusion is not an indication of merit—indeed some are wildly inaccurate—but merely a guide to their relevance.

ANON, *Dordogne martyre*, Paris, 1945.

ANON, *Maquis de Corrèze*, Paris, 1975.

ANON, *Memorial de La Résistance et des victimes du nazisme en Haute-Vieme*, Limoges, 1975.

ARON, Robert, *De Gaulle Before Paris*, Putnam, 1963.

——, *De Gaulle Triumphant*, Putnam, 1964.

ASTIER DE LA VIGERIE, Emmanuel d', *Les Dieux et les Hommes*, Paris, 1952.

BEAU AND GAUBUSSEAU, *R5: Les SS en Limousin, Périgord et Quercy*, Paris, 1969.

BECK, Philip, *Oradour*, Leo Cooper, 1979.

BENNETT, Ralph, *Ultra in the West*, Hutchinson, 1979.

BERGERET AND GREGOIRE, *Messages Personnels*, Bordeaux, 1945.

BEST, Geoffrey, *Humanity in Warfare*, Weidenfeld and Nicolson, 1980.

BROGAN, D. W., *Development of Modern France 1870–1939*, Hamish Hamilton, 1940.

BUCKMASTER, Maurice, *They Fought Alone*, Odhams, 1958.

CALMETTE, A., *Les Equipes Jedburgh dans la Bataille de France*, Paris, 1966.

CAVE-BROWN, Anthony, *Bodyguard of Lies*, W. H. Allen, 1976.

CHURCHILL, Peter, *Of Their Own Choice*, Hodder, 1952.

COLBY, William, *Honourable Men*, Hutchinson, 1978.

COOKRIDGE, E. H., *Inside SOE*, Arthur Barker, 1966.

COOPER, Matthew, *The German Army 1933–1945*, Macdonald and Janes, 1976.

——, *The Phantom War*, Macdonald and Janes, 1979.

DELARUE, Jacques, *Trafics et Crimes sous l'Occupation*, Paris, 1968.

DURAND, P., *Histoire de SNCF pendant la Guerre*, Paris, 1968.

EHRLICH, Blake, *The French Resistance*, Chapman & Hall, 1966.

FARRAN, Roy, *Winged Dagger*, Collins, 1948.

FOOT, M.R.D., *Resistance*, Eyre Methuen, 1976.

——, *Six Faces of Courage*, Eyre Methuen, 1978.

——, *SOE in France*, HMSO, 1966.

GUICHETAU, Gerard, *La Das Reich et le Coeur de la France*, Paris, 1974.

GUINGOUIN, Georges, *Quatre Ans de Lutte sur le Sol Limousin*, Paris, 1974.

HARRISON, D.I., *Such Men are Dangerous*, Cassell, 1957.

HARRIS SMITH, R., *OSS: The History of America's First CIA*, University of California, 1972.

HINSLEY, F.H., *British Intelligence in World War II*, HMSO, 1979.

HISLOP, John, *Anything but a Soldier*, Michael Joseph, 1965.

KRUUSE, Jens, *Madness at Oradour*, Seeker and Warburg, 1969.

LACOUTURE, Jean, *André Malraux*, Deutsch, 1975.

LANGELAAN, George, *Knights of the Floating Silk*, Hutchinson, 1959.

MACKSEY, Kenneth, *The Partisans of Europe in World War II*, Hart-Davis MacGibbon, 1975.

MALRAUX, André, *Antimémoires*

MICHEL, Henri, *Histoire de la Résistance en France*, Paris, 1972.

——, *The Shadow of War: Resistance in Europe 1939–45*, Deutsch, 1972.

MILLAR, George, *Maquis*, Heinemann, 1956.

MINNEY, R. J., *Carve Her Name with Pride*, Newnes, 1956.

MORGAN, William, *The OSS and I*, New York, 1957.

MOUNTFIELD, David, *The Partisans*, Hamlyn, 1979.

NOGUERES, Henri, *Histoire de la Résistance en France*, Paris, 1968–75.

NOIREAU, Robert, *Le Temps des partisans*, Paris, 1978.

PASSY, Colonel, *Souvenirs: 2me Bureau, Londres*, Monte Carlo, 1947.

——, *Souvenirs: 10 Duke Street*, Monte Carlo, 1947.

——, *Souvenirs: Missions secrètes*, Paris, 1951.

PAXTON, Robert, *Vichy France*, Barrie and Jenkins, 1980.

QUAY, Bruce, *Das Reich*, Osprey, 1978.

REMY AND BOURDELLE, *Les Balcons de Tulle*, Paris, 1963.

SCHNEID, Sadi, *Beutedeutscher*, Askania, 1979.

SCHRAMM, Percy (editor), *The OKW War Diaries*, 4 vols., Frankfurt, 1961.

SHULMAN, Milton, *Defeat in the West*, Heinemann, 1963.

SOULIER, A., *Le Drame de Tulle*, Tulle, 1971.

SPEIDEL, Hans, *We Defended Normandy*, Herbert Jenkins, 1953.

STEIN, George, *The Waffen SS at War*, Oxford, 1966.

TERRAINE, John, *The Smoke and the Fire*, Sidgwick and Jackson, 1980.

TILLON, C., *Les FTP*, Paris, 1962.

TROUILLE, Pierre, *Journal d'un Préfet pendant l'Occupation*

VOMÉCOURT, Philippe de, *Who Lives to See the Day*

WALTERS, Anne-Marie, *Moondrop to Gascony*, Macmillan, 1946.

WARNER, Philip, *The Special Air Service*, Kimber, 1972.

WEIDINGER, Otto, *Kameraden bis zum Ende*, Oldendorf, 1978.

WHITE, Frieda, *Three Rivers of France*, Faber, 1952.

ZUCKERMAN, S., *From Apes to Warlords*, Hamish Hamilton, 1978.

Notes and References

p. 1   Some 15,000 men and 209 tanks: The division's total strength on 6 June 1944 was just over 19,000 officers and men. Of these more than 15,000—it is impossible to be more precise—moved north on 8 June. The balance were either in Germany collecting new equipment, or remained at Montauban for training or local security duties. All elements were reunited in Normandy by early July.

p. 1   Professor M.R.D. Foot wrote: *SOE in France* pp. 397, 399

p. 9   Adolf Hitler and his staff discussed: see *Hitler's Führerconferences*, OUP 1950

p. 12   A British Intelligence assessment: PRO (Public Record Office) W0218/114

p. 13   It was a terrible mistake: Weidinger, *Kameraden bis zum Ende*

p. 14   "The military significance . . .": Stein, *The Waffen SS*, p. 288

p. 16   "They laughed at our rags . . .": Author interview with Fritz Langangke, 23 April 1980

p. 16   "Our only concern . . .": Author interview with Heinrich Wulf, 21 April 1980

p. 17   "They were so intelligent . . .": Langangke *loc. cit.*

p. 17   "We asked him his unit . . .": Author interview with Otto Pohl, 23 April 1980

p. 18   Every *résistant* is a terrorist to his enemies, a guerilla to his allies. I have used each word according to the perspective from which the relevant passage is written.

p. 18   "We thought of the Americans . . .": Langangke *loc. cit.*

p. 20   "was in a state . . . : Quoted Stein *op. cit.* p. 271

p. 22   "After all, Lammerding . . .": Author telephone interview with Stuckler, 11 October 1980

p. 22   "I had always wanted . . .": Langangke *loc. cit.*

p. 24   "We were completely unsuited . . .": Stuckler *loc. cit*

p. 25   "On his last evening . . .": Author interview with Karl Kreutz, 22 April 1980

p. 26 Fritz Langangke said: Langangke *loc. cit.*

p. 26 He described an evening: Sadi Schneid, *Beutedeutscher*

p. 30 "The French know . . .": Tillon, *Les FTP*. p. 284

p. 31 "There was no place . . .": Author interview with Selwyn Jepson, 4 June 1980

p. 31 "a new organization . . .": Quoted Foot *op. cit.* pp. 8, 9

p. 32 "I think that the dropping . . .": Ibid. p. 153

p. 32 "I am not at all clear . . .": PRO AIR8/1187

p. 33 One of the chiefs of SOE: Sir Robin Brook

p. 34 SOE's agents were becoming: See Howarth, *Undercover*

p. 34 "Gubbins had all . . .": Jepson *loc. cit.*

p. 34 "because the Allies . . .": Author interview with General Barry, 4 June 1980

p. 35 "He believed that all . . .": Private comment to author

p. 35 "One would hear that . . .": Barry *loc. cit.*

p. 36 money, the last always: By December 1943 £250,000 a month was being dropped into France.

p. 37 "There was no atmosphere . . .": Hiller, unpublished notes

p. 37 "Well, I hope . . .": Author interview with Vera Atkins, 27 March 1980

p. 39 "It is unfortunate . . .": PRO W0219/2388

p. 39 "Assuming 70 trains . . .": PRO W0219/1892

p. 39 Through Ultra they were reading: PRO DEF3/44

p. 40 "It was unthinkable . . .": Durand, *SNCF pendant la Guerre*, p. 437

p. 40 "The weight of air . . .": PRO W0219/82

p. 41 "In the normal course . . .": Author interview with Major C. V. Wintour, 20 May 1980

p. 42 The Glieres: The plateau in Haute-Savoie where German and Vichy troops attacked a concentration of *maquisards* in March 1944, killing 155 and capturing 175.

p. 42 "Massigli handed me . . .": PRO AIR8/1190

p. 42 "This plan gives . . .": Lt. Gen. J.A.H. Gammell in PRO W0219/2387

p. 43 Plan Vert: The principal architect of the railway sabotage plan was an enigmatic railway expert named René Hardy, who was acquitted, in an extraordinary French post-war trial, of betraying fellow-*résistants* to the Nazis.

p. 43 "The immediate offensive . . .": PRO W0219/2388

p. 43 "It cannot be foreseen . . .": PRO W0219/2388

p. 43 "In view of the fact . . .": PRO W0219/2397

p. 44   "We were," said Colonel Barry: Barry *loc. cit.*

p. 44   "It is probable that . . .": PRO W0219/2388

p. 44   half a million active Resisters: For details, see PRO W0219/2387

p. 45   "The Germans will ignore . . .": PRO W0219/2442

p. 46   "The beauty of life . . .": Hiller, unpublished ms.

p. 47   "Her position . . .": Brogan, *Development of Modern France*, p. 543

p. 48   An utterly dedicated minority: It is important to notice that even at the summit of Resistance activity after D-Day, only an estimated 2 percent of the French population was taking any active role, measured by the numbers decorated after the Liberation: 130,000 as *résistants*, 170,000 deportees and the estimated 100,000 who died. It is reckoned that in the spring of 1944, substantially more French men and women were engaged in the struggle to combat Resistance than were working for the Allied cause. See Robert Paxton, *Vichy*.

p. 49   "Il y avait . . .": Author interview with Pierrette Bach, 12 June 1980

p. 50   "Explain how very ordinary . . .": Hiller notes *op. cit.*

p. 50   "A quality of . . .": Ibid.

p. 50   "We were working . . .": Hiller ms. *op. cit.*

p. 50   "Limoges was a dangerous . . .": Ibid.

p. 51   'started fewer schemes . . .": Hiller notes *op. cit.*

p. 51   "Organizing the *maquis* . . .": Hiller ms. *op. cit.*

p. 52   The Groupes Vény's strength. For details, see the magazine *R4*, July 1979, article *Les Groupes Vény et leur Secteur du Lot*

p. 53   "tension and the light . . .": Hiller notes *op. cit.*

p. 53   "The castle chosen . . .": Hiller tapes

p. 55   "Ha, ha, mon cher . . .": Quoted from author interview with Peter Lake, 9 January 1980

p. 55   across the Pyrenees: It is estimated that some 30,000 fugitives successfully crossed the Pyrenees between August 1940 and the Liberation, about one-third of all those who made the attempt. Many reached Spain only to suffer miserably in one of Franco's internment camps.

p. 58   "They lunched on . . .": Quoted Simone de Beauvoir, *The Price of Life*

p. 58   "Have you arms?": Quoted Lacouture, *André Malraux*, p. 288

p. 58   "a German defeat . . .": Lacouture *op. cit.* p. 297, quoting Roger Stephane

p. 58   "old man Churchill . . .": Ibid. p. 309, quoting Pierre Viansson Ponte

p. 58   "the military chief . . .": Malraux, *Antimémoires*

p. 59 "There are a few people . . .": Author interview with Jacques Poirier, 21 March 1980

p. 59 Malraux quoted . . . : Ibid.

p. 59 "André, tonight . . .": Ibid.

p. 60 "Jack, you're crazy . . .": Ibid.

p. 60 "I was always . . .": Ibid.

p. 61 "From February 1944 . . .": Ibid.

p. 62 "More or less . . .": Ibid.

p. 62 "The Dordogne air force . . .": Ibid.

p. 62 "Say nothing . . .": Ibid.

p. 63 "And now, mon commandant . . .": Ibid

p. 63 "For a long time . . .": Ibid.

p. 65 "There's somebody here . . .": Author interview with Philippe de Gunzbourg, 11 March 1980

p. 65 "Because for me . . .": Ibid.

p. 66 "a farmhouse with twenty . . .": Bergeret, *Messages Personnels*

p. 66 "the principle artisan . . .": Ibid.

p. 67 "We'll follow you . . .": de Gunzbourg *loc. cit.*

p. 67 "Oh, M. Philibert . . .": Ibid.

p. 68 "Un homme du métier . . .": de Gunzbourg unpublished ms, *Souvenirs du Sud-Ouest*

p. 68 "Only if I choose . . .": Author interview with George Starr, 24 April 1980

p. 69 "But I didn't . . .": Ibid.

p. 70 "Building a network . . .": Ibid.

p. 70 "We used to discuss . . .": Author interview with Yvette (Annette) Cormeau, 14 May 1980

p. 71 Selwyn Jepson said . . . : To the author, *loc. cit.*

p. 72 veteran named Tony Brooks: Information here from Foot *op. cit.* It is a matter of regret that the author was only able to have one brief meeting with Brooks.

p. 72 "AVERTISSEMENT . . .": see Durand *op. cit.* p. 440

p. 72 "Which did more harm . . .": Ibid.

p. 73 "So English, so careful . . .": Author interview with Prince Michel de Bourbon, 18 June 1980

p. 75 "Barricades are a great . . .": de Gunzbourg *loc. cit.*

p. 75 "With immense enthusiasm . . .": de Gunzbourg ms. *op. cit.*

p. 76 "In spite of the active . . .": Durand *op. cit.* p. 436

p. 76 "General reports indicate . . .": PRO W0219/2342

p. 77 "We knew that every day . . .": Kreutz *loc. cit.*

p. 77 OKW. It is pertinent to the story of the Das Reich to understand that orders descended from OKW—Hitler's Supreme Command -to Von Rundstedt's Army Group B (responsible for the defense of northern France) and Von Blaskowitz's Army Group G (responsible for the south). Within Army Group G, the Das Reich was tactically subordinated to 58th Panzer Corps, also based in Toulouse, and later briefly to 66th Reserve Corps, based in Clermont-Ferrand. On moving north to Normandy, the Das Reich naturally transferred to Army Group B's command, fighting chiefly under the orders of 2nd SS Panzer Corps.

p. 78 "emphasized the desire . . .": Quoted by Shulman, *Defeat in the West,* p. 106

p. 78 "impression growing . . .": Army Group G War Diary, Appendix 153

p. 79 "The departments of Dordogne . . .": Ibid.

p. 80 "Subject: Anti-Terrorist Measures . . .": Ibid., Appendix 339/44g Kdos

p. 81 "The development of the . . .": Ibid.

p. 87 "The first we knew . . .": Hiller tapes *op. cit.*

p. 88 "The men shoot too much . . .": Report loaned to author by regional historian M. Pierre Péré.

p. 90 "Un bruit infernal . . .": Report loaned to author by M. René Jugie

p. 92 "Reports coming in . . .": Army Group G War Diary

p. 95 "Laurent declared . . .": Minutes loaned to author by M. René Jugie

p. 96 "FTP forces . . .": Ibid.

p. 96 "Tulle will pay . . .": Ibid.

p. 97 Pierre has just told me . . .": Ibid.

p. 97 "Some of Laurent's friends . . .": Ibid.

p. 101 "leaders of a local faction . . .": Brogan *op. cit.* p. 646

p. 102 "orthodox communists . . .": Noireau, *Le Temps des Partisans,* p. 141

p. 102 security police and intelligence: The Gestapo/SO had 131 local branches in France; the army's rival intelligence service, the Abwehr, 69.

p. 103 "Here's one . . .": Noireau *op. cit.* p. 149

p. 104 "Those séances . . .": Ibid. p. 158

p. 104 "The first of May . . .": *Maquis de Corrèze,* p. 300

p. 108 "We also know . . .": Ibid. p. 343

p. 108 "We are cut off . . .": Ibid. p. 351

p. 108 "I find a perplexed . . ." : Ibid, p. 352

p. 108 "Towards 8 am . . .": Ibid. p. 355

p. 110 "This great devil . . .": Ibid. p. 357

p. 111 "If the Germans . . .": Ibid. p. 373

p. 115 "They were sitting there . . .": Wulf *lac cit.*

p. 115 "We've got to make . . .": Schneid *op. cit.*

p. 116 "It was a Dante-esque . . .": *Maquis de Corrèze*, p. 379

p. 117 "And what are you doing . . .": Schneid *op. cit.*

p. 119 "We arranged ourselves . . .": Ibid.

p. 119 "We refused to look . . .": Ibid.

p. 120 "Ah yes," he said: Private information to author

p. 121 "I am still ignorant . . .": Quoted from Weidinger unpublished ms.

p. 122 "There was no specific . . .": Stuckler *loc. cit.*

p. 123 "I protested that . . .": Wulf *loc. cit.*

p. 123 "Hascha Kurz . . .": Schneid *op. cit.*

p. 123 "Why are your shoes . . .": Soulier, *Le Drame de Tulle*

p. 123 "I am one of the . . .": Ibid.

p. 124 "My friends . . .": Ibid.

p. 125 "You see this boy . . .": Schneid *op.* cit.

p. 125 "Because our wounded . . .": Soulier *op. cit.*

p. 125 "Terrible look . . .": Schneid *op. cit.*

p. 127 "One basic principle . . .": Stein *op. cit.*

p. 127 "2nd SS Ps . . .": Army Group G War Diary, Appendix 180

p. 129 "We've got a French . . .": Author interview with Tommy Macpherson, 1 June 1980

p. 130 "The British kept . . .": Author telephone interview with Henry Hyde, 8 November 1980

p. 131 "plainly represented . . .": Author interview with Geoffrey Hallowes, 13 May 1980

p. 131 "and it stuck out . . .": Macpherson *loc. cit.*

p. 133 "All those who can . . .": Author interview with Macdonald Austin, 6 November 1980

p. 133 "were shattered to see . . .": Macpherson *loc. cit.*

p. 134 "The great thing . . .": Macpherson *loc. cit.*

p. 134 "They were very conscious . . .": Hallowes *loc. cit.*

p. 138   "Sometimes they would do . . .": Austin *loc. cit.*

p. 138   "I really didn't know . . .": Ibid.

p. 138   "Infinite capacity for . . .": Macpherson *loc. cit.*

p. 139   "With hindsight it was . . .": Ibid.

p. 140   "I felt I had a clear . . .": Ibid.

p. 141   "If an armoured car . . .": Ibid.

p. 143   "The Germans didn't suffer . . .": Ibid.

p. 144   "State of the division . . .": Army Group G War Diary, Appendices 195 and 326

p. 145   "In view of the transport . . .": Ibid.

p. 146   "High transport losses . . .": Ibid.

p. 146   "One man found . . .": Schneid *op. cit.*

p. 147   "1 Area Souillac . . .": Army Group G War Diary, Appendices 27 and 356

p. 148   "Towards 11pm . . .": Quoted Beau & Gaubusseau, p. 383

p. 148   "Terrasson has 3,000 . . .": Ibid, p. 384

p. 149   "I profit from an armoured . . .": Ibid. p. 385

p. 150   "the cycle is simple . . .": Ibid. p. 385

p. 150   "At the end of . . .": de Gunzbourg ms. *op. cit.*

p. 152   "The regiment is greeted . . .": Weidinger *op. cit.*

p. 155   The account of Kampfe's kidnapping and the events leading to the massacre at Oradour are drawn from Weidinger's history, interviews with surviving second-hand French contemporary sources, and the principal published French accounts of Delarue and Beau & Gaubusseau.

p. 157   "She was treated . . .": Quoted by Wache in a sworn statement loaned to the author by Herbert Taege

p. 157   "When I left London . . .": Staunton is quoted by Minney in *Carve Her Name With Pride*

p. 158   "She looked like a little doll . . .": Author interview with an eyewitness in Limoges, 23 June 1980

p. 159   "In the course of . . .": Army Group G War Diary

p. 161   "It was very rough . . .": Quoted from author interview with Weidinger, 11 April 1980

p. 161   "After many delays . . .": Weidinger *op. cit.*

p. 162   "He arrives in an excited . . .": Ibid.

p. 163   The surviving witnesses of the massacre at Oradour were exhaustively examined by post-war tribunals and historians. All quotations in this section unless otherwise stated are drawn from testimony given at the 1953 war crimes trial, or statements recorded in Jens Kruuse's *Madness at Oradour*. I have relied principally upon the published French sources, with some collaborative details from my own interviews in France and Germany, and of course a visit to the ruins of Oradour.

p. 181   "Late in the afternoon . . .": Weidinger *op. cit.*

p. 182   "Mopping up operations . . .": Army Group G War Diary, Appendix 199

p. 183   "There are further . . .": Weidinger *op. cit.*

p. 183   "Action taken during the . . .": Quoted Delarue, *Trafics et Crimes sous l'Occupation*

p. 184   "Turn him over . . .": Schneid *op. cit.*

p. 185   "The German authorities . . .": Quoted by Soulier *op. cit.*

p. 186   "dropped on Billancourt . . .": A reference to a major raid by RAF Bomber Command against the Renault factory, on 9 March 1942.

p. 186   "At 1.30am . . .": News cuttings from private collection of Marcel Racault

p. 186   "Well, let's thank God . . .": Wulf *loc. cit.*

p. 187   "The great thing . . .": Sir Henry d'Avigdor-Goldsmid, quoted Hislop *Anything but a Soldier*, p. 3

p. 188   "Don't use 'em . . .": Ibid. p. 124

p. 188   "I believe that after . . .": Lloyd-Owen, *Providence Their Guide* (Harrap 1980) p. 120

p. 189   "When small successful . . .": Hislop *op. cit.* p. 67

p. 189   "Quite out of his depth . . .": Ibid. p. 125

p. 189   "Where's so and so . . .": Author interview with Peter Weaver, 11 August 1980

p. 189   "He was everything . . .": Author interview with Sam Smith, 6 August 1980

p. 190   "Belted for the bridge . . .": Ibid.

p. 190   "I was in love . . .": Ibid.

p. 190   "The war came . . .": Weaver *loc. cit.*

p. 191   "2nd SS Panzer . . .": PRO W0218/114

p. 191   "This was a serious . . .": Farran, *Winged Dagger*, p. 222–3

p. 192   "You will now concentrate . . .": PRO W0218/114

p. 193   "I can remember . . .": Tonkin in a letter to the author, 11 October 1980

p. 193   "As if, when a boy . . .": Hislop *op. cit.* p. 126

p. 193   "He gave me much . . .": Tonkin letter *op. cit.*

p. 193 "The 5th came . . .": Tonkin contemporary letter to his mother, loaned to author

p. 194 "It is my unfortunate . . .": Tonkin to author, *op. cit.*

p. 194 Hitler's Commando Order: Following the discovery of a German sentry who had been bound and shot by a British commando raiding party in the Channel Islands in 1942, Hitler decreed that all members of the Commandos, SAS and paratroopers captured operating behind the lines were to be treated as saboteurs and shot, whether or not in uniform. More than 200 mostly British prisoners suffered this fate, although the "commando" order was erratically executed. It is only just to add that when operational requirements made it embarrassing to take or hold prisoners, Allied Special Forces were not unknown to kill them. In recent years, there have been an increasing number of revelations of mass executions of German prisoners by Allied units during World War II. The US 45th Division machine-gunned one large group during the summer of 1944. On 4 January 1945, General Patton wrote in his diary: "The 11th Armoured Division is very green and took unnecessary losses to no effect. There were also some unfortunate incidents in the shooting of prisoners (I hope we can conceal this)." The purpose of these remarks is not to excuse the German shooting of prisoners in contravention of the laws of war, but to try to place the matter in a more objective context than was possible in the first, chauvinistic years following the end of the war when many books suggested that only the Wehrmacht and the SS were guilty of breaching the Geneva Convention.

p. 195 "It was the nicest . . .": Tonkin to mother *op. cit.*

p. 197 "A small, very frightened . . .": Tonkin to author *op. cit.*

p. 200 "They hardly knew . . .": Weaver *loc. cit.*

p. 202 "There was nothing . . .": Captain John Sadoine report in PRO W0218/114

p. 202 "should be treated . . .": Ibid.

p. 203 "One point to be . . .": Tonkin report PRO W0218/114

p. 203 Sergeant Eccles . . . : On 28 June 1944

p. 203 Sam Smith and two: On 30 June 1944

p. 205 Soon after first light: On 3 July 1944

p. 206 "almost berserk . . .": Weaver *loc. cit.*

p. 207 "I have always felt . . .": Tonkin to author *op. cit.*

p. 208 "We'd written ourselves . . .": Weaver *loc. cit.*

p. 208 "In comparison with . . .": PRO W0219/2389

p. 209 "In retrospect, it seemed . . .": Hislop *op. cit.* p. 67

p. 209   "Urgent request for . . .": PRO DEF3/171

p. 211   "In spite of efforts . . .": PRO W0219/2342

p. 212   "They couldn't even . . .": Author interview with Ernst Krag, 12 April 1980

p. 212   "After 10pm the Americans . . .": Author interviews with DR survlvors

p. 212   "It was the first hint . . .": Langangke *loc. cit.*

p. 213   "It will be a miracle . . .": Quoted Weidinger *loc. cit.*

p. 213   "Where is the Luftwaffe . . .": Author interviews with DR survivors

p. 214   "Could we allow . . .": Weidinger *loc. cit.*

p. 215   "If we do this . . .": Wulf *loc. cit.*

p. 215   "At Falaise . . .": quoted Stein *op. cit.* p. 225

p. 215   "Aren't you pleased . . .": Kreutz *loc. cit.*

p. 215   "An organization in the . . .": PRO W0219/2342

p. 216   "The movements of . . .": PRO W0219/2389

p. 216   "Poor, tortured . . .": Malraux, *Antimémoires*, p. 213

p. 216   "All things . . .": Churchill to Portal, 2 October 1941, quoted Hastings, *Bomber Command*, p. 141

p. 217   As Professor Foot has said: Foot *op. cit.* p. 441

p. 217   "It has been estimated . . .": PRO W0219/1975 (8 July 1944)

p. 218   "It was only just . . .": Barry *loc. cit.*

p. 219   "In Spain the French . . .": Best, *Humanity in Warfare*, p. 115

p. 219   "We are beating them . . .": See Howard, *The Franco-Prussian War*, p. 251

p. 219   "The truth is . . .": Quoted Best *op. cit.* p. 120

p. 219   "My whole attention . . .": Quoted Nigel Hamilton, *Monty: The Making of a General* (Hamish Hamilton) p. 158

p. 220   "My own view . . .": Quoted Hamilton *op. cit.* p. 160

p. 220   "Levelling everything . . .": Tillon *op. cit.* p. 364

p. 224   "It was necessary . . .": Lammerding post-war written statement to Weidinger, provided to author

p. 227   "Ask the court . . .": Schneid *op. cit.*

Acknowledgments

I AM INDEBTED to many people whom I met or with whom I corresponded during the writing of this book. Some I have already mentioned in the Foreword. Here, I should begin with my wife Tricia and Alan Samson, my editor at Michael Joseph, who endured the trauma of gestation with characteristic patience and understanding. The London Library was as splendid as always. In England I also received generous help or suggestions from Joan Bright Astley, Len Deighton, Geoffrey Lucy, Charles Wintour and the RUSI Library. Without the intervention of David Irving, my inquiries in Germany about the whereabouts of survivors of the Das Reich would have continued to meet with courteous declarations of ignorance from the relevant veterans' organizations.

In France, I am indebted above all to M. and Mme. Louis Bach, M. and Mme. Georges Bru, Marius Guedin, Baron Philippe de Gunzbourg, Réné Jugie, Pierre Péré, Marcel Racault, Marguerite Rollet, Rojé Raveux, Jean Razier, Julien Rouzier, Jean Sennemaut and Marcel Vidal. There are many others, too numerous to list, whom I had the privilege of meeting in southern and central France in 1980.

Among the former staff of SOE in Baker Street: Sir Robin Brook, General Dick Barry, Maurice Buckmaster, Vera Atkins and Selwyn Jepson.

Former agents of SOE in France: Annette Cormeau, the late Amédée Maingard, Peter Lake, Paddy O'Sullivan, Jacques Poirier, the late George Starr, Cyril Watney.

258

The Jedburghs and OSS: Macdonald Austin, Prince Michel de Bourbon, William Colby, Geoffrey Hallowes, Henry Hyde, Tommy Macpherson.

The SAS: John Fielding, Sam Smith, John Tonkin, Peter Weaver.

The SS: Ernst Krag, Karl Kreutz, Fritz Langangke, Otto Pohl, Theo Sorg, Silvester Stadler, Albert Stuckler, Herbert Taege, Otto Weidinger, Gunther-Eberhardt Wisliceny, Heinrich Wulf.

Almost all of these received decorations from their respective nations for their services in World War II.

Glossary

BCRA: *Bureau Central de Renseignements et d'Action*, the Central Bureau for Intelligence and Action set up in November 1940 by Captain André Dewavrin, alias Colonel Passy, at Free French headquarters in London. The BCRA assumed responsibility for all intelligence and sabotage operations in French territory carried out under General De Gaulle's auspices.

Chantiers de la Jeunesse: a Vichy Government-sponsored organization which ran compulsory forest work camps for all twenty year olds, at which they were subjected to intensive political indoctrination.

Cheminots: Railway workers

DMR: *Délégué Militaire Régional*. De Gaulle's headquarters in London appointed six DMRs to act as General Koenig's on-the-spot representatives and deputies in the six Military Regions into which France was divided for the purposes of FFI direction and administration.

FFI: *Forces Françaises de l'Intérieur*. The title given by Free French headquarters in London to all Resistance forces in arms in France under Gaullist command. The FFI allegedly included the men of the Communist

FTP: but in reality these almost everywhere preserved their own command and title independent of the FFI. In March 1944, General Marie Pierre Koenig was designated FFI commander, a role he exercised from London. After the liberation of France, 140,000 men of the FFI were inducted into the French First Army. Most of them spent the last months of the war blockading the remaining German garrisons in the French ports.

FTP: *Francs-Tireurs et Partisans*, the Communist *résistants*, who took their title as "free shooters" from the roving bands of French guerillas who harassed the invaders' lines of communication in the 1870 Franco-Prussian war. Most FTP groups for most of the war accepted orders only from the French Communist Party, although they sometimes formed local tactical alliances with the Armée Secrète or agents from London in order to gain access to parachuted arms and money.

GMR: *Garde Mobile de Réserve*, a Vichyite para-military force.

MUR: *Mouvement Uni de Résistance,* a loose alliance of three noncommunist Resistance groups that had developed in the Unoccupied Zone of France—*Liberation, Combat* and *Franc-Tireur* (not to be confused with the FTP). In the Corrèze the council of MUR included representatives of several other local groups.

Milice: Originally a para-military arm of the Vichy Government in the Unoccupied Zone of France. When the detested Joseph Darnand became Vichy's Secretary-General for the Maintenance of Order—in other words, police minister—in December 1943, he expanded the *milice* into a national para-military force to combat the Resistance, and recruited some 45,000 French volunteers. The *milice* were especially feared by the Resistance because of their local knowledge, and especially detested for their ruthlessness and treachery, although many of their recruits came forward to avoid forced labor in Germany. Some historians suggest that in the spring of 1944 at least as many Frenchmen were working actively to combat Resistance as were working with the FFI and FTP.

ORA: *Organisation de Résistance de l'Armée,* a Resistance group which was originally created within the Intelligence Service of the Vichy Armistice Army, and expanded after the disbandment of the Armistice Army when the Germans took over Unoccupied France in November 1942. It was a non-Gaullist body which accomplished little, but for a time enjoyed the enthusiastic support of the Americans. Many Frenchmen despised the ORA because of its overwhelming dependence on former regular army officers, whom they considered bore a large share of responsibility for the plight of France, and had no claim upon the support of civilians.

OSS: The American Office of Strategic Services created by General William Donovan in July 1941 to build a new Secret Service and sabotage organization to replace that disbanded in November 1942. OSS was the forerunner of the modern Central Intelligence Agency, and after some early blunders and mishaps, caused by the absolute lack of experienced personnel, it developed into a useful weapon of war. Its senior ranks were dominated by lawyers educated at the great American universities—Harvard, Princeton, Yale. Allen Dulles, later director of the CIA, was probably the most successful OSS organizer of the war, running his networks from Switzerland. OSS was dissolved in September 1945.

Plastique: Plastic explosive, the soft, malleable putty-like substance developed by the British and widely used for demolition because of its power and flexibility; charges could be molded into any shape. They were exploded by the insertion of a detonator which in turn was ignited either by electrical impulse or delay fuse.

RAMC: Royal Army Medical Corps

Réseau: network, the standard word for one of the chains of agents created by SOE and the BCRA, meaning a linked group of people rather than a geographical area.

SA: *Sturmabteilung,* the brownshirt "storm-troops," the original elite strong-arm force of Hitler's National Socialist Party, purged and broken in June 1934 when their leader Ernst Rohm was killed.

SAS: The British Special Air Service regiment.

SD: *Sicherheitsdienst*, the SS Security Service operating under the orders of Himmler. The SD possessed some 6,000 agents throughout Europe, and was closely linked with the Gestapo. Most Frenchmen referred to all German police agents as Gestapo.

SHAEF: Supreme Headquarters Allied Expeditionary Force, the controlling staff for the Allied landings in Normandy and the subsequent campaign in North-West Europe, under the command of General Eisenhower.

SNCF: *Societé Nationale de Chemins de Fer*, the national railway organization of France.

SOE: The British Special Operations Executive, forerunner and counterpart of the American OSS's Special Operations department.

STO: *Service de Travail Obligatoire*. The detested forced-labor program introduced in Occupied France in August 1942, and throughout the country from February 1943. Initially the Germans sought French volunteers to man their factories, but although they recruited with some success, the supply of labor was far below their requirements, and compulsion was introduced. By November 1943, 1.34 million Frenchmen were working in German factories (along with millions more Belgians, Dutchmen, Russians, Poles and other defeated nationals). In January 1944 the Nazis launched a new program to recruit a further million Frenchmen, but they met with negligible success, since most of those eligible took to the *maquis*, or went into hiding.

Index